LIFE AT HIGH G-FORCE

THE QUEST OF MAYO CLINIC RESEARCHER

DR. EARL H. WOOD

E. ANDREW WOOD

MAYO CLINIC PRESS

MAYO CLINIC PRESS
200 First St. SW
Rochester, MN 55905
MCPress.MayoClinic.org

To stay informed about Mayo Clinic Press, please subscribe to our free
e-newsletter at MCPress.MayoClinic.org or follow us on social media.

For bulk sales to employers, member groups and health-related
companies, contact Mayo Clinic, 200 First St. SW, Rochester, MN 55905,
or send an email to SpecialSalesMayoBooks@mayo.edu.

Cover design: Brad Foltz

Photos provided by the Wood family and E. J. Baldes.

Illustrations provided by Mayo Olmstead and Bob Golightly.

ISBN: 9781945564635

Library of Congress Control Number: 2022942502

Printed in the United States of America

**Proceeds from the sale of every book benefit medical
research and education at Mayo Clinic.**

This book is published with generous support from John T. and Lillian G. Mathews, founding benefactors of Mayo Clinic Heritage Hall.

Dedicated to my wife, Dr. Krista Coleman Wood,
and my daughter, Karolyn Eide.

CONTENTS

CONTENTS

FOREWORD

BY JAN STEPANEK, MD, MPH, FASMA
Associate Professor of Medicine,
Codirector, Aerospace Medicine and Vestibular Research Laboratory
Mayo Clinic, Scottsdale, Arizona

During my training in internal medicine and aerospace medicine and the clinical practice of medicine, I had the privilege of encountering many gifted teachers and mentors who influenced my approach to clinical care, interaction with my peers, and the science of medicine. When I was asked to work on problems related to acceleration-induced blackout and related protective equipment that was to be evaluated on a human centrifuge in Europe, I reached out to the Mayo Clinic operator and asked if she could connect me to an expert in that domain on staff. She immediately stated that she would connect me to Dr. Earl Wood. A few minutes later I was on the phone with Dr. Wood, explaining my research task and asking if he would be able to provide me guidance. After spending about an hour and thirty minutes in conversation, he asked for a fax number so he could send me pertinent papers. He was very generous with his time and genuinely interested in helping to solve the challenging problems I was having with the design of a valid trial on human subjects under g-forces. I had to restock the fax machine paper supply due to the extensive references and materials he sent. Thus began an extensive correspondence that taught me acceleration physiology and about related life-support systems. During our exchanges, I also came to appreciate the history that Mayo Clinic had in aerospace life-support systems and the tremendous contributions Dr. Earl Wood and his many colleagues had made during World War II and afterward.

When I came to Rochester, Minnesota, I had the opportunity to continue my education under Dr. Wood in countless exchanges in his office and also on several occasions at his family's cherished farm not far from Rochester. It was a privilege to get to know Dr. Wood beyond his many brilliant academic accomplishments and appreciate the extraordinary human being who loved his family, was humble, enjoyed the outdoors, and knew very well what mattered and what did not in life. I also came to realize that I was among numerous fellows who benefited from his generous teaching and education efforts and have gone on to contribute to many areas of medicine in significant ways. His way of teaching was remarkable in that he was fully present and completely focused on the person he was interacting with, as if nothing else existed at that moment. His dedication, focus, knowledge, integrity, and honesty made him more than just a brilliant teacher; he was also an incredible role model. His love and loyalty to dedicated team members who did good work was legendary, and he cherished people for who they were and not for what credentials they had behind their names.

I am grateful to Andrew Wood for compiling this biography to provide a unique perspective on the life of his father, Dr. Earl Wood, that goes beyond the numerous awards, manuscripts, books, and contributions to physiology, aerospace medicine, cardiology, and biomedical imaging, but also shows his important focus on people and family.

While I had the opportunity to benefit from the teaching and mentorship of Earl Wood over several years, I did not appreciate that I was one of the last to take advantage of his immense knowledge in acceleration physiology. I miss him and I think of him often, as do many who had the privilege of crossing his path. I will close this foreword with the unique signature that ended every email and fax communication that I received from Dr. Wood:

"So be it and sincerely . . ."

PREFACE

It has been over ten years since the passing of my father, Dr. Earl H. Wood, on March 18, 2009. As his youngest son, still living in Rochester, Minnesota, in the shadow of Mayo Clinic, I'm impressed by the fact that when my father is mentioned to anyone who interacted with him—be it a Mayo Clinic physician, a clerk at Fleet Farm, or his farming buddies near the small town of Rock Dell, Minnesota, in the southeastern part of the state—the response is the same: "Oh, he was a great person." "One of a kind." "What a great human being." The question I want to answer is *why*. What was it about Earl that made him so special? Why was he loved and respected by so many people?

As I travel the country on business as a health and safety consultant, I frequently glance through airline magazines. Quite often, the headline article or the front page will feature some rich or famous individual, usually a corporate CEO, Wall Street broker, celebrity, politician, or movie star. They're featured in fashionable clothes driving state-of-the-art vehicles, the picture of total success. However, many of these celebrities have a history of scandal or unethical behavior at the expense of their employees, customers, and families. This could include not following organizational policy and procedures, knowingly manufacturing automobiles with faulty ignition switches or poor brakes, producing unhealthy foods, or being unfaithful to their loved ones. In addition, many of these executives may be disliked by their employees, resulting in expensive and high turnover rates.

In contrast, in all my associations with my father's colleagues, employees, coworkers, technicians, and family members, they all say Earl Wood was fair, a good listener who brought out the very best in every individual, whether he agreed with that person or not. Compared with many of today's leaders, these qualities are all too rare and, as such, are worthy of further exploration.

Professionally, Earl Wood was a physiologist, scientist, and world-renowned researcher at Mayo Clinic. He is best known for his groundbreaking research that allowed the G-suit to be used by pilots during World War II, for furthering research in cardiac catheterization, and for the development of the pulse oximeter. He definitely was not a "nerd" as depicted by the character Sheldon Cooper on the television program *The Big Bang Theory*, although he had the pleasure of working with many nerds, leading them toward success as students and research fellows to eventually become scientific and medical colleagues. Earl did not like science fiction, because those stories, movies, and television programs were not supported by scientific data or facts. He was critical of the movie *Top Gun*, since the maneuvers and antics in the movie were for entertainment and not backed up by true-life scenarios he experienced on the human centrifuge and in combat aircraft.

This biography will not focus only on the scientific accomplishments of Earl H. Wood, which are immense: there are more than eight hundred scientific publications covering his career. Rather, it is about Earl H. Wood the person: as a leader, mentor, innovator, and coach. As you will learn, Earl was very humble. He would be the first to explain that he *did not* invent the G-suit or cardiac catheterization, as will be shown later in this book. Earl insisted that he *and his team* made the G-suit and cardiac catheterization better through sharing ideas, better instrumentation, accurate measurement, and data analysis. In fact, it was his unique team approach to medical research that allowed him to be so successful. This biography will focus on those qualities that made him such an inspiring leader. Earl's qualities as a mentor, teacher, and leader are certainly lacking in today's government and corporate worlds. It is my hope that by examining the background, career, and leadership style of Earl Wood, I can offer a role model to our current generation and generations to come.

LIFE AT
HIGH
G-FORCE

PROLOGUE

Tensions were high in the Aero Medical Laboratory at Mayo Clinic in the fall of 1959.

The space race with the Soviet Union to send a human into outer space and eventually to the moon was in full gear. Laboratory personnel were busy preparing the human centrifuge and a human subject for an experiment to evaluate physiological responses to prolonged g-forces. The newly formed National Aeronautics and Space Administration (NASA) had funded Mayo Clinic's Aero Medical Laboratory, directed by Dr. Earl Wood, to study the effects of prolonged g-forces on the human body during blastoff and reentry into the Earth's atmosphere from space. During World War II, Earl Wood and a team of doctors, scientists, and technicians developed the instrumentation to record physiological data from human subjects on a centrifuge experiencing the high gravitational forces pilots experienced in combat aircraft. Now they were being asked to study the effects of gravitational forces on astronauts going into outer space.

That day, Dr. Hiram "Hi" W. Marshall sat strapped into the cockpit at the end of the centrifuge, in the same position as an astronaut in a Mercury space capsule. A research fellow at Mayo Clinic, Dr. Marshall had been chosen as the subject for this study—and he was a little nervous as his coworker went through checklists; he could feel the vibration of two twenty-ton flywheels rotating underneath the superstructure of the centrifuge. A catheter was placed in his arm and ran up to his heart to measure heart pressures while he was subject to the g-forces. An infrared sensor was placed on his ear to monitor his pulse at head level and blood-oxygen saturation. All of this, of course, was being closely monitored by Dr. Wood, his fellow medical researchers, and technical staff to assure Dr. Marshall's safety and get data for the research they were conducting.

In the center seat at the center shaft of the centrifuge, Dr. Earl Wood monitored the physiological responses of the subject plus the functioning of the centrifuge. In a room next to the centrifuge, Lucy Cronin monitored the safety procedures of the centrifuge runs. In a room above Lucy, Bill Sutterer ran the centrifuge's clutch and braking system. Across the hall was Don Hegland, who ran all the analog data-recording equipment. With the two twenty-ton flywheels spinning freely at a prescribed speed for a 4G run, Dr. Wood spoke over the intercom: "OK, Donnie, start your recording." This was to get baseline data on the subject at 1G.

Once the data was reviewed, Lucy began the ten-second countdown for a centrifuge run. On ten, the subject was A-OK. On nine, the flywheels were spinning at the correct rpm; on eight, all tools had been removed from the centrifuge, the doors to the centrifuge room were locked, and so on. When she got to three, the countdown was handed over to Dr. Wood. "Two, Donnie, start your recording; one, Bill, start the run." Bill Sutterer released the brakes on the centrifuge and engaged the clutch on the flywheels, and the centrifuge started to spin, reaching the prescribed G in one and a quarter rotations! After one minute at 4G, Dr. Marshall indicated he was having severe chest pain. Dr. Wood signaled to hit the brakes on the centrifuge, which came to a grinding halt. Frightened, he and the team rushed to the cockpit. They could see only one side of Dr. Marshall's chest rising when he took a breath, and they could hear a gurgling sound with each breath. Dr. Marshall was suffering from a pneumothorax. He was rushed to Saint Marys Hospital, where he recovered, and he was back to work the next day. Although very concerned and worried, Dr. Wood and the team were relieved Dr. Marshall did not sustain any long-lasting injury. The human centrifuge experiments posed some risks that the scientists were willing to take to increase the biological knowledge of aviation, space travel, and clinical medicine.

CHAPTER 1

A GATHERING OF SCIENTISTS, OUTDOORSMEN, AND FAMILY

In September 1981, a scientific and medical symposium was held at Mayo Clinic in Rochester, Minnesota, to honor a soon-retiring Earl H. Wood, MD, PhD. Dr. Wood had been at Mayo Clinic for almost forty years and was reaching the mandatory retirement age of seventy. Medical scientists from all over the world presented at this symposium. Other well-known figures invited to the celebration included Supreme Court Justice Harry A. Blackmun and Earl Wood's high school football coach, Louis Todnem. Also in attendance were farmers from Southeast Minnesota and South Dakota, extended family members, and a group of outdoor enthusiasts with a rather earthy reputation, known as "the Deerslayers."

Earl did not want to retire and would have just as soon kept doing what he loved best, cardiovascular research mixed in with a little hunting and fishing (OK, a lot). It was rumored that if he stayed in the office that he had occupied for at least three decades, the Clinic would remove his phone. The message was clear from the administration of Mayo Clinic: it was time for a new generation of medical scientists to take the lead. He was a humble individual and did not want to go out with a lot of fanfare. However, the chance to meet again and rub shoulders with his close colleagues, former fellows, students, family members, and friends was just too much to resist. For once in his life and career he was a participant, though reluctantly, not an organizer or leader. He simply had to sit back and enjoy the show.

The Earl H. Wood Scientific Symposium covered the latest medical research that spanned Earl's forty-year career at Mayo Clinic. Presentations included "The Human Centrifuge," by **Dr. Charles Code**[1]; "The Investigator as Volunteer Subject," by Dr. Howard Burchell; "Biological Models of Parasystole and Reentry in Isolated Purkinje Fibers," by Dr. Gordon Moe; and "Quantitative Analysis of Structure and Function of the Cardiovascular System by Roentgen-Video-Computer Techniques," by **Dr. Paul Heintzen**. All these and many more covering the latest in aviation and cardiovascular scientific developments—and all in just two and a half days.

Earl's approach to scientific collaborative investigation with multidisciplinary specialties represents an example of "team science." This approach was learned early with the Mayo Aero Medical Unit and similar large scientific projects of World War II, such as the Manhattan Project. Earl understood that bringing together bright young MDs, PhDs, and talented technicians from a wide variety of fields—including medicine, physiology, engineering, physics, math, and computer science—and administrative staff would enable that team to solve problems unsolvable by a single researcher in even the most advanced laboratories. He also relied heavily

---

1.   Names of individuals who played a significant role in Earl's career appear in bold on their first appearance.

on his technicians, who may not have had degrees but knew the equipment better than some of the degreed scientists. Earl always gave credit to his team. Anything that came out of his laboratory that was newsworthy was a product of the team, and he made sure the team received the credit and recognition.

In the last rows of Mann Hall in Mayo Clinic's Medical Sciences Building, where the symposium was held, was a group of nonscientists; Clinic employees, technicians, and administrative staff; and friends and family members, who were also in awe of the scientific progress made during the last forty years and what it meant for the future. These individuals saw Earl not as a world-renowned medical scientist but as a mentor, leader, coach, uncle, and father. During the symposium intermissions, this group shared humorous stories of what went on behind the scenes at the lab and on hunting, fishing, and skiing trips, along with lake house projects.

During the symposium dinner, Dr. Irwin J. Fox, from the University of Minnesota Medical School, a Holocaust survivor and former longtime fellow, gave a humorous reminiscence about Earl. A few excerpts from this speech are in the following paragraphs.

> It is a pleasure and a privilege for me to be asked to speak in the shadow of one of the greatest institutions of this world. One with which I was closely associated for [a] period of seven years during my sojourn in Rochester. An institution which has given ministering to the physical and intellectual well-being of all peoples, regardless of race, color or creed its highest priority, an institution noted for its innovativeness, whose leadership has always

been forward-looking and willing to try new ideas. I am speaking, of course, of Wong's Café. . . .

And then of course, there was Earl, who by the dint of his intellect and hard work had created the foremost human cardiovascular laboratory in the world in which I was privileged to work. But world renowned as it was, Earl's laboratory was really nothing more than a front. A place to do busywork between deer hunting, pheasant hunting, duck hunting, and fishing seasons. In fact, I recall one year in which, in a frenzied fit of hunting mania, the Wood brothers combined all of the above-mentioned seasons into one slam-bang orgy of pheasant, duck, and deer hunting as well as fishing, thereby once and for all removing the cover of the respected occupations behind which they had been masquerading and revealing them for what they really are, incurable hunting and fishing addicts, with many superfluous appendages in the form of doctoral degrees, a kind of plumage totally unnecessary for their prime goal in life, since no deer, fish, pheasant, or duck that I have ever seen cared whether or not their human predecessor had a degree!

Seriously, I greatly enjoyed working in Earl's lab. I must have, for why else did I remain so long that I came to be known as "fellow emeritus"? I sincerely hope that we have not heard the last of Earl's scientific achievements. Finally, over the years, I have had the privilege to come to know personally Earl, Ada, and their children from my participation in family gatherings. I would like Earl and Ada to know that aside from scientific accomplishments, and these are magnificent, they both have much to be proud of in that their hard work and raising their children has come to fruition in the wonderful children that they have brought up.

There were many tributes offered that day, all eloquent and heartfelt like this one. So what was it about Earl? What made people listen to him? Why did people gravitate to him? Why did people follow him, both at work in the lab and in the field? In this biography, I've tried to find out the answers to these questions. The intention of this book is to summarize Earl Wood's scientific accomplishments and look at Earl H. Wood the person, as a leader, mentor, innovator, and coach. In the following chapters, we'll revisit his life together to find out what made Earl such an inspiring, humble leader, beloved and respected by all who knew him.

CHAPTER 2

FAMILY BACKGROUND

For most of us, our family history, upbringing, and environment all play a role in shaping who we become. In order to understand the personality and leadership qualities of Earl Wood, we must first consider his family history. His parents were William Clark Wood and Inez Louise (Goff) Wood. These individuals' background, upbringing, and environment had a substantial influence on Earl Wood, his siblings, and how he approached family matters, work, and play.

Earl Wood's mother, Inez, could trace her lineage back to seventeenth-century Great Britain. The first Goffe who lived in the American colonies was John Goffe. The town of Goffstown, New Hampshire, is named after him. Inez's father, John Anthony Goff, who was born in Herkimer County, New York, acquired a farm near Lake Crystal, Minnesota.

Earl Wood's grandfather Peter Wood was born in Cayuga County, New York, in 1824. Peter and his wife, Emiline, moved to an eighty-acre farm in Faribault County, Minnesota. They had sixteen children. The youngest of the sixteen was William Clark Wood, born in 1874. He was Earl Wood's father.

William Wood and Inez Goff were married on March 22, 1900, and taught school in Delavan, Minnesota. Chester "Chet" William Wood was born in 1902, Delbert Leroy Wood in 1904, and Harland Goff Wood in 1907. The Wood family moved to the "big city" of Mankato in 1907.

Two more children joined the family circle while the Woods were living on Walnut Street: Louise Athena Wood was born in 1910, and Earl Howard Wood took his first breath on January 1, 1912. Earl was named after Earl Osten, a young neighbor and friend. His middle name came from the middle name of the sitting US president, William Howard Taft, the portly commander in chief who had just visited Mankato. The youngest of the Wood children, Wilbur (better known as "Abe"), was born on the family's twenty-acre farm in 1913.

When Earl was born, the family numbered four boys and a girl. Will and Inez decided that it would be advantageous to move their new family out of the city onto a small farm. Will Wood acquired twenty acres just south of the city. There was soil for raising agricultural produce, and there were pastures and buildings for raising livestock. These facilities required work and attention to maintain. Chores had to be done every day, and each child assumed a regular and continuing share of the responsibility. Despite blizzards, heat waves, hailstorms, and tornadoes, cows had to be milked morning and night, the horses and pigs fed and watered, and the barns cleaned out. Each of the Wood children learned how to pull their weight and get the job done day after day, week after week. These were valuable lessons and a preparation for life that wasn't available on the streets of Mankato. The farm was called "the 20 Acres," and it provided plenty of opportunity for physical exercise in the carrying out of agricultural tasks and also in the development of skills in hunting, fishing, and outdoor sports. Sometimes the former suffered because the boys seemed to place an undue emphasis on the latter.

The Wood family, 1914: Inez, Wilbur (Abe), Delbert, Chester, Louise, Harland, Earl, and William

During the winter of 1914, Will Wood's real estate business asked him to relocate to Texas for a year to handle the arrangements for expanding real estate sales in the state. On November 23, 1914, the whole family packed into an open Model T Ford sedan and headed south.

Roads were dirt and gravel. The Interstate Highway System had not been developed, and no numbering scheme of the highways existed. The directional signs were on conveniently located telephone posts and hand-painted signs. The weather was ideal until central Oklahoma. Here the travelers ran into drizzle and an incessant light rain. The dirt roads became a sea of mud and in low places were impassable. They soon became stuck in mud up to the axles.

It was cold and growing dark. They were just four miles from the town of Sunrise, Oklahoma. As fate would have it, they were also nearly in front of a large farm. So, while William and the older boys struggled with the jack, trying to get boards under the wheels, Inez took Louise, Earl, and baby Wilbur, who was in her arms, and walked up the driveway to the large white house. When the lady of the house came to the door, Inez explained the Wood family predicament and asked if they could be given shelter for the night. The woman said, "We are not interested in housing strangers in our home. We have no place for the likes of you!" and the door slammed shut.

When Inez came trudging back, she gave the disheartening news. The wet, shivering, and mud-spattered family held a conference. About this time, a tiny square of light was observed not far down the road, and Will directed his weary contingent toward what they hoped was a beacon in the darkness. It was a small, unpainted wood structure that proved to be an African American sharecropper's cabin. But it was filled with friendliness, generosity, and hospitality. The man and his wife invited the Wood family in, seated them around the stove to dry their wet clothes, and gave them some food and drink. Soon some of the youngsters began to doze off in their chairs. There was minimal furniture and the family could provide only a few thin blankets, but the Woods stretched out on the floor for the night.

As soon as it was light enough to see, the sharecropper led the way across the fields, and they carried two pails of hot water out to the stalled car. It had frozen during the night, which solidified the mud and also thickened the oil in the Ford's crankcase. Starting a car under these conditions was a tough assignment, especially on an empty stomach. Will poured the hot water in the radiator, turned the switch of the magneto, pulled out the choke, and heaved on the cold metal crank handle. The engine coughed a few times, then all four cylinders caught, and the 1914 Model T roared to life to welcome the rising sun. The Wood family thanked their generous hosts and they were soon on their way to Texas. The Woods never forgot the generosity of this African American family on that cold, miserable night; this made a deep impression on all the Wood kids. Later in life, Earl had a diverse workforce in his laboratory, with research fellows, students, technicians, and physicians of all walks of life and racial backgrounds from around the world. He treated each as an equal.

While in Texas, Will Wood pursued his passion for hunting, including quail, turkey, and deer. For shooting at longer distances, he purchased a model 1892 Winchester 38-40 caliber rifle at a local hardware store for eighteen dollars. Will shot his first Texas deer with this rifle. Nearly forty years later, he bagged three Minnesota whitetails in one season with that rifle. Subsequently, his sons, grandchildren, and great-grandchildren, including this author, were introduced to big-game hunting with the old 38-40 Winchester.

The Texas real estate business season ended in early spring, so Will Wood arranged to have his family return home by train. Shortly after arriving home from Texas, Will Wood purchased a shiny new 1915 Model T Ford. He also established a new office in Mankato, in a small brick building a block off Front Street at 113 East Hickory Street.

Back on the 20 Acres, Will and the boys put in a new concrete floor on the basement level of the barn and placed metal stanchions to accommodate eight to ten head of cattle. The second story of the barn was used as storage area for corn fodder. The top level of the structure provided a spacious haymow. There was a three-foot-square open chute on the south side of the barn, which made it possible to drop feed down to the livestock in the basement. They modernized the barn even further by installing a large metal hay fork that operated on a metal track just beneath the peak of the roof. It worked like this: A full pile of hay was positioned at the side of the barn under the big haymow door. This fork was then impaled in the load and pulled upward by a series of pulleys into the mow, where the fork could be tripped and hay dropped at points to evenly fill the storage area. Power to hoist the load of hay was provided by a team of horses at the end of a rope. One of the older kids was always available to drive the team, but the younger ones had great fun jumping around in the hay, sliding and riding an avalanche as a new forkful was unloaded.

One afternoon in late summer, Earl scampered across the south side of the loft area and suddenly disappeared. He had dropped into the open end of the hay chute and fallen three stories, about twenty-five feet, to the basement floor. Luckily, the metal stanchions were not in his line of descent and a mound of hay covered the concrete floor. When his siblings went down to investigate, they met him coming out of the barn door badly shaken up, but otherwise apparently uninjured. He cried and whimpered for a few minutes, and his mother made him come into the house. After cleaning up and tender words from Inez, he was soon back outside, going full speed again.

Despite rainstorms, blizzards, and below-zero weather, the work had to be done, usually by the light of a kerosene lantern before dawn and after sunset. Saturdays were spent plowing, planting, cultivating or picking corn, haying, fixing fences, clearing out the barn or the henhouse, digging potatoes, or doing numerous other jobs that had to be done.

The Wood family's dress on the farm reflected the way of life during the early 1920s. Handmade clothing was a result of both limited income and a do-it-yourself heritage. Inez Wood made a lot of clothes for the family on an old White sewing machine. The boys' one-piece coveralls—or rompers, as they called them—were produced on this equipment. Underwear was made from empty flour sacks, and the original printing on the flour sacks often remained even after repeated washings. The General Mills Gold Medal Flour slogan, "Eventually ... Why Not Now?" reached across the seat of Earl's shorts in bold letters as long as the garment held together.

When Earl was seven or eight years old, the 20 Acres was modernized with electricity. A single light bulb hung from the ceiling of the kitchen where, at night, Inez did most of the food preparation and bathed the young family. This is where light was needed the most. Earl looked at this modern innovation with amazement. First of all, it was the brightness of the single bulb, which gave out more light than several kerosene lanterns. Even more amazing was that it could be lit instantaneously by the flip of a switch; there was no waiting for the glow of the lantern and no adjusting the wick. In addition, there was no need to clean the lantern chimneys and restock the lanterns with kerosene. Earl stood up on a stool, flipping the switch on and off, watching the light come on and then go dark. It should be noted that later in life Earl would be working with machines that switched electrical currents on and off several thousand times a second!

Fall was the start of school, which was not always looked upon enthusiastically. Fall also meant the beginning of football season. All the Wood children participated in athletics in both high school and college. The Wood brothers experienced a lot of hard knocks on the football field and learned the inevitable lessons associated with team play. In those days, everyone on the team played both offense and defense, unlike today when teams are divided into offense and defense. All players playing both ways meant they gained good conditioning, stamina, and a wider range of skills and expertise. In

1923, Louis Todnem took over the athletics at Mankato High School. He coached all the Wood boys with the exception of Chet, the oldest, who had already graduated. Coach Todnem had many championship teams and coached the Mankato Scarlets until the mid-1960s. Earl was an outstanding tackle on the team. Coach Todnem described him as being a little more reckless and carefree than his older brothers. He was a "slashing kind of player," according to Todnem. At the close of the 1929 football season, Earl was elected captain of the 1930 team. But Earl was perhaps best known as one of the top basketball players. He was also captain of the 1930 basketball team. Athletics taught Earl to be a team player. He often gave credit to his teammates Johnny Hearr and Jerry Sullivan for their team's victories.

In 1922, Will Wood negotiated a real estate deal involving the Belvedere Hotel, a former resort hotel on Linder Bay on Lake Washington, about ten miles from Mankato. This meant dividing the family during the summer months between the Lake Washington property and the farm, since work needed to be done at both locations. This situation proved to be untenable, and they decided to leave the farm and move into town. Early in 1925, Will Wood made a deal for a house on Pleasant Street, next to the streetcar line and only two blocks from Lincoln Junior High School.

LAKE WASHINGTON

In the late 1800s, resort hotels were built on many Minnesota lakes, where people could escape the heat of the cities and enjoy the cool, crisp waters of the lake country while having a place to stay and eat. Many large hotels were constructed on surrounding lakes in the Minneapolis–Saint Paul area,

such as Lake Minnetonka and White Bear Lake. Similar
but smaller hotels were constructed on southern Minnesota
lakes, such as the Belvedere Hotel on Lake Washington.

*The Belvedere Hotel on Lake Washington about 1900, which was
purchased by William C. Wood and became Wood's Hilltop Beach*

Construction on the Belvedere Hotel started in the mid-
1890s. The structure was placed on a limestone rock foundation and built with green timbers to allow for expansion and
contraction with the changing Minnesota weather. Timbers
and framing were nailed together with square nails.

The Belvedere Hotel had three floors. The first floor offered a large parlor where guests could gather for socializ-
ing and meals. The kitchen provided access to a large pantry
and a walk-in refrigerator, which was cooled by ice harvested
from the lake during the previous winter. The first floor also
gave access to a wraparound porch, offering a spectacular
view of Lake Washington. The second floor held eight guest

bedrooms. The third floor was an open space used for putting on dances and for storage. The third floor also gave access to a turret.

Many guests from other parts of the country arrived at the train station in Madison Lake and were transported to the Belvedere by horse and buggy. Some people thought that the Belvedere served as a house of ill repute organized by businessmen as far away as Chicago and St. Louis. A picture of the hotel taken at the turn of the century features mostly women on the porch. We can only speculate!

Chester Wood and his friend Walter Dart operated the place as a summer resort during the summer of 1922. Rooms cost one dollar and meals were fifty cents. Full room and board was $2.50 a day. When the Woods moved off the farm into town, they started a swimming-beach business on the Lake Washington property. Summer in southern Minnesota can be extremely hot and humid. This was in the days before municipal swimming pools. As word got around of the smooth beach and cool water of Lake Washington, more and more people flocked to what became known as Wood's Hilltop Beach. The Wood boys built diving docks, rafts, slides, and rolling barrels and installed floating logs and other fun equipment for patrons to use.

During the summer months, the beach was a small-scale gold mine. Family sentiment grew for improved quarters. Chet, Abe, and Earl built a new bathhouse that had an office and dressing rooms. The finished project included a patio for lounging and eating next to the water's edge.

Patrons paid a dime each at the front office and walked down the center aisle to the women's dressing room on the right or the men's dressing room on the left. The front office not only handled the entry fees but also sold soft drinks, candy, cigars, and, on Sunday, ice cream. They even rented out bathing suits, which would be frowned upon with today's safety standards.

The expanding bathhouse business and the people crowding the grounds during the weekends resulted in an increased demand for fishing and watercraft. Will Wood and the boys bought several used boats and canoes and a motorized launch called the *Miss Marie* from a Madison Lake resort that was going out of business. Launch rides at fifty cents per person became a regular Sunday afternoon feature, with Earl as the pilot and motorman.

The Wood kids at Lake Washington, 1925: Louise, Chet, Earl, Buck, Abe, and Harn

The Fourth of July was the busiest day of the summer for Wood's Hilltop Beach, an all-hands-on-deck day for the Woods. One person was in charge of just directing traffic and parking for patrons coming from Mankato, Saint Peter, and other surrounding towns. Abe and Louise spent the entire day in the bathhouse, selling concessions and taking entry fees. Earl handled boats plus gave tours of the lake on the *Miss Marie*. In 1932, the annual Wood's Beach swim marathon was started. This involved swimming from the narrows, better known as "Connor's Point," on the other side of the lake, then swimming nonstop east, finishing at Wood's Beach. Only two people entered the first Wood's Beach Marathon on July 4, 1932: Earl and an unnamed contestant. Earl won the event in one hour and fifteen minutes. The Wood's Beach Marathon became an annual event for many years, bringing in talented swimmers from all over southern Minnesota.

After the summer of 1947, Wood's Hilltop Beach ceased operating. Will and Inez continued to live there during the summer. Hilltop provided a family gathering spot for the various Wood families, giving them the opportunity to meet relatives from various parts of the country.

After the passing of Inez Wood in 1957 and Will Wood in 1959, ownership of the Lake Washington property passed as equal shares to the six Wood kids and the property was retained as a summer rendezvous site for the siblings and their offspring. For the next several decades, the Woods continued to gather each summer for a few weeks' vacation for a period of fun and relaxation. This "relaxation" would invariably develop into work projects, as the old house needed to be modernized. This ensured that the family work ethic was carried forward to the next generation. All the Wood kids seemed to enjoy the balance of hard labor followed by play on the lake. Thus, the old lake place helped keep the Wood family together into the twenty-first century, influencing all three generations that lived, played, and worked on the Lake Washington property.

Like the 20 Acres, Lake Washington had a major influence on Earl. Running a business such as Wood's Hilltop Beach, plus maintaining an old, very large structure, required a team, which included his parents, siblings, relatives, friends, and employees. To keep a place like this running took hard work, which, done well, would provide the benefits of playtime on the lake. Earl and his siblings worked hard and played hard, a philosophy that they carried on into their adult years and professional careers.

Earl was a versatile athlete in high school, but he was an even better student. With former teachers as parents, all the Woods were encouraged to study hard and get into college. In high school, Earl was not a diligent student but had a natural ability to learn, and his grades showed it with straight As. He was also heavily influenced by his brother Harn to pursue the sciences. He graduated from high school as the valedictorian and earned an academic scholarship to Macalester College.

Earl Wood's graduation picture from Mankato High School, 1930

CHAPTER 3

THE COLLEGE YEARS

Earl graduated from high school in 1930 and followed his brothers and sister, Louise, by enrolling in Macalester College, where he'd been awarded a four-year academic scholarship. He also hoped to participate in athletics. Earl started college with a heavy academic load focused on the sciences, taking biology, mathematics, physics, English, and of course physical education.

Earl signed up for the Macalester football team along with his good friend from Mankato, Jerry "Sully" Sullivan. The football team was captained by Earl's brother Harland Wood. Fairly early in the season, one of the varsity star players was injured in a game against St. Thomas, and Earl was brought in as a substitute. It was unusual for a freshman to play varsity. Both Earl and Jerry earned letters in football their freshman year.

At the end of football season, Earl and Jerry tried out for the Macalester College basketball team. The captain of the basketball team was Denny Peterson of Big Lake, Minnesota, who would eventually be Earl's brother-in-law. Sullivan and

Wood became known as "the Mankato Twins" and took a prominent part in the freshman basketball tournament. Earl played guard, showing his great ability to handle the ball.

Earl's early showing on the football field and basketball court, in addition to his academic achievements, probably helped him win the election as class president, representing the sophomore class of 1932.

During the summer months between school years, much of the Wood boys' time was spent working at Wood's Hilltop Beach on Lake Washington—lifeguarding, renting out boats, and working the concession stands for additional money, which was needed during the Depression. Harn and Earl had a second job delivering ice for the Mankato Ice Company. This involved taking ice packed in a wagon insulated with sawdust to various homes in Mankato. In those days, electric refrigerators were not in common use, and many families had kitchen iceboxes. Harn and Earl would drive a horse-drawn wagon full of ice to a house and walk up to the back door carrying a fifty-pound block of ice. They would either open a hinged door at the side of the house to reach the icebox or carry the block through the home and place it in the icebox in the kitchen. In one house they carried the block of ice into a kitchen, then placed it inside the door of the built-in cooler. However, a moment later, they heard the ice crash into the basement; it appeared that they had put the ice into the laundry chute.

In the fall of 1931, Earl returned to Macalester College for his sophomore year. He again took a heavy academic load, with courses in biology, mathematics, and physics. Football consumed most of his nonacademic time. Unfortunately, neither Earl nor Sully could start in the first game due to injuries incurred during the same practice: Jerry hurt his shoulder and Earl fractured his cheekbone. Apparently, their practices were just as hard-hitting as their games.

Earl was at Macalester College during the height of the Great Depression, when financial resources were tight. To supplement his scholarship income and pay for his housing, he secured a job as assistant fireman in Wallace Hall, the women's dormitory. Earl also took a job as a dishwasher—which he called "pearl diving"—at the Dutch Maid restaurant located near campus. As assistant fireman at Wallace Hall, Earl had his own room in the basement. Every morning in winter he had to get up early and load the furnace with coal to heat the building. He loaded it up high enough that he could go to the Dutch Maid to do his morning dishwashing for the breakfast crowd and then head to classes. He would then check on the furnace at noontime and again in the afternoon, before he went to athletic practice. In the evening, he loaded the coal burner high enough that the heat would last through the cold Minnesota night. This worked well for Earl, since he had his own private room in the basement where he could sleep and study in relative quiet.

While living and working at Wallace Hall, Earl became acquainted with Ada Peterson, who lived there with her roommate and sister, Norma Peterson. Earl and Ada were probably first introduced their freshman year by Ada's brother Denny, who was the captain of the basketball team. Earl and Ada soon started dating and attended many campus events and movies. Their favorite activity was dancing to the big bands that were playing at various ballrooms in the Minneapolis–Saint Paul area in the 1930s. They were fortunate enough to listen and dance to live big band music from Jimmy and Tommy Dorsey, Glenn Miller, Artie Shaw, and Duke Ellington. The couple was the hit of the dance floor. One of Earl's most distinctive dance moves was called "the Mankato Pump," and Earl and Ada gladly demonstrated it at the many parties they attended, way into their seventies and eighties.

Back at Macalester in the fall of 1932, Earl took courses in biology, chemistry, mathematics, geology, German, and religion. Ada continued in the liberal arts track, taking English expression, German, philosophy, and sociology. Earl continued his football career. His coach, Al Gowans, in an article in the *Mac Weekly* of October 8, 1932, said, "Earl Wood probably puts in more football in one hour than any man on the field. Dependability is his chief asset. Earl will probably be at right end on offense and at halfback position on defense." Coach Gowans's strategy paid off. In a game against Augsburg, the defensive line Earl led was responsible for Augsburg's failure to make a single touchdown. At the annual end-of-the-year dinner for the football team, Earl was picked to be captain of the 1933 team.

One evening, Earl and a friend had taken two girls to a movie. As they were walking back toward Macalester on Snelling Avenue, three rough-looking individuals came out from a pool hall entrance and fell in behind them, making insulting remarks and kicking snow at their shoes. Finally, the three characters swung around in front of the group, blocking the sidewalk. The leader said, in effect, "You two punk college sissies go on home, we'll take care of the girls." It was apparent to the college boys that a fight was inevitable. Earl stared the lead mugger in the eye and landed a roundhouse punch square in the jaw. The tough one collapsed like a fallen tree. With their leader flat on the snow, his two companions found the one-on-one odds not to their liking, suddenly lost their courage, and took to their heels. The two Macalester boys and their dates went on, stopping to look back at the end of the block. The two runaways were bent over their fallen mugger leader, who was still flat on his back on the snow-covered sidewalk. Earl always remembered his older brother Chet and his dad saying, "Don't start a fight and avoid it if you can, but if you see that a fight is inevitable, get in the first punch and be sure to make it a good one."

Earl's senior year included courses in biology, chemistry, German, physics, religion, and physical education, and in all of them he earned As. At the same time, Ada was taking courses in political science, education, and English, and continuing classes in expression and sociology.

Earl became a member of the Pi Phi Epsilon honorary society, which required members to be formally elected and initiated by college faculty. Many members of the Macalester science faculty had hopes that Earl would become a physicist or an engineer. However, one warm summer evening in 1933, after a particularly busy day at Wood's Hilltop Beach, Abe and Earl were sitting on the dock overlooking the sunset on Lake Washington, discussing their futures. Abe expressed his interest in going into medicine. It was this conversation that inspired Earl to enroll in medical school at the University of Minnesota following his graduation from Macalester in 1934. Who knows what Abe said in that conversation, but somehow, by the end of it, Earl had decided to change his major and apply to medical school. Abe applied and got into medical school two years later.

During fall 1933, the medical aptitude exam was scheduled. This test was administered by the Association of American Medical Colleges and was to be given in December. This examination was one of many requirements for admission to medical school. It is interesting to note it was not necessary that all premedical requirements be completed at the time of the test, as long as they were completed by the beginning of medical school in fall 1934. The test took approximately an hour and a half, and a fee of one dollar was required.

Earl and Ada graduated from Macalester in June 1934, with Earl graduating summa cum laude.

CHAPTER 4

MEDICAL AND
GRADUATE SCHOOL

Earl enrolled at the University of Minnesota in the fall of 1934, after a summer of working at Lake Washington and preparing to move into new living quarters for the long haul of medical school. Initially Earl moved in with his brother Abe in his dorm room at Macalester College. After a couple of weeks of living at Macalester and commuting to the University of Minnesota, he moved to an apartment on Grand Avenue in Saint Paul. It was part of a local funeral home. To reduce the monthly rent, he agreed to assist the mortician with embalming and preparing bodies for burial. The basement was full of empty coffins, and in a separate room were the embalming fluids. This obviously was a dead-quiet place where Earl could get a lot of studying done. He commuted daily to the University of Minnesota by hitchhiking, which was common in those days, or by taking the streetcar toward the Franklin Avenue Bridge and then walking the rest of the way to the university.

Ada, who had graduated from Macalester with a degree in social work, took a job in Winona, Minnesota, working in the emergency relief administration, specifically child protection. Her social work dealt with pregnant single women and their offspring and how best to care for both mother and child through either single parenthood or adoption.

Sometime during the spring or summer of 1934, Earl and Ada became engaged. There was no formal announcement—nor was there any engagement ring, due to a lack of funds. The young couple decided to wait several years to get married, since Ada had many bills from college that she had to pay and Earl was busy studying during his first two years of medical school.

While Earl was studying in Minneapolis and Ada was working and living in Winona, they wrote to each other almost daily. At that time, long-distance phone calls were expensive and not everyone had a telephone. Many letters from Winona were sent special delivery, which meant that if they were mailed in the morning and the mailman was able to get the letter on the noon train to Minneapolis, it would be delivered to Earl's address that afternoon.

Visits were limited to weekends. Most of the time, Ada would take the train from Winona to Saint Paul on a Saturday afternoon, since they both had to work on Saturday mornings. She would meet Earl either at the station or the lobby of the Lowry Hotel. Once Earl and Ada met, they would take the streetcar to whatever destination they were going to, whether it was a movie, a dance, or someone's house.

On one visit to Saint Paul, Ada and several of her friends visited Earl at his apartment above the funeral home. Just for fun, Earl gave them a tour of the establishment. There were no dead bodies there at the time; however, there were several open coffins. One of the gals decided to find out what it was like to be in a coffin, so she climbed in and they shut the lid! As it turned out, the poor girl was quite claustrophobic and jumped out screaming and hollering in fright. Earl and Ada laughed about that incident for years and enjoyed telling that story to their children.

To reduce commuting time, Earl eventually moved to Pioneer Hall on the University of Minnesota campus.

To get back and forth between Winona and Minneapolis–Saint Paul, and also up to Big Lake and Mankato, Earl and Ada talked about buying a car. Due to the depressed economy of the 1930s, this was a financial challenge, especially as Earl was in school and also paying tuition. But Earl did his research and bought a vehicle. He describes the car in a love letter to Ada:

> Ada Peterson
> 223 West Sanborn St.
> Winona, MN
> May 5, 1935, a Sunday at 12 am
>
> My Dearest Ada,
>
> Well "Potato" we're in it now![2] I bought the car this morning. $25.00! A 1926 Model T coupe. Think I got a pretty good buy. All the windows are in, except the one on the driver side. The upholstery is in good condition for a car that old. It has a new license and five tires which are only fair. Has a starter that works but the battery is a little low. The battery looks good however and the generator is

---

2.   One of Earl's endearments for Ada was "Ada Potato" or "Ada Patata."

working good. The motor runs good. It has a heater in it and good floorboards so that if it works okay we could run it next winter if it would start and be fairly comfortable if we had a window put in. The roof needs a little patching but will hold out most of the water! I won't have any time to fix it up now but this summer should have her in tip top shape.

Anyway, we won't be riding the streetcar next weekend! I hope not!! I plan on just leaving it sit until you come up.

I had to borrow $11 to pay for it. I couldn't scrape it up myself. I put in 5 gallons of gas and filled it with oil. Borrowed it from EJ and Don Wright. Hope you've got that much dough as I should pay them within a week. I guess they can wait till you come up though I get paid about five dollars Tuesday so that will help out.

Got a lot of studying done last night. Al came over here and we had a picnic of buns and had a glass of beer. We studied until 11:45, really got a lot done. Going to try to go to town again this afternoon. Should get my regular amount of sleep. I couldn't get my regular amount of sleep last night and don't feel any too ambitious.

Boy! It has been a beautiful morning, only hope it's this way next weekend. Buck was over to see me yesterday afternoon. He certainly thought I was crazy when I told him we were going to buy a car.

Can't wait till next weekend darling. We'll

go on a picnic on Saturday night and maybe
again Sunday afternoon if it's nice. Gosh,
won't [it] be great to have our own car so we
can go where we want to?! Time to go eat.

All My Love,
Earl

According to a letter written in June 1935, Ada wanted
to name the car "Ours," since they had both contributed cash
to purchase it. Earl had driven the car over to Wallace Hall at
Macalester College to visit his brother Abe, and everybody
was laughing at how frequently Earl was getting flat tires on
Ours. Ada eventually sent him some money to get the tires
patched. Note that the tires were not to be replaced; they
didn't have enough cash for new tires.

In letters between Earl and Ada, there was no question
that Earl was quite worried about his upcoming written and
practical exams in the spring of 1935. He was very afraid of
getting a D and failing medical school. In those days, the
freshman class in medical schools was relatively large. The se-
lection process and weeding out of students was done strictly
on grades, unlike the medical schools of today, which invest
so much financially in recruiting good students that they do
their best to maintain their student body.

On one very memorable date, Earl and Ada drove Ours to
a park overlooking the Mississippi River for a picnic. While
setting up the picnic and bringing out the food, Earl noticed
out of the corner of his eye Ours rolling through the grass. He
had forgotten to set the parking brake! Unable to catch the car
and stop it, despite his athletic speed and agility, Earl watched
as Ours rolled over the cliff and met an untimely death below
the bluffs of the Mississippi. It was a long walk to the trolley
stop and ride back to Earl's room in Pioneer Hall. Ada took

the train back to Winona, and Earl went back to studying and looking for another car.

They eventually purchased a 1925 Model T Ford for $17.50. This car was appropriately named "17.50." This old Model T coupe had cracked windows and holes in the floorboards; however, it ran and started on cold Minnesota mornings. One of the memories they have of driving the Model T on the streets of Minneapolis is getting the narrow wheels stuck in the trolley tracks and having a difficult time steering the car out of the tracks before the trolley came.

The summer of 1935 Earl spent at Hilltop working at the beach business, doing some odd jobs in the Mankato area, and studying up for the fall courses in medical school. Meanwhile, Ada stayed in Winona and they continued their frequent visits in Winona, the Twin Cities, and Hilltop.

During the fall of 1935, Earl was again taking courses in anatomy, physiology, and clinical medicine at the University of Minnesota. By the spring semester of 1936, Earl had become an assistant instructor in physiology, earning seventy-five dollars for the academic term.

In early 1936, Ada applied for and got a job in child protection in Hennepin County, working at the courthouse in downtown Minneapolis. Now that Ada was living and working in Minneapolis, the young couple saw more of each other. Both were very busy with work and school and saving money to pay off loans and making wedding plans. On weekends, Earl would pick Ada up in 17.50 for picnics along the Mississippi River and occasionally to go dancing with friends at the Marigold Ballroom.

The summer of 1936 was embedded in the memories of Earl and Ada; they frequently told stories to their offspring about this unique time. That summer was the height of the Dust Bowl and was extremely hot and humid. This made business for Wood's Hilltop Beach very good. However, in the Twin Cities, where people could not escape the heat, entire families were sleeping on cots outside to escape the stifling heat inside their homes. Occasionally the skies would turn a brownish black, blotting out the sun, due to the rising dust storms as far away as Kansas, Colorado, Nebraska, and the Dakotas. Many cars were covered with a thin layer of dust. Dust would also stick to people's skin and faces as they sweated in the stifling heat, and it would seep through the thinnest cracks in the windows, leaving grit and dirt on furniture and clothing.

In March, Earl was approached by his physiology professor, Dr. Maurice (Morris) Visscher, who inquired if he would be willing to enroll in the new MD/PhD program available through the physiology department at the University of Minnesota Medical School. This meant that after taking his basic medical school requirements the first two years, he would delay his medical degree and pursue a PhD in physiology, completing his MD afterward. This decision required a great deal of thought and discussion with Ada, since it would prolong his academic studies and be a continued financial burden on both of them. After long discussions and deliberations, Earl dropped out of medical school and enrolled in the PhD program in the physiology department.

In the fall of 1936, Earl started working on his master's in physiology, taking courses in physiological research and physical chemistry. Because he was pursuing a PhD, he took beginning French as his language requirement. With Ada now so close and the young couple seeing so much of each other, wedding plans were made for the end of the fall semester and a date was set.

Earl and Ada's wedding took place on Sunday, December 20, 1936, at the home of William C. Wood in Mankato. The ceremony took place in the living room, which was decorated with a Christmas tree and ornaments. Rev. Robert E. Dorn performed the ceremony at 1:00 p.m., with relatives and friends observing and participating in the ceremony. Ada wore a lace-trimmed gown with mulberry crepe and a corsage of Talisman roses. Her bridesmaids included her sisters Virginia Hegg, of Minneapolis, and Norma Krampitz, of Lake Crystal. Delbert Wood was Earl's best man.

Earl and Ada spent their wedding night in Minneapolis and the next day drove 17.50 up to Big Lake to visit her parents, August and Hilda Peterson. They then moved into their new apartment at 502 Fifteenth Avenue SE, in Minneapolis.

The hot summer of '36 was followed by an extremely cold winter. The Twin Cities had thirty-six consecutive nights of below-zero temperatures. Earl and Ada often told how they had to get the car started on those very cold Minnesota mornings. Earl would set the choke and the throttle and have Ada step on the starter while he went outside and used the hand crank simultaneously to turn over the engine. With this team approach, the car would start and they would be off to work or school. The only heat in the car was the warm air coming off the cast-iron block of 17.50's engine and the close body heat in the confined space of a Model T coupe.

Winter and spring terms of 1937, Earl enrolled in physiology and physical chemistry classes and took another course in beginning French. His academic advisor, Dr. Morris Visscher, also encouraged him to take classes in research and statistics. By June 1937, Earl had already become adjunct faculty in the physiology department. It is at this time that he met his good friends and future colleagues Dean Collins and Gordon Moe. These three enterprising young scientists assisted each other in their scientific experiments, research data analysis, and writing of scientific papers throughout their academic careers at the University of Minnesota.

While Earl was in medical and graduate school with little or no income, Ada was the breadwinner of the family with her social work job at Hennepin County, earning an excellent wage for the day. Dr. Visscher often said, "With that kind of salary, she will never quit her job." In the summer of 1937, they moved to a small, drafty upstairs apartment on Ontario Street, which was a short walk to the university and a street-car ride to downtown Minneapolis.

Ada did not like driving 17.50 in the city due to the traffic and getting the wheels stuck in the streetcar tracks. Eventually she earned enough money to purchase a used 1936 Ford sedan with a powerful flathead V-8 engine. With no cracked windows or holes in the floorboards, the young couple thought they were riding in luxury! The '36 Ford took them on many trips to Big Lake, Hilltop, and several physiology meetings on the East Coast and down South.

In the fall of 1937, Earl continued his rigorous academic coursework in physiology research, in addition to taking courses in clinical pediatrics and clinical chemistry. Winter and spring terms of 1938, he took courses in internal medicine, psychiatry, and pathology. At the same time, he was busy in the laboratory working toward his master's thesis. By the end of that school year, Earl Wood and Dean Collins published a paper in the *American Journal of Physiology* entitled "Experimental Renal Hypertension and Adrenalectomy." Another publication, written with Gordon Moe, appeared in the *Proceedings of the American Physiological Society* entitled "Studies of the Effect of Digitalis Glucosides on Potassium Loss from the Heart-lung Preparation."

One of the benefits of publishing a scientific paper was presenting the results at a national scientific conference or symposium in a city where these young scientists had never been before. Earl and Ada, along with their good friends Janet and Dr. Gordon "Gordy" Moe, would load up the 1936 Ford sedan and head to locations like New Orleans, Boston, or New York City. These were the days before the Interstate Highway System, and they saw many new and unusual sights on the back roads of 1930s America. On many occasions, the trip was interrupted by a flat tire or an overheating engine. Earl had a tendency to drive faster than the speed limit, which he became noted for later in life.

At each location where the young couples ate or spent the night, they made a point of testing the local beer. After they tasted and enjoyed a bottle or a glass of brew, they would remove the label and rate the beer by taste and quality. Since they were scientists, this was done in a very precise manner, and each beer was cataloged by the state and town in which they consumed the libation and the date on which they consumed it. Most of these breweries have long since gone out of business or been taken over by the large corporate breweries of the twenty-first century. Some of the labels they cataloged are Rock River Brewing Company, from Rockford, Illinois; Polar Pilsner, from Davenport, Iowa; Billings Pale Beer, from Minneapolis, Minnesota; and Old Gross Half and Half, from Cleveland, Ohio. From 1937 through 1941, Earl and Gordy tested and cataloged more than six hundred different beers. One has to wonder if the goal of the trips was to present scientific papers at national conferences or to research beer quality and taste.

Earl finished his master's degree in physiology, defending his master's thesis, entitled "Electrolyte and Water Exchanges Between the Mammalian Muscle and Blood in Relation to Activity." Unlike thesis preparation today, with computerized word processing and computer graphics, this thesis was hand-typed in triplicate and charts and graphs were inserted into the pages with cellophane tape. A great deal of work had to be done not only in the data collection and analysis but also for the presentation of the thesis in a bound book.

At this time, both Earl and Gordon Moe were teaching assistants and instructors working with Dr. Charles F. Code, an assistant professor of physiology. Dr. Code was born in Winnipeg, Manitoba, in 1910. Charlie contracted scarlet fever when he was eight years old and then came down with polio at the age of twelve and was told that he would never walk again. This prediction turned out to be totally wrong, but he did have to wear back and leg braces. Although his first contact with a doctor wasn't until he was treated for polio as a boy, he went on to receive his bachelor's and medical degrees from the University of Manitoba. He decided to turn to research because he was concerned that he would not be mobile enough to treat patients. He completed his PhD in physiology at the University of Minnesota, then continued his training in physiology in London. By the time Earl was working on his PhD, Charlie had already joined Mayo Clinic as a research fellow.

By the spring of 1939, Earl had finished his preliminary coursework in physiology, passed his preliminary examination, and started his laboratory research for his PhD dissertation. His interest and research were focused on the effects of different concentrations of digitalis on the contractility of the myocardium (the heart muscle). Digitalis, an extract of the foxglove plant, was one of the most commonly used medications for treating cardiac disease. It contains cardiac glycosides, whose use for the treatment of heart conditions was first described in the medical literature as far back as 1785 and is considered the beginning of modern therapeutics. Digitalis was used in the control of heart rate and cardiac arrhythmias, particularly atrial fibrillation, and was also used to treat congestive heart failure. Earl's studies revolved around evaluating the concentrations of various electrolytes—such as potassium, sodium, and calcium—as related to cardiac function with various dosages of digitalis. Earl's studies were conducted on dogs, using an isolated heart-lung preparation to study the effects of heart function. Eventually his studies were conducted clinically on patients at the University of Minnesota hospitals.

After struggling for about three years financially and academically to complete a rather massive PhD dissertation, with helpful advice from Charlie Code, Gordy Moe, and Dean Collins and with Ada's typing skills, Earl had almost completed his manuscript, which was ready to be reviewed by his academic advisor, Morris Visscher. Earl knocked on Visscher's door and handed him the large dissertation, which represented a great expenditure of blood, sweat, and tears. He expected Visscher to read it carefully, then criticize and edit the manuscript. Visscher took the manuscript and thumbed through the pages for a minute or two. To Earl's dismay, Visscher handed it back to him and said, "Earl, this looks fine. I'm sure it's OK." Earl was crestfallen since he'd expected the university professor and scientist to review the manuscript very carefully. Disappointed, Earl took the manuscript to Charlie Code, who reviewed it in great detail to prepare it for binding and eventual publication. He also prepared Earl to defend the dissertation for his PhD committee.

Earl completed his research and writing of his dissertation by the end of 1940. The title of his dissertation was "The Distribution of Electrolytes and Water Between Cardiac Muscle and Blood Serum with Initial Reference to the Effects of Digitalis." Unlike his master's thesis, the graphs and charts were professionally done and properly glued into the document. Great care was taken with many editing passes, which were all done on a manual typewriter. Collaboration in his studies included works with Dr. Charlie Code, Dr. Gordon Moe, and Dean Collins. Although the studies and writing were completed months earlier, the final dissertation was not published and placed in the University of Minnesota library until June 1941.

CHAPTER 5

ON THE MOVE: PHILADELPHIA TO MINNEAPOLIS TO BOSTON TO ROCHESTER

With the completion of Earl's PhD dissertation, it was decided that he needed to get experience in another physiology laboratory. Through a fellowship grant, Earl secured a research position at the University of Pennsylvania in Philadelphia, studying under Dr. A. N. Richards.

At the University of Pennsylvania, Earl was studying the relationship between blood sugar level and sugar absorption in the kidney. He wanted to determine if the kidney has a maximum capacity for absorbing glucose, and if it would decrease or even stop once the glucose level was above a particular threshold. This involved a rather tricky and delicate experimental procedure, since he had to enter the lumen (entry point) at the proximal nephron of a frog kidney with a known concentration of glucose and then measure the concentration of glucose on the distal end of the nephron, therefore calculating the absorption of glucose. The pipettes he was using to perfuse the nephrons of the kidney had a tendency to clog due to their small size, leading to some frustration in the data collection. The results indicated that the tubules of the kidney absorb glucose at a constant rate.

Earl and Ada enjoyed their time in Philadelphia. They spent their weekends seeing parts of the country that were unlike Minnesota, such as the Skyline Drive in Virginia. Both Earl and Ada commented that the winters in Pennsylvania were mild compared to what they'd experienced in Minnesota.

With Earl's dissertation completed at the end of 1940, Dr. Visscher offered him a position in neurophysiology back at the University of Minnesota. This quick offer was somewhat of a surprise to Earl, since he had only recently started his studies at the University of Pennsylvania. In a letter written to Dr. Visscher on January 21, 1941, Earl contemplated his future options. He did welcome the opportunity to set up a laboratory and work with ample funds; however, he expressed concern that he knew less than he should about neurophysiology. He also reflected that he would prefer to have an internship in physiology at Minnesota, since he had a warm spot in his heart for his home state, but that he could see the advantage of gaining more experience at other institutions.

There was also the possibility of a position materializing at Harvard University in the pharmacology department, working with **Dr. Otto Krayer**. If that position materialized, Earl would be very tempted to accept it. There was still work to be done on the digitalis research concerning potassium and calcium concentrations—research that he enjoyed working on. Earl also wanted a chance to spend time at Mayo Clinic in Rochester, Minnesota, to gain experience in experimental surgery. Another complicating factor in early 1941 was the completion of his MD degree, which would be easier if he were in Minnesota.

The plans that he discussed in his letter to Dr. Visscher were all good, but there was the issue of what was happening overseas in Europe due to Adolf Hitler and rising conflicts in the Pacific. At that time, Earl's Selective Service number was 294, and he had been placed in Class I, which made him available for immediate service.

Earl discussed these options with his supervisor, Dr. Richards. It was his opinion that Earl should terminate his fellowship at the University of Pennsylvania and return to Minnesota and complete his medical degree, which would delay his induction into the armed services, and that he should instead go into the medical corps.

In a January 1941 letter to Earl, Dr. Visscher wrote,

> I have your letter written yesterday and I hasten to make a few comments. One, have you passed the medical examination for the draft? Ansell [sic] Keys [director of the University of Minnesota Laboratory of Physiological Hygiene who developed the K-rations for the armed services] has told me you have a moderate elevation of systolic blood pressure. This might bar you from service, and if I were you, I should look into it. If you are going to have to spend a year in the Army you should by all means volunteer for some special services in the Medical Corps. I think you should find a way of being assigned to the chemical warfare services or some similar section where you could do physiological

investigation. I might be of some assistance to you in getting such a commission. If it appeals to you, I shall look into it immediately. It would be perfectly futile for you to shoulder a machine gun if you could be doing work of the scientific nature that would be of practical value.

On February 15, 1941, Earl sent a letter to his local draft board asking to have his classification changed to Class III. On February 21, the draft board informed him his appeal had been granted, and he was placed in Class III, which was an indefinite deferment because of dependence. On February 26, Earl received an offer of an internship from Dr. Krayer at Harvard University to begin in September 1941 at a salary of $2,400. On that same day, a letter from Dr. Charlie Code arrived in which he urged Earl to accept a fellowship at Mayo Clinic in Rochester that same year. By this time, Dr. Code had been appointed professor of physiology at Mayo Clinic and chairman of the department of physiology and biophysics.

Earl did send a letter to Charlie Code, stipulating that he would like to go to Rochester in January 1942 if his discussions with Dr. Krayer concerning the start of his internship didn't work out. On March 7, Earl received a letter from Dr. Krayer at Harvard saying the position would be available in January 1942. That same day, a telegram arrived from Charlie indicating that he would do all in his power to entice Earl to come to Rochester. Earl told Dr. Visscher that he was going to accept Dr. Krayer's offer and that he felt that the opportunity to go to Rochester would be available to him in the future, when conditions would be more advantageous.

Earl's plan to return to medical school for six months was

going to place a financial burden on the young couple. Ada would have to secure her old job to make ends meet. They were convinced that this plan of action was the best for them and the easiest one in the long run. In March, Ada wrote her old boss at child protection services in Minneapolis, regarding a position. She immediately got a reply and was offered the job on April 1. They quickly packed their bags and headed back to Minnesota. At last, they arrived in Mankato on April 13, and Ada drove to Minneapolis to start her job a few days later on April 15. Earl then hopped on the train back to Philadelphia. The young couple was going to be living apart for several weeks while Earl finished his fellowship at the University of Pennsylvania.

Earl resigned from his fellowship at the University of Pennsylvania on June 15, 1941. He immediately started his clerkship through the University of Minnesota to complete his MD degree. He worked at the Swedish Hospital and other University of Minnesota hospitals in general medicine, pathology, pediatrics, radiology, surgery, ophthalmology, and public health. These were long, intense hours, including working the night shift and weekends and also being on call. Meanwhile, Ada worked at child protection in Hennepin County to keep them afloat financially. It was exhausting. By December 1941, Earl had completed all of his requirements for his medical degree.

During the first weekend of December 1941, Earl and Ada were in Big Lake visiting Ada's parents, August and Hilda Peterson. It was to be a relaxing weekend, allowing both Earl and Ada to get away from their busy work life in the city. As they were sitting down to eat a leisurely lunch, the regular programming on the radio was suddenly interrupted with the announcement that the Japanese had bombed Pearl Harbor in Hawaii. This came as a frightening shock to the family and to the entire nation. Earl thought he might be needed back at the hospital in case there were attacks in the Twin Cities area. Earl and Ada returned to Minneapolis on back roads, with the lights on low and the door slightly ajar as Ada watched the skies for incoming aircraft. When they arrived back in Minneapolis, there were no streetlights and people were covering their windows with sheets to reduce any kind of lighting that could be used to guide incoming bombers.

Overnight, life changed in the United States, affecting citizens from all walks of life. In a land of abundant resources, there was suddenly rationing of everyday products, such as gasoline, tires, and food. Each citizen was given a book of ration coupons that allowed them so much food per week. Production and raw materials were earmarked specifically for the war effort. Entire industries changed and retooled to manufacture war matériel. For example, Ford Motor Company converted one of their automobile manufacturing plants for producing B-24 bombers. Willys-Overland stopped the production of their iconic coupe to produce the Jeep. Even medical research was gearing up for the war effort. At the University of Minnesota, Dr. Ancel Keys was studying the caloric needs of soldiers in the field to maintain proper nutrition and hydration. The results of this research were K rations, which every soldier took into the field during military maneuvers and battles. Meanwhile at Mayo Clinic, research had already been initiated in aviation medicine.

Citizens from all walks of life were enlisting in military service in an effort to halt the spread of dictatorships and fascism into the free world. Earl felt the need to defend his country and decided to enlist in the Army Air Forces because he had a great interest in flying. During his physical, however, his doctors determined that he was over the weight limit to be a pilot, and he was turned down for flying in the Army Air Forces. Because of his education and medical background, he was deemed essential personnel and therefore could not serve in the fighting services. Initially, Earl felt rejected; however, in retrospect he often stated this was likely a good thing because he probably would've been shot down over the skies of Europe or in the Pacific.

Now that Earl was earning income with his new position at Harvard University, and with a little bit of money in the bank, Earl and Ada finally traded in the 1936 Ford sedan, which had many miles on it and wonderful memories, for a relatively new 1940 Ford De Luxe coupe. This Ford had a larger, more powerful V-8 engine and a new innovation: the gearshift was on the steering column instead of the floor.

Earl and Ada spent the Christmas holidays of 1941 packing and shipping items for the move to Boston and Harvard University. With the 1940 Ford coupe loaded with luggage and scientific papers that Earl needed for his work at Harvard, they left Mankato just after New Year's. The roads were snow packed and slippery. They stopped to take pictures of the massive snowdrifts along the way.

While driving on Highway 30 near East Liverpool, Ohio, about forty miles west of Pittsburgh, a Buick lost control on the slippery road after passing another car on a hill and skidded crossways into oncoming traffic, smashing head-on into Earl and Ada's car. Ada's right arm was broken in the wreck, and Earl had several fractured ribs from colliding with the steering wheel of the Ford coupe. Earl took note that the driver of the Buick was intoxicated—he could smell liquor on his breath. To Earl's disgust and anger, after he pled to the traffic officer on the scene, his mention of the intoxicated driver was totally ignored. The Ford coupe was so extensively damaged that they had to leave it in East Liverpool for major repairs. Earl and Ada hired a taxi to get to Pittsburgh, where they proceeded by plane to Boston. Ada was admitted to the hospital in Boston for treatment of the fracture.

Ada had surgery on her arm on January 16, 1942. It was a more than three-hour procedure using ether as an anesthesia. Five steel screws and a silver band were used to secure loose bone fragments on the right humerus. Following the procedure, she had ulnar nerve paralysis and numbness in the right hand. The ulnar nerve had been exposed in the operative field during the surgery, but according to the surgeon, the nerve did not sustain visible damage and it was hoped that Ada would regain full function. However, she was quite sick and endured considerable suffering due to ulnar neuritis, or nerve pain.

Earl's work in Boston got off to a slow start due to Ada being in the hospital and because many of the scientific papers and references Earl needed at Harvard had been left in the trunk of the Ford coupe back in East Liverpool, Ohio. Nonetheless, Earl started preliminary experiments investigating the effect of calcium and potassium metabolism on the heart and lungs. By March, with the help of Dr. Krayer, he had performed several heart-lung perfusion experiments. One of Earl's papers regarding potassium analysis written from his dissertation was accepted for publication in the *Journal of Laboratory and Clinical Medicine*, which was a bright spot in this time of change and stress. Earl was also very happy with the lab setup at Harvard.

Dr. Otto Krayer, the head of pharmacology at Harvard University, was very influential in Earl's career and life. He was the former managing director of the Institute of Pharmacology and Toxicology at the University of Berlin. Dr. Krayer left Germany after the Nazis took over and worked in the department of pharmacology at University College of London and then at the American University in Beirut. He came to Harvard in 1934.

Meanwhile, while Earl worked in Boston and Ada recovered, their car remained in East Liverpool, Ohio, for months before Earl returned to the town and garage to pick up the scientific papers he needed for work. To his amazement and anger, no work had been started on the damaged vehicle. This was very distressing to the young midwestern scientist with a strong work ethic. Therefore, he went to work on the vehicle himself! After patching the radiator and replacing a tie rod, he wired the hood back on the car to get it running and road ready to drive back to Boston. In Boston he left the car at another shop, where the car was repaired almost as good as new by March at the cost of $400.

By the end of March 1942, the cast on Ada's arm was finally removed. Unfortunately, a couple weeks later several bone chips and nonunion of the fracture were discovered on X-ray. Therefore, the cast had to go back on for another three to four weeks, much to the dismay of the young couple. Adding to this medical complication and restriction of motion, along with the change in environment and job, Ada discovered that she was pregnant. Years later Earl often joked that Ada hadn't been able to defend herself due to her broken arm!

At the same time, Earl continued to receive offers from Mayo Clinic to join their physiology staff on a fellowship. This, of course, left Earl in a period of indecision, since he liked working in the lab and with Dr. Krayer at Harvard. Yet he had a strong love for Minnesota and the Midwest, and the opportunity to work in physiological research at a place so close to home and family was quite attractive. He wrote several letters to colleagues and Dr. Visscher requesting their thoughts on the decision. In a letter to Earl dated May 19, 1942, Dr. Visscher wrote,

> With the regard to your return to Minnesota, it seems to me that you would undoubtedly have excellent scientific opportunities in Rochester. But I am not quite sure about the question of your relation to the Army or Navy in such a situation. I would look very carefully into this problem before moving. . . . As long as you do not have a [medical] internship, you are probably not eligible for research or routine medical work and therefore your 3A classification will probably hold. However, I think this is the only basis on which you can expect to be allowed to carry on research if you go to Rochester. . . . Needless to say, I would be very happy to see you closer to Minneapolis and incidentally a permanent part of the department [at the University of Minnesota].

Earl was still undecided on what to do with his future career in physiology. In a letter to Dr. Charlie Code at Mayo Clinic dated May 13, 1942, Earl wrote,

> At present there are two possibilities for next year which appeared to me to be worthy of consideration. First, to remain here at Harvard and, second, to go to Rochester on a fellowship such [as] you have described to me. Under ordinary circumstances it would undoubtedly be the best for me to remain here, since I am well satisfied with my set

up and believe that Dr. Krayer is certainly
interested in my future. However, it seems
probable that the possibilities of my securing a desirable fellowship abroad or even in
this country will soon be practically nonexistent. Furthermore, in general the budgets for
academic institutions will be progressively
reduced, the teaching load increased, and
consequent research time and assistance cor-
respondingly diminished.

With these thoughts in mind, it appears
to me that a move to Rochester on my part,
if possible, carries every bit as much potential possibility as has been my meeting
here. As soon as the move to Rochester was
made, I would be out of my essential classification, which I have at my present position.
Consequently, after serving in a fellowship
capacity for any mutually agreeable time, I
would be free to apply for a commission in
aviation medicine with the purpose in mind
of entering into or continuing more research
at Rochester or some other active center.

Since it appears to me that the possibilities
for my future are about equal between Harvard
and Rochester, the question of financial remu-
neration becomes the deciding factor. [From]
past conversations I understand that I would
expect a salary of $3,000 a year as a fellow at
Rochester. From experiences with comparative
living expenses between Minnesota and the
East I know that $3,000 in Rochester is equiv-
alent to about $3,600 in Boston. Dr. Krayer has

informed me that due to limitations in pharmacology budget he cannot definitely promise that my salary after September 1 at the end of this appointment will be increased above its present level of $2,400 a year.

I have decided that if the Rochester Fellowship will be available to me at $3,000 a year, I shall grasp the opportunity unless Harvard is willing to pay me $3,600 a year during the tenure of my appointment.

I intensely dislike placing financial considerations in such an important role, but cannot help but feel that I owe a decent place to live along with the relative freedom from financial insufficiency to my wife and prospective family. This debt has been set aside long enough in the cause of my future career. It is about time that my future career pays a few dividends.

Earl turned down the offer at Mayo Clinic. However, one evening Earl and Ada went out to the movies for an evening of relaxation. The movie that they saw was *Dive Bomber*, starring Errol Flynn and Fred MacMurray. It depicted the difficulties pilots were having with the advancement of aircraft flying at higher speeds and higher altitudes. It recognized the difficult problems of aviation medicine as pilots in various maneuvers or altitudes would pass out and crash. This movie also depicted experiments with a pneumatic belt that would keep blood above heart level in an attempt to prevent a pilot from blacking out. Recognizing the physiological challenges of high-altitude flight and prevention of blackout depicted in this movie, and the potential to contribute to the war effort, Earl changed his mind and went in to talk to Dr. Krayer the next day. Dr. Krayer responded, "Earl, if you feel so strongly about this, then you must go." It is interesting to note that this movie influenced another key player in the development of aviation research during World War II: David (Dave) Clark, who was not a scientist but owned a weaving company in Worcester, Massachusetts, noted for the manufacture of women's undergarments. Another coincidence about the movie *Dive Bomber* is that it featured the Douglas Dauntless dive bomber, the same aircraft later used over the skies of Rochester and southern Minnesota to test the G-suit and related scientific experiments.

In the summer of 1942, Earl and Ada once again packed up the Ford coupe and headed west to the prairies of Minnesota. On arriving in Rochester, they rented a small house on Ninth Avenue SW. On November 2, 1942, their daughter, Phoebe, was born.

Ada, Phoebe, and Earl, 1943

CHAPTER 6

THE BIOLOGICAL
CHALLENGES OF FLIGHT

Airplane technology advanced considerably from the time the Wright brothers flew their airplane at Kitty Hawk to the biplanes of World War I. By the late 1920s and into the 1930s, airplanes were flying at higher speeds and higher altitudes. In the 1930s, it was clear that aviation had advanced to the point of exceeding the physiological capabilities of airplane pilots and their crews. A DC-3, which was unpressurized, could fly as high as twenty-three thousand feet. Military aircraft such as the B-17, also unpressurized, could fly up to thirty-five thousand feet and even higher. Although airplanes and aviation technology had made many advances in this short time between the wars, human anatomy and physiology did not change. The human body was now being subjected to changes in pressure, the amount of oxygen taken in by the body, excessive noise, and the forces of gravity. Therefore, we need to review the biological challenges of modern-day flight to understand how and why Earl Wood became involved with aviation physiology.

First, we need to take a look at the air around us. Without it, we cannot live and airplanes cannot fly. The air at sea level consists of 21 percent oxygen, 78 percent nitrogen, about 1 percent of other gases and some water vapor. The oxygen in air is necessary for combustion of any fuel, whether it is gasoline, coal, firewood, or the metabolic respiration of glucose, which gives the human body the energy for life and mobility. Although air is a gas, it's actually quite heavy. At sea level, the atmospheric pressure is 760 mmHg (millimeters of mercury), or 14.7 pounds per square inch. Theoretically, this is the pressure of a column of air one square inch and about one hundred miles high, the approximate thickness of the layer of air or atmosphere covering the Earth. The atmosphere is held to the Earth by gravity. At sea level, the oxygen pressure is three pounds per square inch.

As you go up in altitude—say ten thousand feet—the atmospheric air pressure will drop to ten pounds per square inch and the oxygen pressure will drop down to two pounds per square inch. This is not enough to deliver the normal supply of oxygen to the lungs, but it is enough to keep blood saturation at about 90 percent; this does not have significant consequences for body function. Pilots or people hiking or skiing in the mountains can sense this and compensate by breathing faster and deeper. This phenomenon is known as anoxia, or "oxygen want." As an airplane climbs to over twelve thousand feet, pilots will notice the effects of lack of oxygen in their performance, and controlling the aircraft can be substantially diminished. If the airplane ascends to eighteen thousand feet, the atmospheric pressure will be 7.3 pounds per square inch and the oxygen pressure will drop to

1.5 pounds per square inch, which is about half that at sea level. At this point, oxygen saturation in the red blood cells will drop to 70 percent and the pilot and crew will feel fatigue, drowsiness, a false sense of well-being, overconfidence, faulty reasoning, blurred vision, and poor memory. They may even pass out. Above eighteen thousand feet, the symptoms come on faster, with loss of muscle control, loss of memory, and various types of emotional outbursts. Loss of consciousness generally occurs at about twenty-six thousand feet within three to six minutes. At thirty thousand feet, unconscious-ness occurs within one to two minutes, and at thirty-eight thousand feet, less than thirty seconds.

Oxygen want is not the only thing to be concerned with as airplanes go higher and higher. This is where Boyle's law comes into effect. Simply stated, Boyle's law says a gas will expand or contract in proportion to the pressure put upon it or taken off of it. One can see this on camping trips in the mountains at high altitude. Water will boil at lower tempera-tures than it does at sea level. Therefore, your hot meals will be cooler at altitude than at sea level. It was discovered in the 1930s, in altitude-pressure chambers where the atmospheric pressure is reduced to simulate an altitude of sixty-three thousand feet, blood will actually boil!

Because of the expansion of nitrogen and other gases in the body fluids, they will come out of solution and form bubbles. Nitrogen bubbles inside the body can cause decom-pression sickness, better known as "the bends"—what scuba divers get if they go from the depths of the ocean and rise to the surface of the water too quickly. At very high altitudes—above forty thousand feet—there is the potential of an air em-bolism as nitrogen is released from the blood due to the low atmospheric pressure. This was observed as early as 1934 by Dr. Harry Armstrong at the aeromedical laboratory at Wright

Field in Dayton, Ohio. Using decompression chambers, he observed gas bubbles forming in the arteries of anesthetized experimental animals at an altitude of thirty-five thousand feet. At an altitude of approximately sixty-two thousand feet, which is called the Armstrong limit or Armstrong line, the atmospheric pressure is so low that water boils at a normal body temperature of 98.6°F. At or above the Armstrong limit, exposed body fluids such as saliva, urine, and blood will boil and life is not sustainable.

The famous aviator Wiley Post was the first to use a pressurized suit flying at high altitude. He worked with B. F. Goodrich engineers to fabricate a suit with pigskin gloves, rubber boots, and an aluminum helmet. The helmet was a tall metal cylinder with a glass faceplate. A tank in the cockpit provided oxygen for breathing plus inflation of the suit. Post made brief tests with the suit in a pressure chamber. He then wore the suit in his plane, a Lockheed Vega, and climbed to an altitude of approximately forty thousand feet. His was the first airplane to reach the stratosphere. He attempted to fly from the West Coast to the East Coast at high altitude, but he only made it as far as Cleveland before the oxygen ran out. He did prove the practicality of a pressurized flight at high altitude, since he was approaching ground speeds of 340 miles an hour—more than a third faster than the airplane's normal maximum speed. On Post's final flight, in a seaplane in Alaska, the engine stopped at low altitude and the plane crashed, killing him and his famous passenger, humorist Will Rogers.

Surviving at very cold temperatures at high altitudes is another challenge. For every thousand feet in altitude, there is an average temperature drop of 3.6°F. These temperatures tend to vary depending on the time of year and whether the plane is near one of the poles or the equator. Aircrews flying in nonpressurized, high-altitude airplanes would routinely experience temperatures of twenty to thirty below zero Fahrenheit. In addition, with an airplane flying at 100 to 250 miles an hour, frostbite became an important problem, and electrically heated suits were developed to keep aircrews warm during high-altitude combat missions.

Other issues encountered with high-speed, high-altitude flying involve noise and communication. The usual level of airplane engine noise is 120 to 225 decibels. At a noise volume of 130 dB, a pilot and crew will feel a tingling sensation in their ears. At a noise level above 140 dB, they will experience deep pain. Though airplane noise is somewhat below the pain threshold, it will drown out any human-to-human communication without the assistance of muffled microphones and covered earpieces.

With the increased altitude and speed of the newer aircraft of the 1930s came increased maneuverability and increased gravitational forces on the body with high-speed maneuvers. Gravitational forces (g-forces) and inertia were other physical forces that the body had to endure while in flight in faster aircraft. One way to look at this is to imagine the human body being an elongated bag of blood. If someone were to take you by your ears and spin you around and around, your blood—like water in a swinging bucket—would be thrown to the lower part of your body. This is exactly what happens in a high-speed aircraft when the pilot goes into a tight turn or an inside loop or pulls out of a dive.

Gravitational forces are measured in gravity units, or Gs. For reference, 1G is the force of gravity that you feel while on the ground. You can feel a vertical gravitational force if you are on a roller coaster hitting a dip in the ride, or a lateral G if you take a very sharp turn in a speeding automobile. In flight, a pilot will experience a gravitational force either vertically or horizontally depending on how the aircraft is maneuvered. The pilot can also experience negative G, or even weightlessness, when reaching the peak of altitude and suddenly descending toward the earth.

At 2G, pilots can feel twice the weight of gravity pushing against them in their seat. At 3G, their weight triples and their facial features start to sag, making them look like bulldogs. It also becomes very difficult to lift the arms or legs and for the heart to pump blood up to the brain. The pilot's eyesight will "gray out"—meaning everything will look gray—between 3.5 and 4G. This is because the optic nerve and retina are quite sensitive to a lack of oxygen. If the blood pressure at head level drops to near 0, oxygen in the eye is used up within two or three seconds. At 4G to 5G, the pilot's vision will black out. This blackout is different from passing out from lack of oxygen. When pilots experience a blackout, they are still conscious; they simply cannot see. If the force is maintained over three to five seconds, however, they will pass out completely.

Another way to illustrate the problem is to imagine a column of arterial blood about twelve inches high between your heart and your brain. The heart normally pushes blood up this column at a pressure of around 120 mmHg. When you reach 5G, the downward pull on the blood column equals the upper push from the heart. Meanwhile, the blood pressure in the legs will rise to approximately 240 mmHg. The result of this shift in pressure distribution impairs blood circulation. Blood cannot go up to the brain or return from the area below the heart, such as the abdomen and legs. If the gravitational force continues, the heart cannot pump enough oxygen-rich blood to the brain and the pilot will lose consciousness, lose control of the aircraft, and crash. The goal was to prevent these circumstances from occurring.

CHAPTER 7

MAYO CLINIC
PREPARES FOR WAR

Mayo Clinic has a long history of association with the United States military. Dr. William Worrall Mayo initially started working with the military during the Dakota war of 1862 in south-central Minnesota, attending to the injured, both civilians and soldiers, involved in that tragic conflict. At that time, he was living and practicing medicine in Le Sueur, Minnesota. He treated and attended the wounded from the battle of New Ulm. Shortly after the end of the Dakota conflict, Dr. Mayo became an examining surgeon for draftees during the Civil War and set up his examining services in Rochester, Minnesota. After graduating from medical school, his sons William and Charlie Mayo joined their father's medical practice and eventually developed it into Mayo Clinic.

At the onset of World War I, Drs. William (Will) and Charles (Charlie) Mayo served on the Medical Reserve Corps of the US Army, training nurses, surgeons, and doctors in the treatment of wounded and injured soldiers. They also contributed money to cover expenses of a new mobile hospital in collaboration with the University of Minnesota. The brothers enlisted about one-third of Mayo's personnel to staff the hospital and adopted the latest medical principles for military use. The mobile hospital, called Military Base 26, located in France near the River Somme, served as the surgical unit for a center containing ten hospitals. When the Plummer Building was constructed in 1928, a carillon was built on top of the new skyscraper, and one of the bells is inscribed "Dedicated to the American Soldier."

When the United States entered World War II, Dr. Charles (Chuck) W. Mayo (Dr. Charlie's son) recruited Mayo medical personnel to serve in the 71st General Hospital, which consisted of Rochester physicians, surgeons, and nurses. This portable hospital was set up in the Pacific, in New Guinea. As part of the military's appreciation for the contribution of Mayo Clinic, a liberty ship was named the SS *Mayo Brothers* in honor of Will and Charlie Mayo.

Before the war, Mayo Clinic was a pioneer in the use of oxygen to treat medical problems and administering oxygen for individuals with pulmonary disease. In 1938, **Dr. William Randolph "Randy" Lovelace** worked with **Dr. Walter Boothby** to study how to overcome oxygen want in high-altitude aircraft, which were becoming more common at that time. Together, these doctors devised an oxygen mask that would fit over the face to deliver oxygen at high altitudes. They then elicited the help of **Dr. Arthur Bulbulian**, who specialized in facial and dental prosthetics, and developed a mask that would fit over the nose and mouth to deliver the correct amount of oxygen as the aircraft ascended to altitudes above ten thousand feet. The result was what they called the BLB mask, or the Boothby, Lovelace, Bulbulian mask. This mask was tested on a long-distance, high-altitude flight in the latter part of 1938 from Minneapolis, Minnesota, to Burbank, California, in a Northwest Airlines DC-3. All the crew wore the BLB mask and did not suffer any symptoms of oxygen want at high altitude. The BLB oxygen-delivery mask was used by all high-altitude bomber and fighter crews during World War II. The mask also had an impact in medicine, since it eliminated the use of large oxygen tents to treat pulmonary disease. Using a mask similar to the BLB required less labor than an oxygen tent.

By 1939, there were only a few laboratories in the United States working on aeromedical issues. They included the Harvard School of Public Health, in Boston; the aeromedical laboratory at Wright Field, in Dayton, Ohio; the Naval Air Station Pensacola, in Florida; and Randolph Field, in San Antonio, Texas.

In May 1939, Dr. Lovelace traveled to Europe on a William White surgical scholarship. He sailed on the SS *Normandie*, landing first in England, then going on to the Scandinavian countries, and eventually to Hungary, Austria, and Germany. In Germany, he observed many laboratories working on aviation medicine, including high-altitude flying and depressurization. The German laboratories Dr. Lovelace visited were devoted full-time to aviation medicine, and he was informed that there were at least forty laboratories throughout Germany investigating one or more of the challenges of high-altitude flight and gravitational tolerance. German aviation medicine was headed by **Dr. Hubertus Strughold**, who is known as the father of German aviation medicine. Dr. Strughold was the director of the Research Institute for Aviation Medicine of the Reich Air Ministry in Berlin. Strughold and Dr. Harry Armstrong, director of the aeromedical research laboratory at Wright Field, had met in about 1934 at the annual convention of the Aerospace Medical Association in Washington, DC. The researchers had much in common, having conducted high-altitude physiological research, and had become well acquainted with each other. They met a second time in 1937 in New York, at another medical conference. It is possible that Dr. Lovelace also met Dr. Strughold at international medical meetings both in the United States and in Germany.

Dr. Lovelace had to end his trip early due to the start of the war, when Germany invaded Poland. He returned to the United States on the *Queen Mary*. Lovelace met President Roosevelt's personal physician, Admiral Ross McIntire, and told him in detail about how German aviation science was far ahead of the United States on high-altitude flying. Lovelace insisted that the United States should start on an accelerated aviation-research program. Dr. McIntire relayed this information to the president, and funds were made available for research in aviation medicine. At that time in America, nearly all pilots and flight crews were essentially untrained with respect to the challenges of high-altitude flight and gravitational forces.

The United States military now realized that with the coming hostilities and war, whatever side could overcome the problems of oxygen want, depressurization, and the increase of gravitational forces during high-speed maneuvers would get an edge on their opponent. The opponents were not just the enemy, but anoxia, decompression, extreme cold and noise, and excessive gravitational forces. The winner of this war in the air would be determined in physiological laboratories and tested in the air in simulated combat conditions.

The Mayo Clinic Board of Governors approved a new

scientific and medical facility in the Medical Sciences Building, which was under construction at the time, for the purpose of conducting research studies for the war, many of which were top secret. This was the start of the Mayo Aero Medical Unit. Mayo's services were offered to the United States government in a contract for one dollar a year under conditions of secrecy. Mayo Clinic scientists and researchers were recruited to work on the problems of oxygen want, high-altitude decompression, and gravitational loss of consciousness.

The Mayo Aero Medical Unit was divided between two groups working on oxygen delivery at altitude and acceleration physiology. Dr. Boothby was in charge of the high-altitude laboratory, along with Dr. Randy Lovelace and **Dr. Fred Helmholtz**. This group concentrated on oxygen want and high-altitude decompression sickness. Their laboratory developed a chamber to simulate low barometric pressures at altitude.

In September 1942, famous aviator **Charles Lindbergh**, who was working at the Ford Motor bomber plant in Dearborn, Michigan, came to Mayo Clinic to experience the low-pressure chamber where researchers were studying the effects of decompression and also oxygen want at various simulated altitudes. During one experiment, Lindbergh was in the chamber with technician **Lucy Cronin**. The air pressure and oxygen content simulated high-altitude flying at approximately thirty thousand feet. Wanting to test the bailout bottle Dr. Lovelace had developed for flight crews who needed to abandon their airplanes at high altitudes, Lindbergh removed his mask and passed out within seconds. Realizing the emergency, Lucy placed the mask over his mouth and nose and initiated a gradual emergency "descent." He regained consciousness, and although slightly disoriented, he was all right. Lucy probably saved his life.

To do an actual test of the bailout bottle and abandoning an aircraft at altitude, Dr. Lovelace jumped out of a B-17 at 40,175 feet. When he pulled the cord on his parachute, the shock of the parachute opening blew off his glove and he passed out. He did land but sustained severe frostbite to his hand, ending his surgical career. For his bravery and continued advancement of aeromedicine, he was awarded the Distinguished Flying Cross by the Army Air Forces.

The acceleration laboratory was headed up by **Dr. Edward J. Baldes**, commonly known as E. J. Baldes, with the help of Dr. Charles Code, who had worked with Earl Wood at the University of Minnesota. Their assignment was to study how pilots could withstand gravitational forces during high-speed maneuvers during combat. To simulate the high force of gravity in an airplane, the first human centrifuge and the building that housed it were constructed next to the Medical Sciences Building. Dr. Baldes and **Adrian Porter** designed the centrifuge.

To simulate acceleration forces experienced in an aircraft, the human centrifuge needed to go from 1G, which is the pull of gravity when you're standing still on Earth, to 5G or maybe even 11G within a matter of seconds. This requirement involved not only very fast acceleration but also a strong structure that could withstand high forces and acceleration. The design and construction of the first human centrifuge built at Mayo Clinic is the result of a Midwest farm boy's innovation and building techniques using easily available materials and used equipment, since steel, fuel, and rubber were in short supply due to the Depression and the war effort. The unique design involved a superstructure that would rotate with a simulated cockpit at the end. The power and sudden acceleration were provided by two twenty-ton rotating flywheels underneath the superstructure; they could be clutched to the superstructure, providing the rotation. Adrian Porter designed the clutching and braking system for the centrifuge.

E. J. Baldes with a working model of the centrifuge set up in the basement of the Franklin Heating Station

The superstructure was constructed with steel tubing joined with gas welds, since arc welds had the potential to crack when subjected to high stress. A simulated cockpit was constructed at the end of a forty-foot swinging gantry. Power to the flywheels and superstructure was provided by a used Chrysler engine from a junked car; it was attached to an automobile differential and tire that would spin two twenty-ton flywheels underneath the superstructure. The flywheels provided the power, inertia, and speed to simulate the sudden acceleration that pilots experienced in the cockpit of their combat aircraft.

The final plans for the centrifuge are shown below.

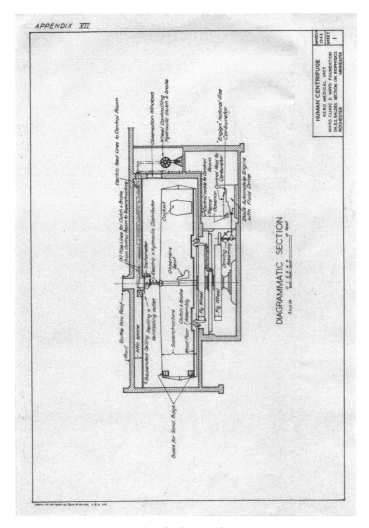

Plans for the centrifuge

Once the design was finalized and approved, the next challenge was obtaining the material for the construction. A search was initiated to find large enough flywheels to provide acceleration for the superstructure. The search started in St. Louis in hopes of getting used flywheels from the Anheuser-Busch brewery. Unfortunately, these flywheels did not meet specifications and had been scrapped. Finally, in January 1942, the City of Cincinnati sold Mayo Clinic two cast-iron flywheels and shafts that had been salvaged from their old Western Hills Pumping Station. They were transported by the Chicago and North Western railway to Rochester. The vertical shaft and bearing housings for the flywheels were completed by the Chicago and North Western railway foundry and maintenance department in Winona, Minnesota.

Drivetrain of a junked Chrysler powering the two
twenty-ton flywheels of the centrifuge

The cockpit of the centrifuge was placed at the end of the superstructure and was designed to swing out as the centrifuge rotated, so the subject would experience vertical Gs pressing down into the seat. When the centrifuge was at a standstill, the cockpit was perpendicular to the floor and the subject would be able to enter and exit the cockpit by climbing over the rails. In the cockpit were a seat and a joystick like a pilot would use to control an aircraft. In front of the subject was a group of horizontally mounted lights. As the lights came on, the subject would turn them off by touching a button on the joystick. The lights were controlled by a scientist sitting in a seat at the center shaft of the centrifuge. Reaction time was recorded from the time the light was switched on by the controller to the time it was shut off by the subject in the cockpit. Both movie and still cameras were mounted in front of the subject, for observation. A timer was mounted behind the subject, to time the centrifuge run. Underneath the timer was a G meter that indicated the number of Gs the subject was exposed to, as well as lights indicating his pulse and when the subject turned off the peripheral-vision lights in front of him. In addition, breathing was monitored using an external mouthpiece. The subject had to wear a nose plug so accurate measurements of respiration could be measured.

It was important to record pulse and blood pressure at head level. It was known at the time that when exposed to G, a pilot or subject would lose vision because the optic nerve and retina are very sensitive to lack of blood flow; vision was lost before the subject or pilot would go unconscious. Initially, blood pressure at head level was recorded by placing the subject's wrist at head level, then inserting a needle into the radial artery in the wrist and connecting it to a strain gauge that would measure blood pressure. This procedure became quite uncomfortable when the subject was exposed to high g-forces. Later, an infrared photoelectric cell device was developed that could be attached to the earlobe to record the pulse in the tiny arteries there. When the pulse at head level was lost, the scientists knew that the subject would soon lose vision and then lose consciousness.

The newly completed centrifuge housed in the circular building on the south side of the Medical Sciences Building. Note the lack of instrumentation.

One of the unique features of the centrifuge was that it simultaneously recorded physiological and physical data from multiple instruments located in the whirling cockpit at the end of the centrifuge. All this data was sent to and recorded on photographic paper in a room across the hallway from the centrifuge. This was accomplished by using copper wire brushes dragging over copper rings on the shaft of the centrifuge. The copper rings were connected to mercury-filled troughs above the center of the centrifuge and sent signals by wire to the recording room across the hall. They used synchronous pen-writing devices, which were available commercially and modified for recording physical and physiological data. In the recording room, a photokymographic recording system used tiny mirrors and galvanometers that shined light on photographic paper, which when rolled across a narrow lighted area would simultaneously record heart rate, arterial pressures, breathing rate, reaction time, earlobe opacity (pulse), g-force exposure, and time of the centrifuge run.

The total cost to Mayo Clinic to build the centrifuge was $50,000.

Mayo Clinic wanted to recruit the brightest and the best scientists to study the effects of gravitational loss of consciousness and how best to overcome these challenges to strengthen the war effort. The goal was to find a way to keep blood flowing to the brain while under acceleration and high gravitational stress. It was at this time that Dr. Charlie Code, who had worked with Earl Wood at the University of Minnesota, contacted him to come to Mayo Clinic to work on these perplexing problems.

It is significant to note that Mayo Clinic physicians, scientists, and technicians were all subjects for the experiments on the human centrifuge. Due to the secrecy of the research, they could not recruit subjects outside the department. Their philosophy was that they would not ask anyone to perform in conditions to which they wouldn't subject themselves.

CHAPTER 8

DAVID CLARK, COLLABORATOR AND MANUFACTURER

In contrast to the highly educated physiologists and scientists who were working in aviation medicine in the late 1930s and early 1940s, David Clark did not have a college degree or even a pilot's license. Although Clark lacked the academic pedigree, he was absolutely key in the research, development, and manufacture of noise-suppression headsets and the G-suit. In fact, without his entrepreneurial spirit and quest for knowledge in aviation safety, the G-suit would not have evolved into what it became during and after World War II and into the jet and space ages.

David Clark was born in Worcester, Massachusetts, in 1903. He attended South and Commerce High Schools and Northeastern University but did not graduate. In the early 1930s, he took a job in the Worcester Knitting factory and soon became superintendent, making undergarments, bathing suits, and outerwear. In late 1934, David developed a new concept of knitting with a two-way-stitch elastic and applied for a patent. He acquired a knitting machine that could handle this particular stitch pattern for manufacturing undergarments such as girdles and brassieres. The David Clark Company was incorporated under the laws of Massachusetts in October 1935. In 1936, his company invented another new method of knitting elastic, and more patents were filed. While continuing the elastic knitting for corset manufacturers, the company developed a new, patented elastic support garment for men called "the Straightaway." The Straightaway was then sold to stores in New York and New England and by direct mail.

In 1941, the Munsingwear Company out of Minneapolis, Minnesota, became interested in Clark's knitting patterns with elastic thread and inquired whether it might be possible to license Munsingwear under the Clark Company's knitting patents and manufacturing. In subsequent negotiations, Munsingwear contracted with the David Clark Company to operate the knitting business for the benefit of Munsingwear.

As events overseas became more threatening, involvement in a European war seemed inevitable, and the company borrowed more sewing machines and even purchased secondhand sewing machines to make tent parts, jungle hammocks, insect netting, and parachutes.

With the threat of World War II in 1941, Clark wanted to do something toward the war effort. Since he was in the corset business, he thought he might be able to develop some sort of protection for the "dreaded blackout" that he had observed in the movie *Dive Bomber*. Clark took one of his Straightaway undergarments, sewed a pocket in the abdominal area, and placed an ordinary football bladder into the pocket so it would inflate inward, to help protect the pilot from a blackout. He started writing letters to the navy and the Army Air Corps in Washington and by pure luck was able to see a **Lieutenant Commander Jack Poppen**. A few days later, Clark received a letter from him praising the garment but saying it would not work because it would not inflate automatically. That is, Clark needed to rig up a valve that would respond and inflate the suit as the pilot was subjected to g-forces and changing directions. At that time, there were no gravity-response valves fast enough to inflate a suit.

Returning to his factory in Worcester, David Clark realized that he'd seen pressure-regulating valves installed on overhead steam lines and heating systems in textile mills, and that he had a good idea how to make a gravity-responsive valve. So he went about making a prototype using a main-line water valve, a miniature bicycle pump, and a half-inch brass pipe. Again he used an old-fashioned football bladder. The bladder would inflate when he swung the bladder and valve around at arm's length, and then when he stopped, the bladder would deflate. He connected the bladder to an eight-foot-long tube and sewed it into the Straightaway underwear. He attached a spring to the valve, which would shut off the flow of the air when the crude swing-and-weight regulator allowed the bladder to empty once the swing stopped. Clark then wrote Lieutenant Commander Poppen about his development of a suit and valve that would respond to increases in gravity. He got a response from a **Lieutenant Commander Leon Carson**, who had replaced Poppen. Carson stated that the navy was not interested and there was no existing data indicating that such an apparatus would be helpful.

Being persistent, Clark wrote several aircraft companies in the fall of 1941 regarding G protection. The only aircraft company that responded was Boeing. Their chief test pilot, Eddie Allen, telephoned him saying that G protection was needed and that he should see **Major Otis Benson** at Wright Field. Allen gave him the details, including how to reach Benson.

Clark did stop at Wright Field on his way home from Minneapolis to Worcester on the train. He inquired at the front desk to see Major Benson, but the security guard indicated that the Army Air Forces was not interested in contracts for producing war-related products. It just so happened that Benson overheard the conversation and granted permission for Clark to speak with him. But first he had to go through security clearance and sign confidentiality agreements. He was fingerprinted and had to explain his intentions to meet with Benson. After Clark showed him the Straightaway with the valve and bladder, Benson suggested that he work with a physiologist. The first name he mentioned was Hudson Hoagland, PhD, who was actually from Clark's hometown of Worcester. The second name was Dr. E. J. Baldes, who was building a human centrifuge at Mayo Clinic in Rochester, Minnesota. This is the first time that David Clark realized that a large centrifuge might be big enough that a human could ride it and be subjected to the same g-forces as someone in a turning airplane. When Clark returned to Worcester, he met with Dr. Hoagland, who indicated that G protection might be feasible but that it would be better to work with E. J. Baldes at Mayo, who could test anything that was in development for G protection. Clark wrote Mayo Clinic and sent one of his Straightaway garments, suggesting that if they weren't interested in G protection, the Straightaway would at least make a good postsurgery abdominal support. Clark did get a letter back from Dr. Charlie Code indicating that it was a nice garment, but nothing else. Clark then wrote directly to Dr. Code, offering to be another set of hands for them in their research and experiments, and mentioning that Major Benson at Wright Field had told him to contact Dr. E. J. Baldes. A short time later, Dr. Baldes responded by inviting Clark to visit him in Rochester. This was the start of a thirty-plus-year relationship between Dave Clark, the David Clark Company, Mayo Clinic, and, within a year, Earl Wood.

David Clark took the train to Rochester and met Drs. Baldes and Code in the Franklin Heating Station. The centrifuge and Medical Sciences Building, where most of the research was to be conducted, were still under construction. Dr. Baldes showed Clark a scale model of the centrifuge and described some of the instrumentation. Clark had not brought his valve contraption with him but described it to Drs. Code and Baldes. They approved of the concept in principle. During their conversation, Clark realized that for his device to work, blood would have to be "milked up" from the legs. A simple belly bladder was just not enough.

Clark returned to Worcester and started working on his second prototype, making smaller latex bladders about the size of a blood-pressure cuff. He devised a system in which a series of bladders were connected: the first near the ankle, the next at the calf, then one at the thigh. The lowest bladder would fill, dumping the excess air into the bladder immediately above it, creating a milking action as the sequence progressed up the leg.

In November 1941, Drs. Baldes and Code visited the David Clark factory in Worcester. They were en route to Boston (Clark later learned) to interview Earl Wood, who was teaching and doing research at the Harvard Medical School.

During the visit in Worcester, Clark and the two Mayo scientists discussed the suit's design; they wanted to have one to test on their centrifuge when it was ready. Dr. Baldes suggested that there should be connections so that pressure gauges might be attached to the bladders at the ankles, knees, and hips, and that the bladder system be extended halfway up the torso. In addition, provisions should be made to inflate only the torso section or the leg sections—in short, an experimental suit that could be easily modified between centrifuge runs. Due to his lack of scientific education, Clark did not want to have a contract between the David Clark Company and Mayo Clinic; he preferred to be a hands-on person at the David Clark Company's expense.

During this time, there was open communication by letter between Dr. Baldes and Dave Clark. One day Dr. Baldes called Clark saying that he was in real trouble. An essential part of the design for connecting an automobile drivetrain to the flywheel on the centrifuge was an automobile tire. At that time, tire rationing had begun and Dr. Baldes was unable to justify the need for a tire without revealing too much about the confidential project. It just so happened that the president of Munsingwear, Ernest L. Olrich, was also chief of tire rationing in Minnesota. Clark got the size of the tire from Dr. Baldes and phoned Mr. Olrich in Minneapolis, and within a couple of hours he had two top-quality tires delivered to Mayo Clinic as a contribution from the Munsingwear Company.

Clark continued working on a valve system to inflate the bladders in his suit. He worked with some friends at the Herald Machine Company, Henry Wilder and Harry Winslow, who both knew something about valves. He wanted a valve that would inflate a bladder using a certain amount of pressure and then shut it off when that prescribed pressure was reached. The result was an initial valve that would inflate the various bladders in the suit; however, it needed to be calibrated to the different gravitational forces once the centrifuge was operational.

Clark connected the valve and experimental suit to a

compressed-air line and calibrated the valve to open at approximately 2G and stabilize the suit at approximately one pound per square inch per gravitational force (G). To see if the system would work, he put on the experimental suit while seated in a chair. He dropped a weight on the valve, and the gauges hit about 20 psi (pounds per square inch) at the ankle, 10 psi at the knees, 5 psi at the hips, and 1¼ psi at the belly bladders, and then stabilized at 1 psi. He could feel the progression of the pressure and felt feverish in his face and neck; his face began to turn pink. The milking system with the progression of bladders from the feet to the abdomen seemed to be working. In June 1942, David wrote Dr. Baldes and requested to come to Rochester to demonstrate the experimental suit and valve system.

CHAPTER 9

THE CENTRIFUGE
EXPERIMENTS BEGIN

David Clark and Ernest Olrich from Munsingwear arrived in
Rochester in July 1942. They went through Mayo Clinic security; they were fingerprinted and told that the projects were
top secret. They were welcomed by Dr. Charlie Code, who
introduced them to Earl Wood, a new member of the Mayo
Aero Medical Unit team. At that time the centrifuge was not
yet operational. However, Clark could demonstrate the suit
with Earl as the subject. Earl was placed on a tilt table, lying
on his back. A tilt table can be placed at almost any angle,
from standing up to horizontal to tilting backward until the
person is almost upside down; if you go from a horizontal position to standing quickly and you're relaxed, you can faint
and lose consciousness. So, Earl put on the suit and Dave connected the valves to an air-pressure line. The tilt table was
cranked to the critical angle, and beads of sweat appeared on
Earl's forehead. Charlie directed Dave to inflate the suit. Earl
recovered quickly. It appeared that the prototype design with

the suit and the valves would provide some G protection and could be tested on the centrifuge.

An experimental subject in the cockpit of the centrifuge with Earl in the center seat

Dr. Ed Lambert joined the team soon after Earl started. Lambert was born in 1915 in Minneapolis. During the Depression, he moved with his family to Chicago, where he received BS, MS, and MD degrees from the University of Illinois. Following his internship at Michael Reese Hospital in Chicago, he received his PhD in physiology. Like Earl, he was recruited by Dr. Charlie Code and Dr. E. J. Baldes.

By November 1942, the centrifuge was operational and **Ralph Sturm** had joined the team. Sturm, an electrical engineer out of Purdue on contract from Bendix Aviation Corporation, was in charge of installing instrumentation on the centrifuge for measuring and recording physical and physiological data such as electrical signals from the heart, blood pressures, breathing rate, rates of response to peripheral lights, and of course G level.

Lucy Cronin, who had worked with the hyperbaric chamber with Dr. Lovelace, had moved over into the acceleration lab. She was acting as safety engineer and observer, plus conducting the checklists of the safety factors along with calibrations of the various instruments before and after each centrifuge run. Lucy lived on a farm east of Rochester with her brothers and sisters. She started work at Mayo in the late 1930s to supplement the farm income during the Depression. Lucy was a down-to-earth, no-nonsense Midwest farm girl with excellent mechanical and technical know-how. She knew how to prepare the instrumentation and surgical equipment when needed. Lucy was a vital member of the laboratory for more than thirty-five years and saw the advances in medical sciences from paper analog recordings to digital computer analysis.

Roy Engstrom operated the centrifuge clutching and braking operation and assisted in monitoring the recording devices in a darkroom across the hall. **Bill Sutterer** joined the team later and assisted Roy with operating the centrifuge and data recording.

The multichannel data sources were recorded simultaneously on the photographic paper in the recording room. These data included when the peripheral lights were switched on and when they were shut off by the subject, so reaction time could be calculated; the electrocardiogram; pulse at the ear; acceleration in gravitational force; arterial pressure at heart and head levels; heart rate; respiration; abdominal/rectal pressure; and pressure inside the G-suit.

So, the experiments on the centrifuge began, with Charlie Code acting as the general manager, Earl dubbed the "coach,"

Ed Lambert the "assistant coach," Ralph Sturm the instrumentation engineer, Roy Engstrom the centrifuge operator, and Lucy Cronin safety engineer and recorder. Dave Clark was in charge of altering and changing the suits and maintaining the pressure valves. At the same time, Dave, Ralph, and Lucy were polluting the place with smoke and ashes since they were chain smokers, with Dave rotating between pipes, cigars, and cigarettes.

On a typical day, Roy would get to the Medical Sciences Building early and start the Chrysler engine, slowly engaging the clutch to the old drivetrain that rotated the tire connected to the two twenty-ton flywheels. The tire would give a loud screech as it slipped on the lower flywheel. To reduce the screeching sound, the clutch had to be slipped, engaged, and disengaged. It was important to limit any noise going outside the building because this was a top-secret scientific project. Bringing the flywheels up to speed took about an hour. Earl, Ed, Charlie, and crew would arrive about 7:00 a.m. to calibrate the instrumentation and get the recording room ready. The subject was suited up, and he climbed into the cockpit. The scientists and technicians then connected the subject to the various instruments, which were calibrated for accurate measurement. This process usually took from 8:00 to 9:00 a.m.

A centrifuge run would start by "overriding the flywheels." That is, they would rotate slightly faster than needed for the prescribed G run, since they would slow down slightly when clutched to the superstructure of the centrifuge. The specific G was achieved with just a one-and-a-quarter turn of the centrifuge. On the following page is a chart showing prescribed G level at the head, the rotations per minute (rpm) of the flywheels before the run, and the rpm when they were clutched to the superstructure.

Acceleration at brain Sitting position in cockpit g units	R.P.M. of flywheels (before full clutch)	R.P.M. of carriage and flywheels (after full clutch)	Ratio: R.P.M. after full clutch / R.P.M. before full clutch
2.0	25.0	19.0	.760
3.0	32.0	24.3	.759
4.0	37.5	28.2	.752
5.0	41.9	31.8	.759
6.0	46.0	34.8	.757
7.0	49.5	37.7	.762
8.0	52.7	40.2	.763
9.0	55.3	42.9	.776
10.0	59.0	45.3	.768
11.0	61.3	47.3	.772

February 19, 1945

Flywheel rpm before and after clutching to the centrifuge superstructure for specific G to be achieved

A scientist—Charlie, Ed, or Earl (if they weren't subjects)—would sit in the center seat to control the reaction lights and monitor the gauges in the cockpit. The countdown for a centrifuge run was called out by Lucy Cronin, starting, "Twenty, nineteen, eighteen . . ." As each number was called out, she would check off an item on her safety checklist. Items to be checked off included the following: Are all loose tools removed from the centrifuge? Are all cables secured? Is the subject strapped in properly? Is the observer strapped in? Is everyone out of the centrifuge room, and are the doors locked and secured? When the count got down to five, the scientist in the center seat would take over. At the count of two, he would call out, "Start your run!" The last two seconds were to let the human guinea pig in the gondola prepare for the run. That is, the subject had to prepare to relax and let himself go temporarily blind and even unconscious, or prepare to strain to retain vision and consciousness. The countdown also alerted the individual in the recording room to start the flow of the photographic paper across the light source to record simultaneous physiological and physical data coming from the centrifuge.

The observer in the chair attached to the center post of the centrifuge would control the lights in the cockpit and switch them on at random. The instrumentation would record when the subject switched them off using the thumb button mounted on the joystick in the cockpit. On a control run—usually 2G to 3G—the subject, usually Earl, would switch the lights out quickly. At 4G, his response time was slower. At 5G, he would leave them on for several seconds, indicating a loss of peripheral vision. Ear pulse was recorded by the photoelectric cell placed on the earlobe. At 3G and 4G, the ear pulse was quite regular. At 5G, no ear pulse would be recorded for several seconds, indicating that the subject most likely had lost vision and would soon become unconscious. Occasionally, the observer would switch on a loud buzzer to monitor the subject's hearing acuity if he did not see the peripheral lights switched off. The electrocardiogram was continuously monitored and was the primary safety factor. If an unexpected irregularity was seen in the electrocardiogram, an emergency stop would be executed. The subject would undergo as many as eight runs at various G levels. He would finally get unhooked about 1:00 p.m. looking a bit ashen and tired.

Earl in the cockpit of the centrifuge, ready for a spin, early 1943.
Note the photoelectric earpiece and strain gauges inserted into the radial
arteries of both wrists, one at head level, the other at heart level.

One of the theories of loss of consciousness in high-speed maneuvers was that blood pooled in the lower body, reducing blood supply to the heart so there was insufficient cardiac output to provide blood flow to the brain. This venous-pooling hypothesis was addressed by surrounding the body with water so the increased hydrostatic pressure in the water matched the increased pressure in the veins; hence, the pooling would be eliminated. This was similar to what Wilbur Franks's water-filled suits tried to accomplish. The water theory was tested on the centrifuge using a steel bath filled with water. They called it the "Iron Maiden." When subjects were immersed in water in the Iron Maiden, their G tolerance did not increase significantly compared to when using air-filled bladders. The scientists therefore eliminated the use of the water bath and Iron Maiden for further experimentation, as they were uncomfortable and exceptionally heavy for the pilot.

Earl at 1G (control run without the centrifuge running)

Earl at 7G

The Iron Maiden

A TRIP TO THE HARDWARE STORE

By late 1942, the valves and the initial G-suit were routinely tested and monitored on the centrifuge. Dave Clark's initial valve was bolted onto the gondola of the centrifuge and connected to the prototype G-suit that Dave had brought with him from Massachusetts. Earl was the first subject to ride the centrifuge with the suit connected to compressed air regulated by the valve. All the scientists present were surprised that the system with the valves did indeed provide some measurable protection compared to the controlled, relaxed runs. Earl made two or three runs and then was followed by Ed Lambert, who also experienced measurable protection.

However, when they put the suit on another subject, that individual got little protection. They surmised that the size and fit of the suit, plus the inflation of the bladders, were making the difference. Dave Clark was then asked to try the suit. While riding on the centrifuge, Dave found that the inflation of the bladders was much slower than he expected, compared to what he experienced at home in Massachusetts. The suit was supposed to reach prescribed pressures at the same time the centrifuge reached a specific G level. It just so happened that the air-pressure line was just a one-quarter-inch hose connected to a 50-psi pressure tank. The lack of "come on pressure" in the bladders (or the rate that the bladders are filled with air) was solved by changing the quarter-inch air-pressure hose to a three-quarter-inch hose that Dave purchased at a local hardware store.

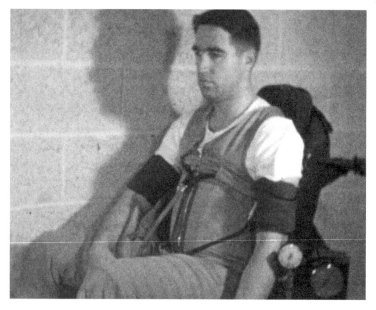

Earl in a Progressive Arterial Occlusion Suit monitoring
blood pressure as the suit is inflated

By early 1943, the G-suit was altered so the bladders in the calves would inflate first, progressing up to the thighs and eventually toward the abdomen, with the valve opening at 2G at 3 psi. They would provide increasing pressure at 1.5 psi per G up to a prescribed pressure, and the excess air would be dumped. This created a milking action of increasing pressure from the calves to the abdomen. This suit was called the Progressive Arterial Occlusion Suit and was first made in Worcester and modified in Rochester by David Clark and one of his assistants using a sewing machine borrowed from Munsingwear in Minneapolis.

Many modifications were made to the pressure valves going to the suit so it would inflate depending on the increments of Gs experienced. The valves tended to chatter audibly at perhaps five times per second, which could annoy the subjects and the scientists. This was due to a slight overinflation and dumping of air, which meant that the gradient pressure in the suit had been maintained but then released, creating the chatter. Earl told Dave Clark that he needed a simple valve preset to open at 2G at 6 psi, with increments of 1.5 psi per G, and then hold that pressure in the bladders. Dave worked with one of his engineers to redesign a valve. The idea came of incorporating a venturi-like scheme within the valve that would provide all the source volume and pressure until it encountered resistance and built up back pressure enough to match 1.5 psi per G; then the valve would shut off. They didn't realize it at the time, but this was the same type of valve that would be used on every gas pump that appeared after World War II. If Dave and his engineers had applied that same design for a valve to the petroleum industry, they would've been multimillionaires.

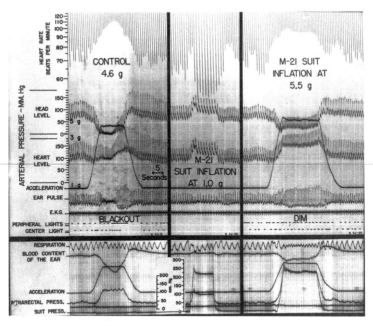

Multichannel analog graphic data from the centrifuge

AN IMPORTANT MANEUVER

One of the most important concepts of G protection was getting enough blood to head level to maintain vision and consciousness. The problem did not result from lack of venous return to the heart because of blood pooling in the lower extremities, but more from the need for increased arterial pressure to get blood up to the head and brain during exposure to G. Some pilots demonstrated they could tolerate high-G turns by yelling during the turn. At this time, Earl was working on developing a straining maneuver that would increase intra-abdominal pressure and therefore increase the blood pressure and blood volume going to the head. This was done by tightening the abdominal muscles and closing the epiglottis—the flap at the base of the tongue—in quick succession, while simultaneously contracting the muscles of the calves and thighs. When the maneuver is done properly in a sitting position, individuals can increase their systolic blood pressure to 200 mmHg. Initial experiments were done in a chair, not using the centrifuge. These experiments progressed to the centrifuge, and using the straining maneuver, known as M-1, offered protection up to 6G without a G-suit. The amount of protection varied by individual, depending on their physical condition and if they conducted the maneuver correctly.

Earl performing a straining maneuver before high-G run

G MEASLES

In an attempt to reduce the vertical distance blood had to flow from the heart to the head, different angles of the pilot seat were evaluated for G tolerance.

Earl got the idea that further protection could be provided if inflatable arm cuffs were added to the G-suit. The Progressive Arterial Occlusion Suit with arm cuffs was tested on the centrifuge on February 16, 1943, with Earl as the subject. The test included a series of fifteen-second control runs at 3G, 4G, and 5G, and up to 8G, with the suit inflated, starting at 200 mmHg at 1.5G, an increase at 1 psi per G above that level. Complete blackout occurred with loss of ear pulse in the first eight and a half seconds of the control exposure at 5G without the suit inflated. Ear pulse was maintained throughout the exposure to 8G with the suit inflated. However, there was about a two-second loss of vision that occurred about four seconds after reaching 8G. Then another run, up to 9G, was carried out with both the suit inflation and the progressive M-1 straining maneuver. The ear pulse and clear vision were maintained throughout that run. The photographic recordings obtained during these high-G exposures showed that the combined use of the suit and the M-1 maneuver increased blood content at the ear and head level during exposure to 9G. In other words, the combination resulted in "overprotection" against loss of blood at the head—verified by the fact that color motion pictures of the subject during this exposure showed flushing of the skin on the neck.

After exposure to such high g-forces, the nonpressurized areas of Earl's skin around the arm cuffs and his abdomen were covered with small hemorrhages; this became known as "G measles."

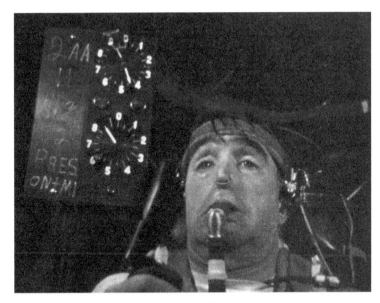

Earl at 9G

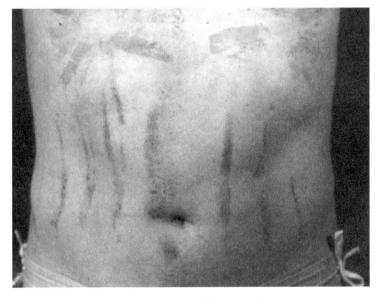

Earl with "G measles" following a 9G run

E. J. Baldes, who conceived the idea that Mayo Clinic should have a centrifuge and be at the forefront of aviation medicine, was seldom around to direct any of the experiments. Instead, he turned over the direction and implementation of these very complicated experiments to the new boys, which included Charlie Code, Ed Lambert, and Earl Wood. Dr. Baldes put a lot of trust in the people that he hired and let them know what needed to be done, so he could go on to develop something else that interested him. He knew that his dreams would materialize without his help. Later in Earl's career, he may have been influenced by Dr. Baldes, letting a younger scientist in his laboratory take charge of a project. In the meantime, other laboratories and manufacturers were working on G protection and G-suits. Dr. Franks, in Toronto, had developed a similar suit that had compartmentalized bladders filled with water, which was effective but very heavy. Berger Brothers, out of New Haven, Connecticut, was also producing similar suits and had sold some to the US Navy. The Berger Brothers suit was being tested at Wright Field in Dayton, Ohio, which had just started operation of their centrifuge. The advantage of the Mayo system was the simultaneous recording of the multichannel data, which other laboratories did not have. Mayo began testing other suits also. Since they were under government contract, their goal was to find the best suit and G protection regardless of manufacturer. However, since Dave Clark was working locally in Rochester using Munsingwear equipment, he and his team were able to change the suits and orientation of the bladders relatively quickly based on directions from Earl and the Aero Medical Unit. They designed a suit to reduce or eliminate unpressurized areas between the bladders to increase its efficiency when exposed to G. As a result, another suit was developed, the Arterial Occlusion Suit, or the AOS.

CHAPTER 10

FLIGHT TESTING IN THE G-WHIZ

When Earl Wood and Dave Clark saw *Dive Bomber,* little did they realize that they'd someday be using one of the planes featured in that movie to test for G protection.

It had been established in the laboratory setting that significant G protection could be accomplished with the M-1 straining maneuver plus the use of the G-suit with properly functioning valves to inflate it to the pressure necessary to maintain blood flow at head level. The challenge was to prove this technique and equipment could work in an actual aircraft. The navy and Army Air Corps were skeptical. In those days, pilots and aircraft designers would rather have the capacity for three more gallons of gasoline than the additional weight of a G valve and a G-suit attached to the aircraft. E. J. Baldes and the Mayo Aero Medical team convinced Colonel Harry Armstrong at Wright Field of the need for an aircraft for testing. The Army Air Forces furnished an older, slightly used Douglas Dauntless dive bomber without the armaments so that comparisons might be made between G effects in an aircraft and those obtained on the centrifuge. Many Douglas Dauntless planes had seen action in the Battle of Midway and were also featured in the movie *Dive Bomber.*

Ed Lambert was in charge of installing instrumentation on the dive bomber to provide the same physiological and physical data obtained from the centrifuge. The rear cockpit contained a G meter, a timer, and wiring for a photoelectric cell to be attached to the subject's ear to monitor his pulse. A film camera recorded the subject's head and background data during each of the G runs. The G valve was mounted in the cockpit with a quick-release connection to the G-suit. Pressure was provided to the G valve through the vacuum pump from the engine.

They named the experimental aircraft and flying laboratory "the G-Whiz." The pilot of the G-Whiz was Captain Kenneth Bailey of the Army Air Corps. During the war, Rochester was a refueling stop for flying fighter planes from their manufacturing facilities to the West Coast, Alaska, and eventually Russia. Captain Bailey agreed not only to maintain the dive bomber but also to fly it for the G-suit tests. Ken perfected a flying technique to closely duplicate the fifteen-second centrifuge runs. He'd fly up to an altitude of ten thousand feet and put the dive bomber into a spiral dive. He could then readily produce runs from 3G to 8G, as requested by the scientists. These flights proved that centrifuges adequately simulate the Gs experienced in aircraft. Aircraft engineers had long doubted that was possible. More than one hundred experimental flights were conducted over the skies of Rochester and Southeast Minnesota with different configurations of different G-suits and valve adjustments in straining maneuvers. Ken Bailey was trained in the use of the G-suit and straining maneuvers and wore full G-suit protection during all the flights. Meanwhile, the subject in the rear seat was subject to the same g-force turns and dives without a G-suit, or using variations of different G-suits, with or without performing a straining maneuver. As on the centrifuge, Ed Lambert, Charlie Code, and Earl Wood were the subjects in the rear seat of the G-Whiz.

Earl as subject in the G-Whiz. Pilot Ken Bailey at the controls.

On one occasion when Earl was the subject, he had Ken fly the G-Whiz over Lake Washington so that his parents, Will and Inez Wood, could see their son in action. This was the first time Earl had seen Lake Washington from the air. It had to be quite a spectacle for his proud parents and the farmers in the area to see a speeding aircraft making circles over the skies of Blue Earth and Le Sueur Counties.

It was thought then that all fighter pilots should be tested for G tolerance and trained in straining maneuvers to increase G tolerance during high-speed maneuvers. Many pilots were coming to Mayo, Wright-Patterson, and other aviation-medicine fields, such as Naval Air Station Pensacola and Brooks Field, in San Antonio, for this testing and training. They were also being trained in the use of the oxygen mask for high-altitude flying at all of these institutions.

A MORE COMFORTABLE SUIT

G-suits from various manufacturers were undergoing continuous testing for both G protection and comfort. To test two different types of G-suits, the Mayo AOS and the Berger Brothers suit, the Army Air Corps set up two aircraft with pilots wearing the different suits. One was the lead aircraft; the other was the pursuit aircraft. Both went through a series of dives and turns. Both pilots got adequate G protection by using straining maneuvers and the G-suits. The pilot wearing the Berger Brothers equipment was ahead, and the pilot wearing the AOS from Mayo and Clark had to quit the chase because he could no longer tolerate the discomfort of the compression between the thighs and abdomen. It turned out that the sudden inflation of the AOS was compressing the pilot's testicles, resulting in another type of unintentional straining maneuver. From that point, Dave Clark and his staff looked at ways to add comfort to the suit without sacrificing G protection or the pilot's private parts.

At this time, the navy was purchasing a limited number of G-suits and valves from both the David Clark Company and Berger Brothers. Apparently, the navy had a greater interest in G protection than the Army Air Corps. Dave Clark brought in employees from Munsingwear to help with the growing production orders. He also worked with Dick Cornelius and his company out of Minneapolis for the production of G valves and quick disconnects to attach the G-suits to the valves.

In early 1944, there was a scientific meeting at Wright Field in Dayton, Ohio, of all the experts in aviation medicine, including Charlie Code, E. J. Baldes, Randy Lovelace, Ed Lambert, Ken Bailey, and Earl Wood from Mayo Clinic, plus some top brass from the Army Air Corps and the navy. This high-level group had decided to go with a simplified Berger Brothers suit, which offered the same type of protection as the Mayo AOS but was lighter and more comfortable.

After the meeting, Earl took the train to Worcester, Massachusetts, to discuss the results of the meeting with Dave Clark. Earl told Dave they had learned a great deal about G protection but the manufacturing of the G-suit would probably go to Berger Brothers, despite all the blood, sweat, and tears Dave had put into the project. Earl had a going-away dinner at the Clark home that evening. Dave took Earl to his hotel and invited him to come by the factory the next morning to say goodbye to many of the company employees that Earl had worked with over the last couple of years. Earl's train would not leave for Chicago and Rochester until 1:30 that afternoon. After dropping Earl off at his hotel, Dave went to his factory and started working on a simplified AOS. He had resisted the simplified design initially because he knew the AOS gave better G protection. He put together a one-piece bladder system combining the legs and the abdominal area and inserted the hose for quick inflation. Taking what he'd learned from the pilots at Wright Field, that comfort was the prime consideration, he shaped the belly bladders very carefully, using himself in the seated position as if flying an airplane, so the bladders would compress his stomach without uncomfortable contact with his pelvis or ribs.

He then put the suit together with lightweight vinyl-coated fabric that the Clark Company had been using for the roofs of jungle hammocks. The next morning when Earl came by, he tried the newly designed suit on even while the cement on the connections was still wet. It leaked like a sieve, but Dave had plenty of compressed air to keep the bladders full. Earl was immediately impressed but indicated that the belly bladder was not big enough. Seeing the potential for a better, more comfortable suit, Earl canceled his train back to Rochester and told Charlie Code that he would be delayed. Earl stayed in Worcester three more days as Dave and his seamstress worked to modify the suits based on Earl's direction. The suit became known as the model 2. Earl took the prototype suits of different sizes back to Rochester to be tested on the centrifuge and the G-Whiz.

A week later, Earl phoned Dave Clark from Rochester to report that the suits had worked and provided good G protection. He asked for more suits of various sizes. Variations on the valve were being made by Dick Cornelius so that bladders could be inflated with no obstructions. In this way, the pressure inside the suit would increase in increments of approximately 1 psi per G starting at 1G, and the air could flow freely through the valve until the suit reached the prescribed pressure, and then it would shut off.

They also learned that many pilots refused to take off their flying uniforms or coveralls, wearing the G-suits outside their pants, and they still worked. As a result, a cutaway design was started so the G-suit could be pulled on and off with ease, as requested by the pilots. Pockets for knives and other items were also added. In testing the cutaway G-suits, it was found out that G protection was about a half a G less than the model 2 G-suit that Earl and Dave Clark had designed earlier. With the decreased weight and increased comfort, these were the suits that were accepted most widely by the Army Air Corps and the navy during World War II. It is this same design as the skeleton suit—designed to keep the bladders in place over the legs and abdomen—which airmen preferred and is still in use by fighter pilots worldwide. The cutaway design was also placed in coveralls in the same configuration.

By the end of 1944, the David Clark Company was supplying both the navy and the Army Air Corps with G-suits and Cornelius-Clark valves along with installation kits for the P-51 Mustang, the P-47 Thunderbolt, and navy Hellcats and Corsairs, which were in air-combat service in both the European and Pacific theaters. Fighter pilots quickly realized that with the combination of the straining maneuver and the G-suit, they could outmaneuver enemy airplanes in aerial combat. It was suspected that pilots who did not wear a G-suit and did not return from their mission simply "dove in." Although German aircraft at the end of the war, such as the Me 262 jet fighter-bomber, were faster and far more advanced, the G-suit made it possible for Allied pilots in their propeller-driven fighters to outmaneuver their jet opponents. Famed American pilot Chuck Yeager was noted saying to Dave Clark, "The G-suit made the impossible possible."

POSTWAR G-SUITS

With the German surrender in May 1945 and the eventual surrender of the Japanese, many government contracts for war research were soon ended. That was not the case, however, with the production of G-suits and related equipment; the advancement from piston-driven fighter aircraft to jet aircraft made G protection even more important. In addition, aircraft were flying higher, and the development of full-pressure suits was needed. Research studies and training continued on the Mayo centrifuge until 1947. It is not known what happened to the G-Whiz. However, the wings of the G-Whiz were severely warped due to the metal stress from repeated high-G turns and dives.

Following VJ Day in August 1945, and with the instrument of surrender pending, E. J. Baldes received a letter from an H. F. Wagner, the purchasing agent for the City of Cincinnati. The letter states,

> Dear Dr. Baldes,
> You will recall that in January 1942, we sold to Mayo Clinic two cast iron flywheels and shafts which were salvaged from the Old Western Hills Water Works pumping station. At that time you advised us that the wheels would be used in a research project being launched by the Mayo foundation in the interest of national defense under your general supervision and with the cooperation of the aeromedical research unit under Major Otis Benson at Wright Field in Dayton, Ohio.
> With so much being written about the research work performed leading up to the manufacture of the atomic bomb, we are curious to know whether or not these old flywheels in some way played a part in the development of the bomb or whether they were used in some other project.

If you are not revealing any confidential information we should like to be advised accordingly.
Very truly yours,
H. F. Wagner City Purchasing Agent

It is not known whether E. J. Baldes answered this letter, since research being completed for aviation medicine at Mayo Clinic at that time was strictly top secret.

One of the first contributions to general medical practice as a result of postwar experiments on the centrifuge was inflatable trousers that could be used both in the operating room to increase blood pressure and for emergency medical technicians to stabilize lower-extremity injuries and fractures, enabling them to transport injured individuals to a medical center without further injury or blood loss.

In 1946, Earl was appointed associate professor of physiology for the Mayo Foundation and a physiology consultant for the University of Minnesota. Later, in 1947, he was named head of the Cardiovascular Respiratory Research Laboratory at Mayo Clinic.

In October 1947, Earl Wood, E. J. Baldes, Ed Lambert, Charlie Code, and David Clark were awarded a certificate of merit signed by President Harry Truman "for outstanding fidelity and meritorious conduct in the aid of the war effort against the common enemies of the United States and its allies in World War II." Dr. Baldes and Dr. Code received their awards in Washington, DC, while attending a meeting. Earl, Ed Lambert, and David Clark received their presidential certificates of merit from Rear Admiral F. L. Conklin at a ceremony in Balfour Hall in the Mayo Foundation House in May 1948. Some thirty Mayo Clinic and Mayo Foundation staff members witnessed the presentation of the awards.

Rear Admiral Conklin stated that the work done by the Aero Medical Unit enabled the United States to keep the human body in pace with the advancement of aviation.

Dave Clark ran the David Clark Company until his retirement in 1964. He continued working on antipressure suits and valves and developed the first operational pressure suit for the X-1 rocket, when Chuck Yeager broke the sound barrier. He also produced pressure suits for the X-15 along with the spacesuit worn by Ed White for his first spacewalk during the Gemini program. David Clark pressure suits are still worn by pilots in high-altitude aircraft such as the F-4, the F-15, the U-2, and the SR-71 Blackbird. They were also worn by the astronauts on the space shuttle. The David Clark Company today is best known for aviation technology including headsets, microphones for communication, and hearing protection.

Following the war, Ed Lambert built EMG (electromyography) equipment using some of the basic techniques he learned with the instrumentation on the centrifuge and the G-Whiz. By the late 1940s, Dr. Lambert began studies on electrophysiology of neuromuscular diseases. Working in Mayo Clinic's Department of Neurology, Dr. Lambert and Dr. Lee Eaton studied neuromuscular transmission associated with lung cancer. This disorder became known as Lambert-Eaton syndrome. Dr. Lambert's pioneering research led to electromyography and nerve conduction studies becoming an integral part of the evaluation of the neuromuscular disorders. He evaluated a wide variety of neuropathies such as facial neuropathies, traumatic neuropathies, and carpal tunnel syndrome. In 1975, he was appointed professor of neurology at the Mayo Clinic School of Medicine and the Mayo Graduate School of Medicine.

At war's end, Charlie Code started working on histamine and the role that histamine plays in mediating acid secretion in the stomach. In the 1950s and '60s, he carried out pioneering studies using radiological methods to film patterns of movement of the esophagus, stomach, and intestines in dogs and healthy humans during digestion and between meals. In the early 1970s, Dr. Code helped lead an effort to form the medical school at Mayo Clinic, where he served as the first director for education research and became a member of the board of governors.

Without the understanding of physiology from the objective recordings from the centrifuge and G-Whiz experiments, the evolution from the various gradient-pressure suits to a very simplified single-pressure suit would not have occurred in such a short period of time. The team approach and the lessons learned in the war years in the Aero Medical Laboratory at Mayo Clinic launched these individuals into long-term successful careers in medical research and business. These studies also propelled Earl's future research in cardiovascular physiology, which will be described in more detail in upcoming chapters.

The first public display of the centrifuge in the Medical Sciences Building was held in April 1947 as part of the Mayo Foundation's postwar demonstration day. Pictures of the centrifuge and scientists were included in an article in the *Minneapolis Sunday Tribune* on April 20, 1947. Since most of the experimental research on the centrifuge was complete, the centrifuge was mothballed in 1947, but it came back into service during the space race in the 1950s. Much of the data from the Aero Medical Laboratory was held top secret and not declassified until the mid-1990s. The results of the initial studies on the centrifuge and the G-Whiz are actually more important in today's aircraft due to higher speeds and prolonged high-G turns.

CHAPTER 11

OPERATION PAPERCLIP

In the last year of World War II, it became apparent that German aviation technology was quickly surpassing the Allied effort with the deployment of the jet-powered Messerschmitt 262, as well as the V-1 rocket (known as the "buzz bomb") and the V-2 rocket, which both rained terror on London and other Allied positions during the final months of the war. In addition, the Germans had developed chemical and biological weapons, and there was a fear of the potential of atomic weapons. The Germans thought these unique weapons would render their enemies defenseless; they called them *Wunderwaffen*, or "wonder weapons." Many were manufactured in secret, abandoned underground salt mines by slave laborers from nearby concentration camps. Even before the end of the war, the United States was sending military and scientific personnel into the European fighting theater in search of the scientists and technologists who were developing these weapons.

It was the general feeling that if America didn't recruit these scientists, the Soviets would and these weapons would eventually be used against the United States. In addition, the United States government figured that acquiring equipment, scientists, and technologists from the Germans would close the gap between the more advanced German technologies and the current Allied technologies and could save millions of dollars in research and development. The US military wanted to act quickly to capture Nazi armaments and to hire the German scientists and engineers who had created those weapons. The goal was to prevent resurgence of Germany as a war power and also to advance American technology and know-how for the upcoming battles in Japan and potentially with the Soviet Union.

Operation Paperclip was a top-secret program directed by the US State Department and the US military to bring German scientists and their families to the United States. The most controversial issue was State Department approval of certain individuals who had been members of the Nazi Party, including members of the secret police in Nazi Germany. It was also speculated that some of the scientists had conducted human experiments on unwilling inmates in German concentration camps. Army intelligence officers reviewing reports on the scientists would attach a paperclip to the files of individuals suspected to be more troublesome, so the program was called Operation Paperclip. It soon became apparent that the program had to focus not just on whether these individuals were Nazis, but also on whether they were of some interest to the Russians. If these scientists went to the Soviet side, they would eventually work against American political and military objectives after the war.

The most famous German scientist brought to the United States as a result of Operation Paperclip was the rocket scientist Wernher von Braun. He designed and developed the V-2 rocket on the German North Sea island of Peenemünde.

The V-2 was the first long-range ballistic missile and had the capability of striking England within minutes after launch. When he got to the United States, Wernher von Braun was the key scientist who designed the Saturn rocket that propelled American astronauts to the moon in the late 1960s.

German aviation medicine and research was known for decompression- and high-altitude-sickness studies and for studying pilot performance in extreme cold and at extreme altitude and speeds. In addition, the Germans were conducting work on air-sea rescue programs and recovery from severe hypothermia.

The two United States military officers attentive to Nazi-sponsored aviation research were Major General Malcolm Grow and Colonel Harry Armstrong. These scientists, who cofounded the Aviation Medical Laboratory at Wright Field in the 1930s, had collaborated with Mayo Clinic researchers on many major medical advances, such as oxygen-delivery systems at high altitude, decompression sickness, and gravitational loss of consciousness, which included the development and testing of the G-suit. They knew the German offices of aviation medical research institutions were in Berlin.

After the fighting stopped in 1945, Colonel Armstrong went to Berlin, hoping to find the Third Reich's most important aviation researchers. The director of the Luftwaffe war-aviation research programs was Dr. Hubertus Strughold, whom Armstrong had met before the war at the Aerospace Medical Association conference in 1934, after Strughold conducted aviation research and physiology at Case Western Reserve University, in Cleveland, and the University of Chicago. These scientists had much in common, having conducted high-altitude experiments on themselves. They met again in 1937 at a medical conference in New York City. Both were the directors of major laboratories in their respective countries. Armstrong was the director of the aeromedical research laboratory at Wright Field, while Strughold oversaw the Research Institute for Aviation Medicine of the Reich Air Ministry in Berlin. Strughold had also given a lecture on German aviation at a physiology and biochemistry symposium at the University of Minnesota in collaboration with Mayo Clinic in August 1929. The title of the presentation was "Aviation Physiology: Nervous Mechanism Involved in Airship Control." At the time, Strughold was working with the University of Würzburg.

Harry Armstrong arrived in Berlin in 1945, shortly after the hostilities stopped, in search of the German aviation scientists. He found that the ones he was interested in had left the city, which was mostly destroyed by Allied bombings and the invasion by Soviet troops. Many scientists wanted to avoid being captured and arrested by the Soviet or American troops, so they went into hiding in the countryside or smaller towns. Through several contacts and some luck, Armstrong was able to locate Dr. Strughold in Göttingen, in the British zone. Being an old acquaintance with mutual scientific interests, Armstrong was able to convince Strughold to work with the Americans to bring other German aviation scientists to work for the Allies.

Together Major General Malcolm Grow and Colonel Harry Armstrong were able to use the Kaiser Wilhelm Institute for Medical Research, in Heidelberg, Germany. Before and during the war, this institute was used by chemists and physicists under the direction of the German Reich. The former Kaiser Wilhelm Institute was complete with machine shops, carpentry shops, and electrical shops, along with photographic and research laboratories. It was built in 1929, and additional wings for physics and pathology were constructed in 1936. It also had an extensive library, which contained all the important German research journals along with many American and British chemical, physics, and physiological periodicals. This two-story building became the Army Air Forces Aero Medical Center in Heidelberg. Its mission was to bring back from Germany everything of aeromedical interest to the US Army Air Forces and all information of importance to medical science in general. In the summer of 1945, Dr. Howard Burchell, then a major in the Army Air Forces, was initially put in charge of finding and interviewing the German scientists.

Howard Burchell was born in Athens, Ontario. He received his medical degree in Canada and studied physiology at the University of Minnesota, where he earned a PhD. He studied for a year in England, in 1940, and then returned to the United States and became a naturalized American citizen before the attack on Pearl Harbor. Dr. Burchell worked in the aeromedical laboratory at Mayo Clinic, studying low-pressure environments and oxygen-delivery systems with Randy Lovelace and Walter Boothby. At the start of the US involvement in World War II, Dr. Burchell volunteered for the Army Air Forces. He was stationed at Randolph Field and taught aviation physiology to new pilots and bomber crews. He was eventually transferred to Britain, where he worked with the Eighth Air Force, treating and studying the physiological and psychological trauma encountered by bomber pilots and crews following their missions over Europe. He also conducted medical consulting in surrounding hospitals in England, where the air force personnel might have been treated.

Following the German surrender in April 1945, Dr. Burchell—by then a major—was preparing to head to the Pacific theater. However, since he was already stationed in Europe and was an expert on psychological and physiological stresses of flight, he was transferred to Heidelberg to evaluate the progress on the new laboratory and set up interviews with the German scientists. Being a scientist and a physician, he was quite uncomfortable with this new assignment. He took the position that army intelligence was better qualified to determine whether the German scientists in question should be brought to the laboratory or be arrested and tried. Several German scientists who were well known for their work in aviation medicine came to Heidelberg to conduct research in which the Army Air Forces was interested.

Dr. Otto Gauer was the first to come, arriving on September 20. He was followed shortly by Drs. Theodor Benzinger and Siegfried Ruff. On October 16, Dr. Strughold joined Major Burchell's staff. In November 1945, the Aero Medical Center in Heidelberg was put under the command of Colonel Robert J. Benford, and Dr. Burchell returned to Rochester and Mayo Clinic in January 1946. On his return home, he stopped in London and was able to observe a cardiac catheterization procedure being done at several hospitals; this idea and its potential for future research he brought back with him to Mayo.

With Mayo Clinic's involvement in aviation medicine during the war, it was only natural that its scientists would become involved with Operation Paperclip. Dr. Randy Lovelace, now a colonel in the US Army Air Forces, went to Germany shortly after the war and interviewed Dr. Strughold and several of his colleagues. One of them was Dr. Theodor Benzinger, who ran the Reich's Luftwaffe experimental research center. Dr. Lovelace, of course, had an interest in Benzinger's work involving high-altitude parachute escapes, which Lovelace had himself experienced after jumping out of a B-17 at forty thousand feet. Benzinger told Lovelace that he had performed his studies on rabbits. Lovelace had no idea that some of Benzinger's experiments were conducted on human beings, inmates from a concentration camp.

It was through the connection to Harry Armstrong that Dr. E. J. Baldes, who directed the Mayo Aero Medical Unit and Mayo scientists, was sent to Europe in late 1945. In a letter dated September 15, 1945, Howard Burchell wrote from Germany to E. J. Baldes at Mayo:

> Dear E. J.,
>
> I'm delighted to hear that you are coming over to Europe on a trip and I think that I will be definitely seeing you as some of your "targets" will be in the city where I shall be stationed. . . .
>
> From the more purely physics point of view you will be most interested in the work at the Helmholtz Institute which is located on the top of Mt. Wendelstein a few miles south of Rosenheim in Bavaria. It is here that they have been attempting to study the effect of supersonic energies on the human organism, but as of yet not many experiments have been completed. They have also been working on natural periodicity of various parts of the body when exposed to various frequencies.
>
> The Air Corps in Europe is setting up a laboratory in Heidelberg in the Kaiser Wilhelm Institute and it will probably be getting functioning at the time you arrive. Dr. Otto Gauer will be at the place and it is he who was working on the centrifuge in Berlin. He is [a] very knowledgeable fellow but he never had a centrifuge that would compare in performance to those in the states. Nevertheless, you would be interested

in his ideas and the work that has been accomplished. At Heidelberg also there will be Dr. Ruff who did most of the medical work on the catapult seats and Dr. Benzinger who was chief of testing station of the Luftwaffe in Rechlin.

Personally, I feel that it is a very bad policy to set up the German scientists in the Institute, as they were all party members. It makes me very unhappy to see it done as my training has been in clinical medicine and not in basic physiology, you can imagine that my assignment is an uncomfortable one. But I have [put] considerable constructive effort into the general problem of aviation medicine research in Germany and suggested alternative plans to the Institute, but I have always been a minority option.

Amending among the men I have listed above, Rein [sic] is the only person you will meet who is not a Nazi party member. Some will say it was forced upon them and among the most verbose individuals that you will meet is Strughold.

Very Sincerely,
Howard

In November 1945, Dr. E. J. Baldes made his initial visit to Heidelberg to discuss further interviews with the German scientists, Dr. Burchell, and the new commanding officer, Colonel Benford. Plans were being made to bring laboratory equipment and scientific apparatus to the aeromedical center from Luftwaffe laboratories and research institutions throughout Germany. This included the more than twenty tons of equipment salvaged from the human centrifuge being constructed at Tempelhof airport in Berlin. Further plans were made to have civilian scientific consultants conduct the searches and interviews of the German scientists so the Army Air Forces could work specifically on intelligence matters.

Under the command of Colonel Benford, the American personnel were looking specifically at the German researchers' scientific qualifications and contributions before and after World War II to determine whether the scientists should be hired to work in the laboratory. Dr. Strughold became the co-director at the Aero Medical Center in Heidelberg and was put in charge of hiring scientists who were considered authorities in aviation and medicine. German research workers would be able to organize their material, which had been dispersed throughout Germany in the last years of the war. The plan was to establish a laboratory so that certain unfinished experimental work might be conducted and completed by the same German scientists who initiated it.

In February 1946, General Grow visited the Aero Medical Center in Heidelberg. He was accompanied by Colonel Otis Benson, now the commanding officer at the headquarters of the US Air Force School of Aviation Medicine, who had encouraged David Clark before the war to work on G protection. Colonel Benson suggested that a compilation of the German scientific work in aviation medicine be written and published for the benefit of all aviation scientists in the United States. Before his return to the United States, Colonel Benson contacted E. J. Baldes at the Mayo Foundation to assist in the recruiting of German scientists and the compilation of their scientific works during World War II.

THE INVITATION

In early 1946, General Grow spoke with Dr. Donald Balfour at Mayo Clinic. Dr. Balfour, who was the head of the Mayo Foundation, informed General Grow and Colonel Otis Benson that it was possible for Dr. Baldes and another civilian scientist to return to Germany in March. Two other candidates for this trip were not able to leave their university positions; therefore Colonel Benson extended the invitation to another researcher, preferably a physiologist, to accompany Dr. Baldes.

In early February 1946, E. J. Baldes invited Earl Wood to accompany him to Germany, France, Switzerland, and Holland, in search of and to interview German scientists as part of Operation Paperclip. They were to be headquartered at the Aero Medical Center in Heidelberg. Why Dr. Baldes did not ask Charlie Code, codirector of the acceleration laboratory, or even Ed Lambert, who directed many of the experiments on the G-Whiz, is still a mystery. Earl had to think twice about agreeing to go on this extended trip, due to obligations in the laboratory plus at home with his young family.

In a letter to Dr. Morris Visscher dated February 11, 1946, Earl wrote,

> Dear Dr. Visscher,
>
> As a relatively interested party who is familiar with my background, I would appreciate your advice on a decision which I have to make before Thursday, February 14.
>
> I have the opportunity to make a trip to Europe with Dr. Baldes as a civilian representative of the Army Air Forces. The trip would

be for two to three months duration, most of which time would be spent in Germany at the scientific centers under Allied control excluding the Russian zone. Some of the time would be spent in scientific centers in England, France, Switzerland and Holland.

We would be civilians in Army uniform, transportation and maintenance furnished by the Army, and also pay.

The purpose of the mission is, from what I can make out, exploration of German scientists' scientific equipment and ideas. EJ plans to bring back all the scientific equipment obtainable which, in his opinion and perhaps mine, might be of value to the United States. Evidently, many Army personnel are very pessimistic about the future relations with Russia; this mission stems from that pessimism.

As you may know the Americans own the German research centers, which are being run under U.S. Army supervision. We are also to visit the centers and give our opinion as to the research being carried on, etc.

Our only responsibility to the Army, as far as I can learn, is to make a memorandum report summarizing our activities in Europe and outlining whatever conclusions and recommendations we might have.

That about outlines the setup, as I know it.

I'm very skeptical of the scientific value of this mission and hence count that practically zero in attempting to arrive at a decision as to whether or not to grasp this opportunity. However, such a trip would be of considerable value to me personally from the broad educational viewpoint and from what I could pick up in a scientific way from visiting a good many European laboratories and interviewing many scientists. From reports I have heard from several sources, the German scientists are very cooperative with the Americans and are actually anxious to make available to the United States all of their ideas, results and equipment. This attitude, evidently, is largely due to their capacity and fear of the Russians.

The cost of the trip to me as I see it would be a serious disruption of our plans to get our war research written up and published this year and similar disruption in our plans for future research. The disruption of my family life as a consequence of three months absence is also a major stumbling block. Charlie would be pleased, I surmise, if I didn't go since it would change somewhat his plans for the year. Clinic personnel as a whole will accept without too much concern one way or another whatever decision is made.

That is about the story. I would very much appreciate if you would give me a call or drop me a note before Thursday as to your opinion of whether or not these months of my time are worth what I would gain from the liberal education obtained from touring Europe at this time.

Very sorry to hear that you have been ill

recently and hope your health is on the mend
by this time.

Best wishes to Mrs. Visscher and your
family.

Sincerely,

Earl

P.S. Needless to say, most of the above for
my good should be confidential.

On the receipt of this letter, Dr. Visscher phoned Earl immediately, expressing his thoughts that visiting the laboratories and interviewing the scientists in Europe would broaden
Earl's horizons and enhance his future career in physiological
research.

By March 1946, Earl was receiving forms to complete
from the War Department and requests going to the secretary of war for his appointment as a civilian consultant. A
civilian consultant could serve no more than 180 days in a
year and no more than ninety consecutive days. Therefore,
the orders were cut for Earl for approximately ninety days.
Once the paperwork was completed, passport procured, and
arrangements with Mayo Clinic made, Earl was permitted to
accompany Dr. Baldes to Europe. They were to leave shortly
after the close of the physiology meetings in Atlantic City on
March 15. While Earl was away in Europe, Ada and Phoebe
went to Big Lake to live with Ada's parents so they would not
be alone and so Phoebe could be around loving grandparents.

By the spring of 1946, several German scientists had already been employed at the Aero Medical Center in Heidelberg.
They included Hubertus Strughold, who was in charge of compiling the various research projects conducted by the German
scientists; Dr. Theodor Benzinger, who was summarizing
and studying the effects of temperature and oxygen-delivery

change on the human body with altitude; Dr. Otto Gauer, who was looking at venous return and blood dynamics during high-acceleration flight, similar to what was being done at Mayo Clinic; Dr. Ulrich Henschke, who was working on new advances in prosthetics for the hands and lower extremities using hydraulics; and Dr. Siegfried Ruff, who was working on physical and physiological responses due to high-velocity seat catapults and ejection seats in the latest jet aircraft.

Earl Wood and E. J. Baldes arrived at Orly Field in Paris about 1:00 a.m. on Thursday, April 18, 1946, on a TWA Constellation airliner. They were required to report to the US embassy, but unfortunately it was closed and they were not able to report in until that next Monday. This gave them time to see the sights of Paris, including the Eiffel Tower and the Arc de Triomphe on the Champs-Élysées. While in Paris, Earl was lucky enough to contact his sister, Louise, who was working with the American Red Cross in Europe at the time. True to Wood form, Earl had Louise arrange to get an M-1 rifle and a semiautomatic twelve-gauge shotgun through her contacts in the Red Cross and the military, so he could go hunting in Germany.

HEIDELBERG

Earl and Dr. Baldes finally arrived in Heidelberg on April 25, 1946, and reported to Colonel Benson. At this time the two Mayo scientists were introduced to Dr. Strughold and his team of German scientists. Work had been initiated to bring in equipment from the Graf Zeppelin Research Institute and the Helmholtz physiological laboratories, formerly in Berlin, but which had been moved to Bavaria before the end of the war.

In a progress report written on May 21, 1946, Earl and Dr. Baldes summarized their activities since arrival in Germany, most of which involved contacting scientists throughout Germany, but which also included combining the Helmholtz physiological group with the Graf Zeppelin Research Institute, where much of the acceleration research had been done during the war. Drs. Ruff and Gauer had also given them blueprints of the centrifuge that was under construction in Berlin. In addition, they were obtaining the design for a catapult for studying ejection seats from jet aircraft and deceleration studies, simulating the effects of a plane crash on the human body. The number one priority of the project was starting a comprehensive monograph covering the accomplishments of German aviation and research during the war. The project was underway, and deadlines were set for turning in completed German manuscripts by September 1 of that year. Dr. Strughold was the chief German editor of the monograph and estimated the printed edition would be at least six hundred pages.

That same evening, after the progress report was sent to Army Air Forces command, Earl wrote a letter to Ada and Phoebe. The letter was written on stationery from the Army Air Forces Aero Medical Center headquarters, Third Central Medical Establishment, APO 172 US Army. The envelope had a return address of American Air Force Aero Medical Center, Third Central Medical Establishment, New York, NY. It was postmarked US Army, May 23, 1946, with a six-cent airmail stamp. There was no indication from either the envelope or the stationery that this letter was written in Germany. This is an indication of the strict security surrounding Operation Paperclip.

The letter was addressed to Mrs. Earl H. Wood, Big Lake, Minnesota USA. No street address, which was typical when addressing an envelope in those simpler times. In the letter,

Earl in Heidelberg, Germany, 1946

Earl indicated that he was packing his bags to leave the next morning for Frankfurt to see a Dr. Wetzler and then on to Wiesbaden to see people at the Army Air Forces headquarters. From there they were going to drive to Göttingen by way of Bad Nauheim and then Fulda, where they were to see a couple of physicians, a Dr. Schaeffer and a Dr. J. Schneider. Earl was looking forward to seeing and meeting a prominent physiologist by the name of Dr. H. Rine, who was the head of the University of Göttingen physiology department and was a good friend of Dr. Otto Krayer from Harvard University. Dr. Krayer had a letter for Dr. Rine that Earl was to deliver to him. Earl wanted to spend some time in his laboratory; however, time would not allow him to do so. Earl also mentioned he was looking forward to being in Westphalia and the possibility of going hunting. He had purchased a pair of combat boots in the post exchange, along with an army jacket, for being out in the woods.

Operation Paperclip gave the two Mayo Clinic scientists a unique opportunity to visit and explore the landscape, culture, educational system, and university scientific research centers in postwar Germany. The Army Air Forces provided a four-door Chevrolet sedan for Earl, E. J., and Dr. Strughold to travel to the various university and research centers in Germany.

In the early morning of May 23, 1946, Earl wrote a letter to Ada and Phoebe discussing their travels so far. That morning they set out for Fulda on their way to Göttingen. The roads, which were not good for fast travel, passed through some beautiful country. From Fulda, they went north toward Kassel and were soon on the Reich autobahn.[3]

---

3.   In later years, Earl said this was the first time he had driven on the autobahn, and he talked about how impressed he was with the construction and the smoothness of the pavement. No question he tested the top speed of that army-issue Chevrolet sedan!

They drove very close to the Russian-occupied zone, where the army was checking all vehicles as they traveled by. Earl noted that as they came closer to the Russian-occupied zone, Dr. Strughold started to tear up and throw away his identification papers in fear that he might be captured and detained by the Russians.

They were unable to pass through Kassel due to several blown-up bridges on the autobahn and had to go through Hannover and Münden and a small village on the Weser River. Arriving that evening, they visited Professor Rine, who taught physiology at the University of Göttingen and was the university's acting director.

On Friday, May 24, they attended a lecture on muscle physiology given in German. The amphitheater was crowded and every seat was filled. Several experiments were performed before the class. Textbooks for college students were unavailable, and most of them depended on their lecture notes. Paper was also a scarce commodity. In schools there were no books either, since the occupational armies had confiscated all textbooks, even Shakespeare.

Dr. Baldes noted that the caloric intake in the British zone was a little over one thousand calories per day. One thousand calories will maintain life metabolism if one is in bed, whereas it takes thirteen hundred calories if one is up and moving around but doing no work. The visiting scientists were invited out for supper with Dr. Strughold's cousin. The evening meal was the first they had in a German home, and it offered them their first taste of pumpernickel bread. (As Dr. Baldes noted, there is no doubt that the US can learn much from German breads, of which there are several varieties involving rye, wheat, and various mixtures.) Besides pumpernickel there were *schwarzbrot* (black bread), *weissbrot* (white bread), and *graubrot* (gray bread), all which tasted good and were very nutritious. The visitors were informed by the Germans that the daily rations consisted of only three slices of bread per day, but the bread definitely had more body and higher caloric content than American bread. The eating technique was to take a piece of bread, spread a layer of butter on it, cover it with a thin slice of sausage or ham, and eat it with a knife and fork. They were served coffee, so there was coffee available in the British zone.

The next morning, Saturday, May 25, they attended a lecture by Professor Pohl, who taught physics in Germany. His lecture was on lenses, and Dr. Baldes noticed that the Germans had better teaching and instruction on lenses than corresponding schools in the United States. Of course, German lenses and cameras were superior to what was made in the US at that time.

WESTPHALIA FARMLANDS

After lunch, the three scientists loaded up in the Chevrolet sedan along with two relatives of Dr. Strughold, who were hitching a ride home, and set out for Westphalia, his homeland. They passed through beautiful country, traveling along the Weser valley for many miles until finally reaching the city of Paderborn, which was almost completely destroyed in the war. This area of Germany is known as the Sauerland and is quite mountainous. In the small village of Eikeloh they stopped at a farm owned by Dr. Strughold's aunt, Frau Fredricka Schulte Beehuhl, or "Tante Fredricka," for supper and to spend the night.

Earl was particularly interested in the farms, since he'd grown up on a farm in southern Minnesota. In this area, the houses and barns were basically built together. The buildings were made of brick and the walls were very thick, topped with tile roofs. The barn side of the houses had large doors to allow for a horse and wagon with a full load of hay to enter. The farm was about one hundred acres, and there was good hunting for wild boar as well as deer. Later that evening they drove to another farm owned by the Hinchey family. Frau Hinchey was Frau Schulte Beehuhl's sister, and this farm had been in the family since about 1600 and consisted of some eight hundred acres, most of which were forested. Frau Hinchey and her husband had five sons and a daughter; all the sons were great hunters.

On the morning of May 26, Dr. Baldes went for a long walk in the woods while Earl tried his luck at hunting with one of the Hinchey boys. The hunting was both interesting and enjoyable. Earl was successful in shooting a partridge with a twelve-gauge shotgun. The noon Sunday dinner consisted of canned venison, boiled potatoes, rhubarb sauce, and a fruit mixture for dessert.

In the afternoon they went to the Möhne Dam on the Möhnesee, a big lake on the north edge of the Sauerland. This large dam was destroyed by a direct hit from a Royal Air Force Lancaster bomber. The damage done, even the Germans would admit, was more than the loss of a major battle. When the torpedoes from the Lancaster hit its target, within minutes the entire reservoir was empty. The water totally submerged the town of Neheim within twelve minutes, engulfing more than fifteen hundred residents. It came so fast that observers could see the headlights of automobiles still on under the rushing waters.

On Monday, May 27, the group set out for the towns of Lippstadt and Minden in an attempt to contact some British officials in regard to procuring optical equipment for the laboratory. Unsuccessful, on Tuesday they drove north across the border into Holland, passing through the town of Emmerich, which was almost completely destroyed in the war; the devastation, in Earl's words, was "unbelievable." Along the road they stopped by a shot-up German tank. There were six graves scattered around it marked with crosses and helmets, both German and Canadian. They passed through the city of Rotterdam, noting many vacant spaces in the downtown. Rotterdam had been bombed by the Nazis six years previously. The rubble had been cleaned up, yet the rebuilding had only just begun. From there they went on to The Hague, staying at the Grand Hotel Terminus.[4]

The next day they visited with a Dr. Formijne in Amsterdam and toured his clinic and laboratory, then spent the evening with Dr. Formijne and his wife at their flat, which they had lived in during the war. It was a single room with a stove just large enough for a teakettle. With the stove they were able to keep warm and do their cooking and washing. There was no electric light, so they had to make do with a flashlight and were able to change the battery just once a month. The Dutch diet during the war consisted mostly of sugar beets, with an approximate intake of three hundred calories a day. This was an attempt on the part of the Nazis to starve the Dutch into submission. The loss of lives because of malnutrition during the last year of the war was between 50,000 and 150,000.

MÜNSTER

On Thursday, May 30, they set out for the city of Münster, where Dr. Strughold had gone to medical school. In a letter to Ada following the trip, Earl noted that "the city of

---

4.   It is interesting to note that eating in a hotel in Amsterdam in 1946 was considered relatively expensive at four dollars per meal.

Münster was officially 80 percent destroyed. You can't imagine what that means until you see it. It looks like 100 percent! It is the worst large city I have seen yet." As Earl later wrote in the letter to Ada, "Prof. Strughold went to school here, I walked with him through some of the ruins and he pointed out where some of the buildings used to be." Münster, with its beautiful cathedral, famous town hall where the treaty was signed ending the Thirty Years' War and giving the Netherlands its independence, and arcades along its main street. Around twenty thousand Münster citizens were killed in the bombardment, and in 1946 the remaining eighty thousand inhabitants were just getting by with food rations, living in buildings with no roofs or windows. Here they visited Professor Schuz, a friend of Dr. Krayer's, at the Physiological Institute at the University of Münster, and they also had a demonstration using X-rays to locate foreign bodies in wounded soldiers.

This initial visit to Münster was the start of a decades-long relationship between the town, the university, and the young visiting physicians, and lifelong friendships for the Wood family. Future cardiovascular fellows who came to Mayo Clinic to work with Earl went to medical school in Münster. These individuals included Dr. Franz Bender, Dr. Paul Heintzen, and Dr. Thomas Behrenbeck.

On Friday, May 31, they drove to Dortmund to visit the Arbeitsphysiologiesche-Institut, or "work physiology institute." They had difficulty locating the building because many landmarks and buildings had been destroyed. Some of the equipment had been moved during the war to the town of Ems, which was now in the French zone. At that time the French would not let the equipment return to Dortmund because Dortmund was in the British zone; therefore, the visiting scientists could not procure the equipment for the aviation laboratory in Heidelberg. That afternoon they drove back to Münster to visit Dr. Sigmund, the head of the pathology department, and with a Dr. Schnetz.

HUNTING THE REHBOCK

Earl explained in a letter to Ada and Phoebe,

> We got back to Eicheloh [*sic*] about 7 pm. I got my hunting clothes and Dad Eichof and his son Rudolph went hunting with me in the mountains for Rehbock (a small type of deer we don't have in the United States) and also for wild boar. EJ and Strugie [Strughold's nickname] left me there for the night and they drove back to Strugie's sister a few miles away. We walked up into the mountains, which was plenty of exercise and hunted until about 10 o'clock when it gets dark here. We had no success, but it was very interesting. They do a good share of their hunting for deer and boar from high platforms erected in strategic spots so that you get a good view of the countryside. These are known as a "Jagtturm" or hunting towers. The family has a "Jagthaus" or hunting house up there in the mountains where they stay when they concentrate on hunting for several days in a row. We got down from the mountains about 10:30. We had a little dinner and sat around and talked and drank a little wine until 12:30 am. They spoke very

little English and I very little German so we had some difficulty making ourselves understood but got along okay. Two of his sons were in the German Army from 1940 and were Tiger Tank drivers. They were in Russia, Holland and France.

Got up the next morning at 3:30 am. Rudolph and I went up into the mountains. It was very windy with occasional showers and quite cold. He put me in the best Jagtturm and I sat there with a pair of binoculars looking for game. About 6 am, I spotted a Rehbock on the hillside quite close by. It was a female so I couldn't shoot it. They shoot only bucks here. I watched her on the hillside eating until about 8 am. She came within 30 yards of the tower for a time and for a while there were two of them in sight but no bucks so I did no shooting.

We returned to the house about 9 am. EJ and Strugie were there waiting. I ate breakfast, shaved and we took off for Eicheloh [sic]. The Eichofs were very insistent that I come back to go hunting for several days so I would be sure to get a buck.

By June 2, they were on their return trip to Heidelberg, taking the scenic route through areas of the Sauerland that Dr. Strughold wanted them to see.

Between June 22 and June 26, Earl and E. J. Baldes made a trip to Switzerland. On the way, they stopped in Köndringen, Germany, had lunch in the Rebstock Restaurant, and met Dr. Otto Krayer's parents, who owned the establishment.

Dr. Hubertus Strughold and Earl Wood, Germany, 1946

On June 24, they spent the day at the University of Bern, inspecting the physiological institute headed up by Professor Alexander von Muralt. This institute specialized in neurophysiology and muscle physiology and was a contact for future collaborative research in which Earl participated two decades later. During their stay in Bern, Earl purchased a Le Phare Swiss watch at a watch store on the Kramgasse. This mechanical chronograph had a stopwatch and indicated date, day of the week, month, and current time. Perfect for scientific research! This watch was worn by Earl for several decades and was passed on to his son.[5]

On June 25, they drove to Grindelwald in the Berner Oberland and took the cog railway through the tunnels to the Jungfraujoch. The Jungfraujoch is a saddle between two

5. The watch still works and keeps good time more than seventy years after its purchase.

mountains, the Jungfrau and Mönch, and is only accessible by the cog railway. The purpose of their visit was to evaluate the high-altitude experimental station. The high-altitude laboratory at the Jungfraujoch is active only during the summer months due to the harsh winters at altitude. Unfortunately, during their visit, the laboratories were vacant except for pieces of equipment that were stored there during the winter months.

According to his letter to Ada and Phoebe dated July 7, 1946, Earl was staying in Louise's quarters in Wiesbaden. Earlier that day he had driven to Frankfurt, where he picked up his plane reservations to London. The next morning, Earl got up at 8:30 a.m., worked at the institute, said goodbye to Strughold and all the staff, and headed for Frankfurt. He packed two large bags, about a quarter of which was food and candy for his contacts in England. When he was done visiting the laboratories and universities in the UK, he would fly from London to Paris, where he could catch a plane back to the States on July 21.

In a letter from London dated July 15, 1946, Earl stated he had a reservation to fly home from Paris on July 22 or 23 on a TWA Constellation. Unfortunately, all those planes had been grounded due to mechanical issues and therefore he had to make different reservations, possibly going on a cargo plane.

On July 22, Earl was back in Paris for meetings and to arrange his trip back to the United States. Earl met up with his sister Louise in Paris and went out to dinner at a nice restaurant overlooking the River Seine. As they were dining on fine French cuisine, Earl asked, "What are two farm kids from Mankato, Minnesota, doing in a fine, luxurious restaurant in Paris, France?" Earl also mentioned to Louise that he dreamed of bringing his family to Europe, a goal that did materialize about twenty years later.

Earl flew out of Paris the evening of July 23, landing in

Westoverfield, Massachusetts. Earl planned to visit Dave Clark in Worcester and Mrs. Krayer in Boston prior to his trip to Washington, where he had to report to the air force surgeons' offices and meet with Colonel Otis Benson before proceeding to Minnesota.

For Earl, Operation Paperclip was an introduction to scientific research in foreign countries and different viewpoints and cultures, which had a lasting effect on him and his growing family. But one can also say that Operation Paperclip, for Earl, was a joyride through postwar Europe and gave him the desire to return to work and live in Europe. He and E. J. Baldes completed their mission for Operation Paperclip by interviewing many German, Dutch, Swiss, and British scientists and creating an outline for the monograph summary of German aviation medicine during the Second World War. At the end of their visit, plans were initiated for the compilation and publication of all the important accomplishments in aviation medicine made by the Germans during the war years of 1939 through 1945. Forty-nine German scientists, all authorities in particular fields of aviation medicine, contributed manuscripts to this project. Translation of the documents began in late 1946. By the end of 1947, a two-volume set of books was published in English highlighting German medical-aviation research.

There is no question that Earl wanted to return to Europe. In a letter to Colonel Otis Benson dated August 13, 1946, Dr. Baldes requested arrangements for Earl to spend a year in Germany starting early that next spring. Earl wanted to become familiar with the physiological work done at Dr. Rine's laboratory in Göttingen. Mayo Clinic would assume all financial obligations so that Earl could work in the capacity of scientific advisor to the Army Air Forces, independent of any financial considerations of the Army Air Forces. This was subject to the approval of General Grow and Colonel Benson and the aeromedical group at Wright Field, along with the State Department. Unfortunately, Earl was denied for the work in Europe in the spring of 1947, since the activity in Heidelberg was winding down.

CONTROVERSY

Operation Paperclip's mission was controversial. Some of the scientists that Earl and E. J. Baldes interviewed and worked with in Germany were arrested and tried at Nürnberg. Some of them were acquitted and came to the United States to work. Earl never mentioned the controversial activities of these scientists during the war. He viewed these individuals strictly from a scientific perspective. He did mention that some of the German scientists did poor science. One can only speculate whether he knew of the atrocities that took place before and during the war. Like Howard Burchell, he left the intelligence work up to the military justice system.

Hubertus Strughold came to the United States in 1947 as part of Operation Paperclip. He was assigned to Randolph Air Force Base, in San Antonio, Texas, and the US Air Force School of Aviation Medicine. He became a US citizen in 1956 and worked with the National Aeronautics and Space Administration (NASA), where he helped design pressure suits and life-support systems for the Gemini and Apollo astronauts and spacecraft. In 1962, the Space Medicine Association of America established the Strughold Award, honoring individuals that had made outstanding contributions in the area of aerospace medicine.[6] Strughold had been a

---

6. Earl was a recipient of this award in 2002.

subject of numerous investigations into the war crimes committed in World War II. A 1958 investigation by the Justice Department fully exonerated him, and he denied any involvement in human experimentation. It wasn't until after his death in 1986 that US Army Intelligence documents were released linking him with the atrocities that took place at Dachau. His name and picture were eventually removed from the library at Randolph Field, and by 2013 the Strughold Award was no longer given by the Aerospace Medical Association.

Theodor Benzinger was arrested in September 1946 as part of the Nürnberg trials and was released several months later. Following his work in Heidelberg, he was transferred to Randolph Air Force Base in 1947. He then worked in Bethesda, Maryland, at the Institute of Naval and Medical Research. He became an American citizen in 1955. He was credited with the development of the ear thermometer.

Siegfried Ruff was also arrested and tried at Nürnberg. Ruff acknowledged human experimentation but denied that it resulted in any deaths. He was acquitted of all charges and remained in Germany, practicing medicine.

Otto Gauer continued his work on gravitational physiology and came to the aerospace medical laboratory at Wright Field in 1947. Later he taught physiology at Duke University, in Durham, North Carolina. His research surrounded weightlessness and space medicine. He was globally recognized as a circulatory physiologist and became an associate professor at the University of Giessen in 1956. In 1962, he was appointed a full professor at the Free University of Berlin.

The debate about Operation Paperclip continues to this day. On the one hand, Operation Paperclip was wrong to bring Nazi scientists to the United States who should've been tried and jailed. On the other hand, it's not known what would have happened if these Nazi scientists had gone to the

Soviet side. What can be said, however, is that many of these scientists assisted in the advancement of aerospace and clinical medicine and helped the United States launch a man into space, land him on the moon, and safely return him to Earth.

CHAPTER 12

THE 1950S: CARDIAC CATHETERIZATION, DYE DILUTION, AND OXIMETRY

When Howard Burchell was in England in 1945, he visited various hospitals and saw a cardiac catheterization (placing a flexible tube in a vessel and up to the heart) done by Dr. Sharpley Shafer and thought this was a coming thing. The procedure was relatively easy, and it opened up a new frontier to a better understanding of cardiac physiology. The first cardiac catheterization in the United States was performed by Drs. André Cournand and Dickinson Richards at Bellevue Hospital, in New York City, in 1945. When Howard Burchell returned to Mayo Clinic in January 1946, he wanted to sell the idea to Mayo Clinic. At the time, Dr. John Pender, an anesthesiologist, was putting catheters in veins to inject anesthetics more efficiently. In the 1940s, when a cardiac patient came along, the diagnosis was determined by the different heart sounds, along with X-rays. However, doctors did not know the amount of oxygen in the blood or the extent of the malfunction of the heart. In November 1946, Dr. Pender, Dr. Howard Burchell, and a technician performed the first cardiac catheterization at Mayo Clinic in the metabolic laboratory, to assess the cardiac condition of a patient undergoing surgery for gallstones. They convinced their colleagues at Mayo that the procedure was feasible and safe and had great diagnostic value.

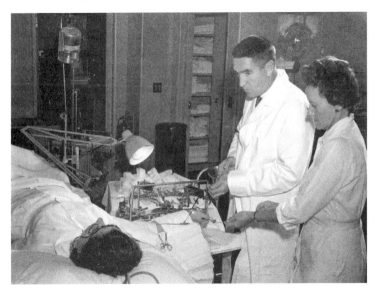

Earl in the cardiac catheterization lab in the 1950s

It just so happened that the Aero Medical Laboratory at Mayo Clinic was winding down at the end of the war and Earl was looking for something else to do. Howard Burchell suggested that Earl might take on the cardiac catheterization laboratory, and he jumped at the opportunity. In the process, he revolutionized the way cardiac catheterization was done and helped develop a world-renowned cardiovascular diagnostic center.

The cardiac catheterization laboratory was set up in the Medical Sciences Building, in the same rooms where the aviation scientists had prepared the subjects for the centrifuge runs in the Aero Medical Laboratory. Much of the instrumentation needed for studying the physiology of the heart was already set up, including an electrocardiograph, pressure gauges, and a blood-analysis laboratory. This instrumentation was used for cardiac catheterization, and the data was recorded in the same recording room and on the same photographic paper that had been used for the experiments with the centrifuge.

The Medical Sciences Building was connected by a tunnel to the main Mayo Clinic and the downtown hospitals in Rochester. Patients were transported through the tunnels from the hospitals or the main Mayo Clinic building to the Medical Sciences Building. Some changes had to be made to the Medical Sciences Building, since it was initially built for nonclinical purposes.

One of the interesting observations the scientists made while working with subjects on the centrifuge was that the photoelectric earpiece device for monitoring blood content and pulse showed a change in signal due to the passage of a bolus of saline solution, which was injected to flush the needle in the radial vein to prevent a potential blood clot. This observation was the basis for utilizing a dye-indicator dilution to study the flow of blood through the heart and the circulatory system and, eventually, measuring blood-oxygen content.

The photoelectric earpiece device was modified and manufactured by the Waters Conley company in Rochester. Earl worked with Waters Conley to produce the cuvette oximeter, which could be connected directly to a cardiac catheter. Infrared sensors to measure the light transparency of the blood indicated not only the dye that went through the instrument but also the oxygen saturation in the blood.

EARPIECE OXIMETER DEVELOPED IN DR. EARL WOOD'S LABORATORY
AT MAYO CLINIC, ILLUSTRATING LIGHT SOURCE AND PLUNGER IN
FULLY RETRACTED POSITION, WITH AIR TUBE TO SUPPORT
INFLATION OF RUBBER MEMBRANE AGAINST PINNA, CIRCA 1942

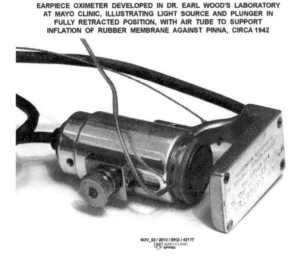

NOV_02/2010/BKG/42177
MAYO CLINIC
SPPDS

The ear pulse oximeter

With the development of flexible catheters, direct blood pressure could be measured in various chambers of the heart and vessels. Ralph Sturm modified the strain-gauge manometer that was on the centrifuge. Connected directly to the catheter, it would send a signal to the recording room, recording a direct pressure wave that varied depending on the location of the catheter tip in the heart. Each chamber of the heart has its unique pressure wave. Pressure-wave recording was a diagnostic tool to determine the efficiency of the heart muscle and to identify heart-valve issues such as aortic stenosis, narrowing of the aortic valve, or mitral regurgitation (when a mitral valve does not close completely and blood flows into the left atrium).

Cardiac catheterization gave cardiologists the ability to study both the right and left sides of the heart. With a left-heart catheterization, the catheter was inserted through an artery, usually the femoral artery in the groin, and fed up the descending aorta through the aortic arch and aortic valve into the left ventricle. Using the correct techniques, the catheter could be maneuvered into the left atrium through the mitral valve. The pressures in the left ventricle and the left atrium could be directly measured using the strain-gauge manometer, which was attached to the catheter outside of the body. Radiopaque dyes could also be injected through the catheter to view the inside of these chambers on X-ray. A right-heart catheterization involved placing a catheter into a vein, usually the brachial vein or radial vein in the arm, and feeding the catheter up to the right atrium and, with the correct maneuvering techniques, into the right ventricle.

The pressures in the chambers of the right side of the heart could be measured directly through catheterization techniques. Using the correct maneuvers, the "catheter pusher" could place the catheter from the right ventricle into the lung to directly measure the blood pressure in the lungs. Blood-oxygen saturation could be measured at any point by drawing blood from the tip of the catheter, which went through the cuvette oximeter for an instantaneous, real-time readout of oxygen saturation. A dye could be injected through the catheter and then detected downstream to evaluate the efficiency of the heart and whether there was a potential shunt or mixing of oxygenated and nonoxygenated blood, indicating a potential heart-chamber defect.

THE DYE CURVE

One of the problems facing pediatric cardiology was the location of heart defects in children. When the chambers of the heart fail to close during fetal development, creating a hole between the atria or the ventricles, nonoxygenated and oxygenated blood mix, causing the baby to turn blue (what was called a "blue baby" at the time). To remedy this, the earpiece used on the centrifuge to monitor blood flow at head level was modified to monitor hemoglobin oxygenation by continuous withdrawal of blood through a catheter positioned in various sites within or near the heart, to locate the heart defects. This instrument could measure oxygen levels in the blood directly without the need to send a blood sample to the laboratory for analysis. Blood flow could also be measured by injecting a dye into the vascular system; it would then be detected downstream by the oximeter, creating a curve indicating the efficiency of blood flow at the site being studied. This became known as a dye curve. A short circuit in the blood flow caused by an atrial septal defect or ventricular septal defect could be diagnosed by the early arrival of the dye at the sampling site. Initially, the dye that was used, called Evans Blue, was affected by oxygen concentration and reduced the specificity and the accuracy of the blood flow and also the curve generated.

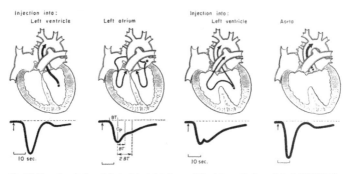

Wood EH. Diagnostic applications of indicator-dilution technics in congenital heart disease. Circ. Research. March 1962;X:531-568.

Dye curves showing different locations of heart defects

Dr. Jesse Edwards started at Mayo Clinic in 1946 when he got out of the army. Dr. Edwards was a pathologist and was interested in cardiac diseases. He worked with Earl in determining the anatomy of various congenital heart defects and assisted Earl in maneuvering the catheters into the various vessels and chambers of the heart and with analyzing and diagnosing cardiac pathologies.

The ear oximeter picked up pulse at head level and also oxygen-saturation levels. Both these parameters will change with exercise and physical activity. Therefore, an in-floor treadmill was installed in the room next to the catheterization laboratory to study the effects of blood-oxygen saturation and heart rate with physical activity, for both research purposes and clinical diagnoses. During exercise, a dye could be injected into a vein and then picked up by the photoelectric oximeter at the ear, and a dye curve could be produced, calculating cardiac output and evaluating if there was a potential shunt or cardiac dysfunction.

In the process of writing the publication about this new diagnostic procedure with exercise, Earl wanted to get a picture of one of his kids on the treadmill with the ear oximeter. Ada had Phoebe and her little brothers Mark and Guy dressed up in their Sunday best, since she knew that this picture was going to be published in an international scientific journal. As a reward for the occasion, Mark and Guy were given cowboy outfits complete with cap guns and holsters, to look like real cowboys. On a Sunday afternoon, they went into the Medical Sciences Building and into the cardiovascular laboratory. The oximeter was first placed on Phoebe's ear; however, it was too hot and uncomfortable and messed up her hair. Mark would have nothing to do with either the oximeter or the treadmill. So, the oximeter was put on Guy and he walked on the treadmill, looked over at the camera, and gave a big smile. This picture ended up in several medical journal publications and was also on the wall of Earl's office in the Medical Sciences Building for many years.

Guy Wood with an ear pulse oximeter, walking on the treadmill

Soon, medical researchers, research fellows, graduate students, and physicians came to Mayo Clinic from all over the world to learn about the latest in cardiovascular physiology and diagnostic techniques, including cardiac catheterization and analyzing dye curves. These budding scientists and physicians came from different countries and backgrounds and had differing views of the world. This was shortly after World War II, and the scars of war were still on the minds of many of these young students. However, in the laboratory, differences were set aside for the sake of learning and medical science. It was a unique atmosphere where French people were working with Germans, Japanese were working with Chinese, and Democrats worked with Republicans. Many of these individuals went on to other institutions as laboratory directors or stayed at Mayo Clinic. These individuals included Dr. Homer Warner, from the University of Utah; Dr. Dan Connolly, from Ireland; Dr. Irwin J. Fox, from Princeton and New York University; Dr. Hiram W. Marshall, from Michigan; Dr. Franz Bender, from Münster, Germany; Dr. Claude Puthon, from Annecy, France; Dr. Wilhelm Rutishauser, from Basel, Switzerland; and Dr. Hugh Smith, from Canada, who eventually became the chair of the Rochester Board of Governors.

Dr. Homer Warner, from Salt Lake City, Utah, came to the laboratory in 1951. Warner had flown navy Corsairs off aircraft carriers and experienced aerial combat during World War II. As a navy pilot, he wore a G-suit. Following World War II, he received his medical degree from the University of Utah, started work toward his PhD in cardiovascular physiology, and was granted a fellowship at Mayo Clinic. He worked on analyzing the pressure waves generated in the atria and ventricles during cardiac catheterization. Following his stay at Mayo Clinic, he returned to Utah, where he established the cardiac catheterization department at the University of Utah and LDS Hospital, in Salt Lake City. This also led to a long collaboration between cardiovascular laboratories in Salt Lake City and Earl's laboratory at Mayo Clinic, exchanging ideas, equipment, and computer technology and research fellows. Dr. Warner's laboratory was responsible for initial computer analysis of electrocardiograms and physiological data coming from the catheterization laboratories.

One of the most influential research fellows working in Earl's lab in the 1950s was Dr. Irwin J. Fox, whom Earl affectionately called "IJ." IJ was born in Germany in 1926. Being Jewish, his parents were well aware of what was occurring politically in Germany with the rise of Adolf Hitler and the Nazi Party. So they decided to take a vacation. His mother sewed all their money into the lining of the clothes they were wearing, they packed their bags as if they were going on vacation, and they fled Nazi Germany for Holland and eventually Great Britain. From there they sailed to the United States, settling in Trenton, New Jersey. IJ was an academic scholar, receiving his undergraduate degree from Princeton University and then his medical degree from New York University. He arrived at Mayo Clinic as a research fellow in the cardiovascular laboratory in 1953. IJ had a vast knowledge of biology, chemistry, mathematics, and physiology, along with data analysis and statistical evaluation capabilities. What he had in academic knowledge, he lacked in mechanical ability and sometimes basic common sense about how things worked, such as light switches, valves, stopcocks, and even locks on doors. In addition—and unlike Earl, who was brawny, athletic, and physically active—IJ was relatively skinny and had minimal interest in athletic endeavors or outside activities. During experiments in the lab, IJ was known for throwing the wrong switch, opening or closing the wrong valves, and misplacing equipment. Earl once said, "You can make things foolproof, but you can't make them Foxproof!" What made IJ unique was his willingness to try new things and a sense of humor that could leave everyone around him laughing until tears rolled down their cheeks. Despite IJ's clumsiness, Earl leveraged IJ's scientific strengths and data analysis capabilities for physiological studies being conducted in the cardiac catheterization laboratory in the 1950s and early '60s. IJ became a close personal friend of the entire Wood family, participating in multiple family activities and hunting and fishing trips. IJ stayed at Mayo Clinic for almost ten years and became known as "fellow emeritus." But his reasons for staying at Mayo as a research fellow so long are simple: he enjoyed the scientific challenges, and, most of all, he enjoyed working with Earl Wood. There is no question IJ Fox's success in academic science is a result of Earl's understanding and compassion for this humble first-generation immigrant. He would have had a difficult time in any other laboratory. Earl often said, "IJ Fox is one of the smartest people I have ever met."

Dr. Irwin "IJ" Fox

FOX CARDIO GREEN

In the mid-1950s, Dr. IJ Fox was on an airplane, traveling to a physiology meeting. Sitting next to him was a chemist from the Kodak Company. The two began discussing the issues of working with various dyes in the human body and, specifically, the circulatory system. IJ discussed the drawbacks of working with Evans Blue, because it was affected by oxygen in the blood and it also turned the subjects and patients blue. It just so happened that this chemist was working on a green dye that was not affected by oxygen concentration. After several months, IJ worked with this chemist at Kodak and developed a dye that became known as Fox Cardio Green, or indocyanine green dye, which gave more accurate blood flow information and a clearer dye curve and increased the accuracy of determining cardiac output and diagnosing cardiac abnormalities. This dye is also used in other fields of medicine, including ophthalmology.

In the mid-to-late 1950s, X-ray fluoroscopy was being used to help the physician guide catheters through the veins and arteries and into the chambers of the heart. Initially, single-frame X-ray pictures were taken as the dye was injected into the heart chamber. This was very cumbersome because the doctor had to inject the dye and call out to the technician when the X-ray picture needed to be taken. The process was improved by using a movie camera to record both the radiopaque dye-injection process and the movement of the internal walls of the heart chambers. The disadvantage was that the movie film had to be developed and the diagnostic analysis had to be done following the procedure. This drawback was taken care of in the early 1960s with the use of videotape recording and eventually videodisc. The advent of image intensifiers, developed by Ralph Sturm, allowed for video-based recordings to be made during the passage of a radiopaque dye injected into a heart chamber so that the physician could quickly view the interior walls of the heart without having to wait for film development.

HEART-LUNG BYPASS

In the 1940s, cardiologists and cardiovascular surgeons were dreaming of direct surgical inner-cardiac repair. However, performing this type of surgery on a beating heart with blood flowing through it seemed an impossibility. Researchers looked at how they could bypass the heart while keeping the blood flowing and also oxygenating the blood. The main problem was preventing the blood from frothing or foaming as oxygen was added to the bloodstream. A heart-lung machine would divert blood away from the heart temporarily into the machine for oxidation and then back to the body while the heart was not moving. During the surgical procedure, the heart would be relatively free of blood so the surgeon could see while he was working. The first successful human open-heart procedure utilizing the heart-lung machine was performed by Dr. John Gibson in Philadelphia in 1953.

Development of a heart-lung bypass machine at Mayo Clinic started in 1952, headed up by cardiac surgeon Dr. John Kirklin and Earl Wood. The Mayo proposal was for a complete heart-lung bypass apparatus, adding a pump-oxygenator device or artificial lung. This would assure a relative absence of blood in the heart as the surgeon worked. Since the human body requires blood that contains fresh oxygen and is free of carbon dioxide, the apparatus would provide the respiratory exchange of oxygen and carbon dioxide and return it to the body via a temporary route while the surgeon completed his work. Approval was granted and the personnel for the project were assigned. This included Dr. John Kirklin, Dr. Dave Donald in surgical research, Earl Wood and Dr. Jeremy Swan in physiology, and a group from engineering. The project was divided into two parts. The first part was the design and engineering of the machine, and the second part was developing the surgical techniques necessary for utilizing the device.

The first phase of the project took almost a year, incorporating research from other laboratories and models modifying the engineering plan. The second phase was largely devoted to the construction of the device itself. Other Mayo personnel involved in this were Dr. James Duchenne, who worked on preoperative and postoperative management; Dr. Robert T. Patrick, an anesthesiologist; Dr. Howard Burchell, the cardiology advisor; Dr. Fred Helmholtz, advisor on respiratory problems; Jim Fellows, the technician assisting in the proper operation of the bypass device; and Lucy Cronin, technical assistant. Dr. John Kirklin's and Earl Wood's teams worked together to develop a heart-lung machine with a better oxygenation system. The first open-heart operation using the modified Mayo heart-lung machine was successfully performed March 22, 1955, by Dr. Kirklin at Rochester Methodist Hospital, on a patient with a ventricular septal defect.

In September 1955, a live television broadcast was done documenting open-heart surgery at Mayo Clinic. The local television station, KROC, was an NBC affiliate and had to get special permission to carry the program from ABC, which was broadcasting the event. The program was called *Medical Horizons* and was sponsored by Ciba, a pharmaceutical company. This was before satellite transmission. Live television was transmitted by telephone lines, so good rehearsals were a necessity. After a day and a half of rather ragged rehearsals, the show went off with little or no trouble, with Mayo Clinic personnel taking part in the telecast as the physicians were interviewed by ABC moderator Quincy Howe. During the broadcast, Dr. Kirklin explained the challenges of open-heart surgery using wax models of the heart constructed by Dr. Art Bulbulian (who helped design the BLB oxygen-delivery mask for high-altitude pilots, along with Drs. Boothby and Lovelace, during World War II). Using a mannequin, Earl demonstrated the cardiac catheterization procedures employed for accurate diagnosis prior to the open-heart operation. The function of the heart-lung machine was described by surgeons Dr. James Duchenne and Dr. David Donald as Jim Fellows oversaw the functioning of the machine during the surgical procedure. The sponsoring company and television stations estimated that six to nine million viewers watched the telecast. The only hiccup during the broadcast occurred when a fly settled on the hand of Dr. Howard Perry as the camera closed in for a picture of needles being inserted into his arm for the demonstration.

A team approach to cardiology was formed at Mayo Clinic. In the 1950s, weekly cardiovascular conferences were held on patients and research protocols. Dr. Howard Burchell read the electrocardiograms, which were his expertise. Dr. Jesse Edwards discussed the patients' clinical pathological issues. Dr. John Kirklin discussed surgical procedures, and the reviews of the cardiac catheterizations were done by Earl Wood.

In October 1955, **Don Hegland** joined the technical staff of the cardiac catheterization laboratory in the Medical Sciences Building. Don (or "Donnie," as Earl used to call him) was from Bemidji, Minnesota, and was a Korean War veteran. One of Don's first assignments working in the lab was to remove Earl's glasses during the cardiac catheterization procedure so that Earl could view the X-ray or oscilloscope without them, since Earl needed his bifocals to concentrate on the close work of maneuvering the catheter in the patient's arm or leg while viewing the electrocardiogram or pressure waves on the monitors next to the patient. Since Earl was in a sterile field, he could not remove his glasses himself and required Donnie to assist him.

Don also worked closely with Lucy Cronin in the cardiac catheterization laboratory, assisting with the instrumentation, including the strain-gauge manometers and oximeters. He eventually ended up in the recording room with Bill Sutterer, working with the same photographic instruments used for recording the data from the centrifuge. Don soon became an expert in recognizing the various pressure waves as seen on the instruments in the recording room. Through an intercom, he could direct the physicians maneuvering the cardiac catheter tip in the vascular system or the chambers of the heart, based on the pressure tracings in the recording room. From the hallways of the Medical Sciences Building, you could hear Don's voice over the intercom stating, "You're not in the ventricle yet," as he looked at the aortic-pressure wave on the recording paper. Don became very well known among the medical fellows, since he knew the pressure waves better than they did, and they often watched him during the experiments to gain knowledge of the various pressure waves generated by the chambers of the heart. When movie cameras and video were used during cardiac catheterizations to record angiograms, Don was responsible for turning the cameras on and off. Over the intercom, during cardiac catheterization, Earl would state, "OK, camera on, Donnie!" And after the dye was injected, "Camera off, Donnie." Along with Bill Sutterer and Lucy Cronin, Don became an integral part of the cardiovascular laboratory team at Mayo Clinic. Don Hegland also became a good friend of the Wood family. He participated in several Canadian fishing trips along with pheasant and deer hunting, in addition to working on projects at Lake Washington.

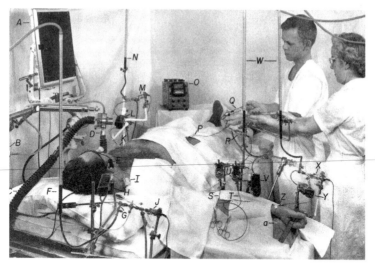

Don Hegland and Irene Donovan assisting with
a left-heart cardiac catheterization

POTENTIAL COMPLICATIONS AND RISKS

Cardiac catheterization procedures were run much like the experiments on the centrifuge. Lucy Cronin did all the preparation and safety checks. She also arranged the surgical instruments needed and made sure everything was clean and sterilized. Don Hegland and Bill Sutterer assisted with data collection and recording. It was a well-oiled machine.

Cardiac catheterization was not without its risks, however. A catheter tip could rub against a sensitive structure of the heart, such as the A-V node or the S-A node, which are the pacemakers of the heart, and cause arrhythmia. With a cardiac patient, even irritating the walls of the ventricles or atria with a catheter could cause the heart to go into tachycardia or fibrillation. One evening, Earl came home late for dinner. When he took off his coat and jacket, he had blood all over his shirt and tie, which caused quite a reaction from his kids, who were already at the dinner table. During a cardiac catheterization procedure, a patient had gone into cardiac standstill and was not able to be revived by shock or medication. Earl had cut open the chest, reached in and performed hand cardiac massage to start the heart, and continued hand pumping until the cardiac surgeons arrived to close the chest.

In another incident, Dr. Marshall was performing a cardiac catheterization and the patient's electrocardiogram started to show pre-ventricular contractions, or PVCs. The patient then went into ventricular tachycardia. Lucy Cronin phoned Earl's office, stating, "Dr. Wood, you need to get down here right away!" Earl rushed down from his office on the second floor of the Medical Sciences Building like he was running a hundred-yard dash at Macalester College. When he got to the cath lab, the patient had already slipped into ventricular fibrillation. Earl pulled some of the equipment away, raised his fist high in the air, and came down hard on the patient's chest, like he was pounding dock pipe at Lake Washington. This was known as a precordial thump. The heart went into normal sinus rhythm. One of the surgical assistants asked Dr. Marshall after Earl went back to his office, "Do you think it'll go back into ventricular tachycardia?" Dr. Marshall replied, "With a sledgehammer-fist like that, it wouldn't dare!"

In 1959, **Julijs Zarins** joined the team of cardiovascular technicians in the Medical Sciences Building. Zarins had emigrated from Riga, Latvia. During World War II, he had the choice to join either the Russian or the German army. He chose the German army; he hated the Russians. Eventually, he was captured by the Americans, spent time in a prisoner-of-war camp, and was released. After returning to Latvia, he took part in a small revolution against the Soviets when Russia took over the Baltic countries, and he was arrested. Taken out of Latvia in a railcar, he was imprisoned by the Soviets for at least a year. Julijs was lucky enough to escape the communist prison and ended up in West Germany. He worked on a farm near Munich for a couple of years. Dr. Charlie Code sponsored Julijs and his sister to come to the United States and Rochester.

Julijs worked as a painter and at the Pine Island Cheese Company before taking his job at Mayo. When Julijs arrived at Mayo, he oversaw the experimental catheterization laboratory in room 456 of the Medical Sciences Building. This room was used for conducting experiments on a smaller scale not suitable for the human catheterization laboratory or the centrifuge, which was on the first floor of the Medical Sciences Building. Julijs would set up the laboratory according to the protocols set forth by Earl and his research fellows. This involved working with the latest experimental equipment, including X-ray machines, ultrasound, monitoring equipment, video, and movie cameras. Room 456 on the fourth floor was directly hardwired to the data-recording room on the first floor, between the cardiac catheterization lab and the centrifuge. Therefore, Julijs and Don Hegland had to be in constant communication before, during, and after experiments were conducted in room 456. Julijs, whom Earl called "Joe," became another integral part of the technical crew that made the cardiovascular lab so successful from the late 1950s into the 1980s. Julijs was a quiet, gentle soul and a very hard worker. He was an outstanding chess player and an even better volleyball player. He happily showed killer spike shots playing volleyball at many lab picnics in the summers at Lake Washington.

A multitude of scientific investigations and publications were being produced in the physiology department in the Medical Sciences Building in the 1950s and '60s. An organized, dedicated secretary was needed to handle all of the paperwork and administrative tasks that came with the lab. That person was **Jean Frank**. Jean had the capability of perfectly typing 150 words a minute while carrying on a conversation. She had a filing system from which she could retrieve papers at a moment's notice, yet no one else understood it. She was extremely loyal to Earl Wood, Charlie Code, and Ed Lambert. She was a no-nonsense individual, and along with Lucy Cronin, ran the laboratory. Jean Frank was one of those individuals a fellow needed to get along with in order to be a success in the lab. She gave the young fellows a hard time, mainly because of their writing styles and their habit of submitting their papers for typing at the last minute. This was in the days before word processing, and she used carbon paper so that multiple copies of the manuscript could be produced for editing.

Most of the time Jean was quite approachable, with one exception: when a grant request was due. She needed to give those documents her undivided attention until it was complete. Technical staff were known to get their "heads bit off" if they asked Jean for something when grant requests were due. Jean was married to Carl Frank, a local banker. They didn't have any children; however, they were very active in animal rescue. She was particularly fond of Boston terriers. Jean and Carl purchased several plots of land within the city of Rochester and donated the land for dog parks, where people could play with their dogs without a leash in a controlled environment. These dog parks still exist in the city of Rochester.

THE DAWN OF THE DIGITAL AGE IN MEDICINE

It became increasingly evident with the physiological studies that data analysis could not be carried out by the conventional manual methods of the time, which included mechanical adding machines and slide rules. Multichannel data was still recorded on the photographic paper system used in the 1940s for the centrifuge experiments. To record even more data, the lab installed multichannel magnetic tape-recording equipment in parallel with the old photographic-recording equipment. The output from the magnetic tape was in a format suitable for direct input into an IBM 650 general-purpose digital computer, which was available at IBM in Rochester. IBM personnel were willing and anxious to work on the biomedical projects on a limited basis, but only after working hours. By the 1960s, the cardiovascular laboratory in Salt Lake City headed by Dr. Homer Warner was one of the most sophisticated electronic diagnostic laboratories in the world, using what were then state-of-the-art Control Data computers. A collaborative effort was initiated between Mayo and the University of Utah using a first-generation Control Data computer to evaluate physiological data.

The recordings from Earl's laboratory were suitable for direct input into Dr. Warner's Control Data computer. His lab technicians were able to analyze recordings of aortic pressures and other parameters obtained in the Mayo catheterization laboratory or the human centrifuge, which provided beat-to-beat values of stroke volume and cardiac output. These were the first laboratories to use computer technology in evaluating cardiovascular parameters for diagnostic and research purposes. This was in the days before Silicon Valley in California led the tech world. From the early 1960s through the early '80s, Minnesota was the tech leader, with headquarters for Control Data Corporation and Honeywell and eventually Cray Research computers in Minneapolis. To IBM's shock, Earl chose to have Control Data computers in his lab so that he could collaborate with similar equipment and studies being conducted in the Salt Lake City cardiovascular laboratory.

Willis Van Norman was a biology teacher in Byron, Minnesota, in 1960, when he was alerted by his next-door neighbor that a friend of his, Bill Sutterer, was leaving Mayo to pursue a master's degree in Florida. The neighbor thought Willis would be a great candidate to fill Bill's position in the cardiovascular laboratory in the Medical Sciences Building. Willis applied for the job and got it. Earl was very impressed with Willis due to his knowledge and his Midwest farming know-how and background, which made him a good fit in the entrepreneurial-research culture of the laboratory. Early in his career, Willis attended a computer-programming class in a language called Fortran with Earl and Ralph Sturm. Both Earl and Ralph realized they didn't have significant time for computer programming, and they gave Willis the responsibility for programming the computers in the laboratory.

By the late 1950s, Mayo Clinic cardiovascular surgeons wanted cardiac catheterization procedures to be performed at Saint Marys Hospital, close to the surgical suites. Earl performed the catheterizations in the Medical Sciences Building, away from the clinic and surgical suites. In addition, some of the surgeons did not like the long-duration studies conducted by Earl, who made each clinical study more of a research protocol.

Earl had a full plate at the time, with his research activities in the cardiac catheterization laboratory and the acceleration studies he conducted using the human centrifuge for the air force and NASA projects. It was his wish to work full-time in physiology research and turn over the time-consuming clinical diagnostic procedures to capable physicians he had trained in cardiac catheterization. As a consequence, Dr. Jeremy Swan was selected to head up the new Saint Marys catheterization laboratory.

The 1950s to the mid-1960s could be considered the grand days of cardiac catheterization at Mayo Clinic. The science and techniques had been developed in Earl's lab in the Medical Sciences Building, and the torch had been passed to the clinicians at Saint Marys Hospital. At the same time, Earl had assembled a top-notch staff, which he called his "crew," to continue groundbreaking physiological research in the decades to come.

CHAPTER 13

THE CENTRIFUGE SPINS AGAIN

Late on a chilly night in October 1957, Earl woke up the whole family to go out in the backyard and look up at the night sky. Looking toward the north, they saw a small object that resembled a star move from the western horizon toward the eastern horizon. This was Sputnik, the first satellite, and its launch by the Soviet Union caught the US Department of Defense and the scientific community completely off guard. The launching of Sputnik created public fear in the United States and the Western world that the Soviets could launch satellites or ballistic missiles that could carry nuclear weapons from the USSR into the United States or Europe. In November 1957, the Soviets launched Sputnik II, which carried a heavier payload, including a dog named Laika. Immediately following the launch of the first Sputnik, the Department of Defense responded to immense political pressure by approving funding for a US satellite project. Wernher von Braun and many of the Operation Paperclip scientists began working on the Explorer project.

The Explorer project launched the first US satellite into space on a modified Redstone rocket, which was the first American ballistic missile and, one could say, a direct descendent of the German V-2 rocket. Sputnik also led to the creation of the National Aeronautics and Space Administration, or NASA.

One of the objectives of NASA was to get a man in space. The physiological questions were what would be the stresses on the human body with prolonged exposure to G during launch and reentry into Earth's atmosphere, and what other physiological requirements were there for space flight at 0G? Through Mayo Clinic's relationship with the Defense Department, research funding became available from NASA and the United States Air Force. Gravitational physiological research was of vital importance, and so was the need for the centrifuge. In addition to studies of the effects of space travel, research to address new aircraft designs was necessary. Jet aircraft were faster than the piston-propelled fighter aircraft of World War II, and unlike those planes, which could make sharp turns quickly, the faster jet aircraft made high-speed arcs. Consequently, pilots were exposed to increased gravitational forces for longer periods of time. In early 1958, a request came from the US Air Force to "unmothball" the centrifuge that had been dormant since the end of World War II. There were other centrifuges available for use, such as the one at Wright-Patterson Air Force Base. But the advantage of the Mayo centrifuge was the instrumentation and the scientific expertise that resulted from advancements in cardiovascular physiology during the postwar era.

In an article in a *Mayovox* newsletter from December 5, 1959, Earl stated, "This type of investigation will almost certainly increase our knowledge of the circulation and is particularly important for improvement in the diagnosis and treatment of disease."

UPDATING THE CENTRIFUGE

Bringing the centrifuge up to speed was no easy task. One challenge was that research on the centrifuge could not interfere with the primary purpose of the catheterization laboratory, which was clinical medicine. Initially, the centrifuge was located in a building south of the Medical Sciences Building. In the late 1940s, an addition was made to the Medical Sciences Building that surrounded the centrifuge to accommodate the cardiovascular laboratories and additional recording rooms. This added a particular challenge during the construction, since the centrifuge took up at least two floors, with the flywheels on the lower floor and the superstructure at approximately street level. It also had to be protected during the construction. A silo structure was built around the centrifuge as the building addition was constructed around it. Two floors were added above the centrifuge, and a steel bridge was constructed to support the additional weight of the building and the shaft of the centrifuge. Since the centrifuge had been idle for such a long time, the entire structure had to be examined for potential cracks in the welds and metal structures. One particular concern was the weight of the two twenty-ton flywheels pressing down on the ball bearings. If any of the bearings had dented or warped during the idle time period, a bearing could fail during a centrifuge run. The results would be catastrophic, sending a fractured steel structure, equipment, and people flying at a high rate of speed. The old Chrysler engine and transmission were replaced by an electric motor, which was connected to the same drivetrain and tire that were connected to the flywheels.

The instrumentation on the centrifuge also had to be updated, including the addition of oximeters, new strain-gauge manometers for catheterization, and cameras. New methods to study the physiological effects of acceleration had been developed since the centrifuge was last used. The measurement of cardiac output—that is, the volume of blood the heart pumps per unit of time—was being done by indicator-dilution techniques employing the new dye-curve analysis using Fox Cardio Green developed in the Mayo physiology laboratory in the mid-1950s. The recording room was also remodeled with a multichannel magnetic tape recorder that let the investigator play back studies at will to observe the physiological responses of the subject during the centrifuge run. The centrifuge cockpit was modified to have the subject seated as though in an aircraft or spacecraft and an observer lying in a prone position above the cockpit.

Earl was assisted by personnel from physiology and engineering sections of the air force. These individuals included Drs. Robert Headley and Evan Lindbergh from Wright-Patterson Air Force Base in Dayton, Ohio. In August 1959, rehearsals for the experiments began, with one individual (the experimental subject) in the cockpit; another lying prone up above, controlling the valves for the catheters and dye injection; and a third sitting in the center seat of the centrifuge, observing the entire process. On the first run, which was to test the efficiency of the recording apparatus in the renovated centrifuge, the centrifuge did not exceed 28 rpm and the subject was exposed to 2G to 3.5G for a period of two minutes.

The subject in the centrifuge cockpit was attached with instrumentation that made it possible to directly observe and record his responses during acceleration. Electrodes were taped in position for EKG determination, a thermocouple unit was placed in the mouth to measure both depth and rate of respiration, and a pulse oximeter was attached at the ear to measure pulse and blood flow at head level. Arterial- and venous-pressure levels were determined by strain-gauge manometers attached to catheters. Cardio green dye was injected into a vein and withdrawn downstream to create a dye curve that would determine the amount of blood flow through the heart plus cardiac output (the volume of blood pumped through the heart in a minute). The physiological data was transmitted electronically to the recording room across the hall from the centrifuge and recorded photographically and on magnetic tape by a multichannel recording assembly. Bill Sutterer was the chief technician in charge of the centrifuge operation. Don Hegland was in the recording room, and it was his responsibility to turn on and off the photoelectric recording and multichannel magnetic tape recorder before and after the centrifuge runs. Lucy Cronin, now the supervisor of the cardiovascular laboratory, made sure all the surgical instruments were in the proper place and ran the safety checks for each centrifuge run. These technicians were vital to the success of the experiments on the centrifuge and for the safety of all personnel involved.

In an article published in the Mayo Clinic *Mayovox*, Earl stated, "The objective is to learn as much as possible of the effects of acceleration on the human subject, particularly in relation to the function of the heart, circulation and the central nervous system. We want to know the factors which limit tolerance to increase acceleration. We want to know just how the heart and blood vessels react to compensate for these factors and at what point a pilot would become insufficient in performance. We want to study ways to protect him and increase limits of tolerance."

"I see they're running the G-Wheel again."

Cartoon from the December 5, 1959, Mayovox *newsletter*

On November 1, 1959, the *Minneapolis Sunday Tribune* described an experiment on the centrifuge. The subject in this case was Dr. Terrence McGuire from the air force. He was taped, strapped, belted, and wired into the cockpit. Needles and catheters were placed in the arteries and veins in his arms and advanced far into his body. One catheter went all the way into the heart. Chest leads were attached for the electrocardiograph. An oximeter was clipped to his ear to record blood flow and blood pressure at head level. A plastic cap was placed over his head to keep the equipment in place when exposed to G. Another tube was placed in his throat, opposite the heart, to monitor intrathoracic pressure. (Not mentioned in the *Minneapolis Tribune* article: another transducer was placed up the subject's rectum to monitor intra-abdominal pressure.) All these devices were connected to the recording room, with tape recorders, cameras, and electrical devices transmitting all the physiological data to be recorded simultaneously. Another scientist described in the article, Dr. Lindbergh, climbed above the cockpit and lay flat on his stomach. He would stay there during the runs, manually operating the valves to flush the catheters and turning the switches on the essential test devices. All the preparations for the run usually took more than two hours. With preparation almost complete, Bill Sutterer would ask, "Want to start the flywheels now, Doc?" Earl would say, "No reason why not." With a great squeal from the rubber tire, the two twenty-ton flywheels beneath the centrifuge would begin turning, but the centrifuge gantry itself remained still.

Blood samples were taken from the subject by Dr. Hiram Marshall and lab tech June Shervem. The puncture site on the arm was also the site where the Fox Cardio Green dye would be injected during the run to determine the blood flow through the heart. The first experiment and data gathering was a static run, with the centrifuge stationary to establish baseline data at 1G. Earl sat in the aircraft seat beside the center shaft of the centrifuge to observe the subject and the top rider, Evan Lindbergh. Then Earl would speak into the microphone, saying, "Well, we're all set to go." In a tiny room overlooking the centrifuge, Lucy Cronin would pick up a stopwatch. She was now "the quarterback" as she ran through the safety checklist that would regulate the whole operation. She gave several directions to the top rider and the recording technicians (Bill Sutterer, Roy Engstrom, and Don Hegland). After going through the checklist protocol, she would say, "All right, you can start the countdown!" Earl would give the countdown from the center seat: "Five, four, three, two, one," and technician Wilford Hoffman would turn the switch in the control room, engaging the clutch onto the two twenty-ton flywheels, and the centrifuge would begin to turn around and around counterclockwise, while the cockpit, the subject, and the top rider began tilting forty-five, fifty, then about sixty-five degrees at 2G, twice normal gravity.

Dr. Hiram Marshall pointed out that everyone in the lab had been both human subject and top rider. "Being on top is just plain miserable," he said. "Your head hangs down, blood rushes to your face, your hands hang down and blood runs down the vessels making your hands ache. In addition, your mouth will open, spraying saliva all over the subject and instrumentation in the cockpit!"

When the centrifuge reached the prescribed G, within one and a quarter turns of the superstructure, Wilford Hoffman called out, "Peak!" and the centrifuge would start to slow down. The whole run lasted only a minute and twenty seconds, but it seemed like three or four hours to the subject and top rider. The centrifuge runs would continue throughout the day at different intervals, sometimes up to four minutes at 4G.

At 4G, a subject's face began to be strained and his cheeks began to flatten; occasionally, the subject would black out from lack of blood supply to the brain. Subjects did, however, recover quickly, similar to what was observed on the centrifuge and the G-Whiz in the 1940s. On this particular day, there were seventeen runs. On some runs, the subject was protected from blackout with the inflation of the G-suit, and on others they were not protected. By about the fourteenth run, the subject threw up. Earl would say, "Just a little motion sickness, that's all." Earl's colleagues said that he had been a subject on the centrifuge so often that it was like driving his car. (Maybe that's why he liked to speed.) The experiments were carried on until around 1:00 or 2:00 p.m. (and sometimes into the evening). At the end of the study, the subject was disconnected right away. Lucy would offer the subject, and sometimes the top rider, a wheelchair. Most of the time, these macho air force men and young researchers would say, "I'm OK." Regardless, Lucy would accompany the subject down the hallway to the other room and "give him a drink of whiskey and put him to bed," she would say jokingly.

At the end of the article, Earl mentioned that a new cockpit was being constructed so the subject would lie on his back the way project Mercury astronauts would be positioned in space. "We will keep the 4Gs for five minutes, maybe longer," he said. "My interest as a physiologist is in studying the human body and the compensating reactions of the heart and blood vessels while exposed to different stresses. To me the centrifuge is to produce severe stress on the system. One of the best ways to study the heart's compensatory mechanisms is to change the system and see what happens."

With funding from NASA and the air force, a new cockpit was constructed on the superstructure of the centrifuge, on the opposite end of where the human subject cockpit was. This new cockpit was constructed so that the subject could lie supine, or on his back, the way Mercury, Gemini, and Apollo astronauts would lie as they experienced the g-forces on rocket blastoff and reentry into Earth's atmosphere. The new cockpit could accommodate humans as well as animals. Special molds were fabricated by the David Clark Company to fit a chimpanzee or a dog. X-ray fluoroscopy was also added, along with automated

injectors so that angiography and dye curves could be performed remotely while the centrifuge was spinning. In the
recording room, broadcast-quality videotape machines were
added for instant playback of the angiograms and multichannel
data recording. Last, a large IBM computer, which filled an entire room, was added for data analysis and automated synchro-
nization of the EKG and dye injection for either an angiogram
or dye curves. With the more sophisticated instrumentation
and data collection and multiple G runs, experiments on the
centrifuge would last thirty-six to forty-eight hours.

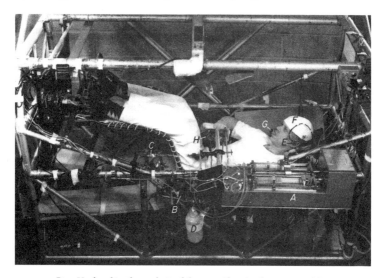

*Don Hegland in the cockpit of the centrifuge in the same position
as a Mercury or Gemini astronaut, in about 1962*

NEAR MISSES

Conducting experiments on the centrifuge was not without
risk. A forty-foot-wide superstructure whirling at any rpm
poses a significant safety risk. In addition, the two twenty-ton

flywheels were designed to rotate vertically when initially installed in the water plant in Cincinnati, Ohio. These flywheels
were now mounted horizontally, and it was unknown if and
when they might fail while rotating. It is noted that one Mayo
Clinic building engineer would leave the Medical Sciences
Building during a centrifuge run, in fear that the flywheels
might fly apart, causing a catastrophic failure. Add to this the
significant risk posed to the subjects while they were spinning at the end of the superstructure, sustaining major stress
to their cardiovascular, neurologic, and musculoskeletal systems. Yet with the multitude of centrifuge runs during World
War II and into the late '50s, '60s, and early '70s, there were
no significant injuries or death. There were two near-miss in-
cidents worth mentioning.

On one prolonged 4G run, Dr. Hiram Marshall was
the subject. Halfway through the run, Hiram had difficulty
breathing and significant pain in his chest and gave the signal
to stop. In an emergency shutdown, the superstructure could
be stopped with the clutching brake within a turn and a half.
When the physicians and scientists got out to the cockpit,
they noted that only one side of Hiram's chest rose when he
inhaled. He was quickly released from the cockpit and rushed
to Saint Marys Hospital, where he was treated for a pneumothorax, or collapsed lung. He was in the hospital overnight
and returned to the lab the next day, although he declined to
be a subject for the next few months. Nonetheless the incident did cause significant concern among all members of the
cardiovascular research staff.

The second near-miss episode occurred in the late 1960s,
when they were conducting experiments on chimpanzees. As
they were preparing for a centrifuge run and disconnecting
power equipment to the cockpit, Don Hegland was the last
person in the room and was walking toward the exit when

the superstructure started to spin. Don quickly ran to the exit and began knocking on the door, plastering himself up against the wall as the superstructure swung past him. An emergency shutdown was initiated and a potentially fatal accident was avoided. More safety procedures were implemented after this incident, with more safety checks and an interlock installed on the door to limit anyone entering the centrifuge room during a run.

In addition to the human volunteers, experimental subjects included dogs, monkeys, and eventually chimpanzees, since they so closely resemble humans. Special casts were fabricated by the David Clark Company for each chimpanzee so it could lie supine in the cockpit of the centrifuge, in the same position as an astronaut in a space capsule. The experimental animals were kept at Institute Hills, southwest of Rochester, and were under the expert care of veterinarian Dr. Paul Zollman.

The space race was now on, and more research was needed on the exposure of astronauts to gravitational forces during blastoff into space and also during reentry into Earth's atmosphere. The experiments became more complex, with multiple catheters and more sophisticated X-ray equipment and techniques, including the use of radioisotopes. Research using the centrifuge continued through the Apollo and Spacelab eras. The resurrecting of the centrifuge after the Sputnik wakeup call paved the way for the use of high-speed computers in data analysis and, eventually, mathematical video reconstruction of intact anatomical structures in Earl's laboratory in the 1970s.

CHAPTER 14

FAMILY LIFE IN ROCHESTER

Earl, Ada, and Phoebe took up residence in a small rental house on Ninth Avenue SW after moving to Rochester in 1942. But in 1946, when Ada learned she was expecting a second child, it soon became apparent that this house would not be adequate for a growing family. They purchased a modest home on the edge of town, on Second Street NW next to Kutzky Park and Cascade Creek, where their kids would have ample places to run and play. On the other side of the park and creek was a cornfield and, beyond that, the Chicago and North Western train tracks. From the back windows, they could see the farmer working in the fields and twice a day watch the Chicago 400, a passenger train to Chicago, pull into the depot near downtown Rochester.

Unlike most Mayo Clinic staff doctors, Earl Wood and his family did not live in a large house on Pill Hill in Southwest Rochester. The name Pill Hill was given to the neighborhood where many of the Mayo Clinic staff had houses in the 1930s. These were large, beautiful homes with many rooms and lots of space. The physicians who did not live on Pill Hill had homes with land southwest of Rochester, in an area called Bamber Valley. The Wood family home was much smaller and decidedly modest in comparison to the typical home of Mayo Clinic medical and administrative personnel.

Mark Goff Wood arrived on the scene on October 8, 1946. Much to the young family's surprise, Guy Harland Wood arrived on August 15, 1947, just ten months later. Obviously, this was a very busy household, with two active boys, though Phoebe assisted with some of the chores that could be done by a five-year-old.

In another surprise, Earl Andrew (Andy) Wood arrived on a bitter-cold night in January 1953. The modest little home on Second Street was full and active. Phoebe had her own room, while the three boys shared another room. Things got a little crowded, particularly in the mornings when they were getting ready for school, since there was only one upstairs bathroom, with a bathtub, and a small bathroom downstairs.

Life on Second Street with four active kids was chaotic at best. Earl was always first to wake up in the morning, usually around 4:00 a.m. He would get up, put on his bathrobe, go down to the kitchen, and heat some water for instant coffee (Nescafe). He would then sit down at the dining room table and have quiet time to work on scientific manuscripts and correspondence. About 6:30 a.m., he would go upstairs to nudge the family up to get ready for school. The house became a buzz of activity, with three or four kids vying for the single bathroom upstairs and figuring out what to wear for the day. Breakfast on weekdays was usually cold cereal or, occasionally, eggs and bacon. Ada would not let the kids out the door unless they looked respectable. They usually walked or biked to Lincoln Elementary School, five blocks away. This occurred rain or shine and in the dead of cold Minnesota winters.

Mark, Phoebe, Andy, and Guy in 1958

Later, when the kids were going to Central Junior High, Earl might give them a ride and drop them off on his way to the Medical Sciences Building. Once the kids were out of the house, Ada had a few moments of quiet time. She also had to deal with a ton of household work, including laundry, making beds, vacuuming, grocery shopping, planning meals, and getting ready for the kids to come home between 3:30 and 4:00 p.m. Often, she would go out for coffee with friends. Occasionally, her good friend Louise Lambert, Ed Lambert's wife, would come over and they would sit in the kitchen and chat, drinking coffee and smoking Kool cigarettes. By 4:00 p.m., all hell would break loose, with kids coming home with their books and homework and changing clothes to go outside and play with friends before dinner. The kids were also encouraged to practice their musical instruments or perhaps start on homework during this time. Most evenings Earl arrived home between 5:30 and 6:00 p.m., in time to watch part of the *Huntley-Brinkley Report.*

Some evenings Earl did not come home until very late due to experiments in the lab or physiology or cardiovascular meetings at the Foundation House. If Ada didn't know about his dinner plans beforehand, it usually led to a heated discussion upon his arrival home. Most evenings after dinner, the kids would go upstairs to do their homework and Earl would take off his shoes, loosen his trousers and belt, and lie on the sofa reading the evening edition of the *Rochester Post-Bulletin.* He always made himself available to assist with homework in subjects such as mathematics and science. All the Wood kids said they never would have passed algebra, chemistry, or physics without Earl's help. Earl did get frustrated, however, helping with these subjects, which were simple and obvious to him but confusing to his kids. Once the dishes were complete, Ada would assist with homework assignments in English literature and history. Ada was particularly concerned about Andy, who had to cope with severe dyslexia and a learning disability. She read most of his school assignments to him. Earl was in bed by no later than 9:00 p.m.; he would fall asleep reading the latest edition of *Scientific American* or *Circulation.* Earl followed Ben Franklin's advice: "Early to bed, early to rise, makes a man healthy, wealthy, and wise." Meanwhile, Ada occasionally joked, "Early to bed, early to rise, will make your gal go out with other guys."

Having gone through the Great Depression of the 1930s

and the food and material rationing of World War II, Earl and Ada were very frugal. When the kids asked for something new, such as a television or a bicycle, the answer came back, "What's wrong with what we've got?" If something still worked and was serving a function, there was no reason to replace it. Vehicles were not traded in for something newer; they had to last at least ten years. The black-and-white television was not replaced until 1969, when Apollo 11 went to the moon.

Although the family grew up in the 1950s and early '60s, this was not a *Leave It to Beaver* household. Ada had her hands full as a stay-at-home mom with four kids and a busy husband. The guys coming home with dirty hunting clothes after days away often led to heated exchanges. Being late or missing a dinner that Ada had worked hard to make would also lead to some friction. She had issues with the Wood relatives who came in from out of state to hunt, fish, or visit the clinic for medical checkups. Although Ada loved her family, it was not easy being married to Earl Wood, who received most of the attention professionally, socially, and within the family. She also had an issue with some of his fellows who worshipped the ground he walked on. Like many housewives at that time, she was smart and well educated and she did let her frustrations be known.

Earl and Ada insisted that their kids be physically and socially active. Phoebe was in Girl Scouts and played clarinet in the band. All the boys were in Boy Scouts and attended summer camp at YMCA Camp Olson near Longville, Minnesota. Mark was a champion tennis player, Guy played tight end on the football team, and Andy swam competitively in high school and college.

Christmas, of course, was a special time at the house on Second Street. Ada and Earl threw great Christmas parties, inviting friends and people from the lab. They enjoyed cocktails and danced to big band music on the hi-fi. Earl and Ada enjoyed reliving their dancing days in college, doing the Mankato Pump. Ada usually prepared a formal dinner. No one left hungry, and the party went on way after the kids headed upstairs to bed.

When the kids were older, the Christmas holidays were a family gathering time, since they were away in college or graduate school or at work. Sometimes it was the only time of the year all six were together in one place. After spending Christmases during Earl's sabbatical years in Switzerland and England, the Woods would meet in other locations to spend the holidays, including Mexico, Colorado, California, the Grand Canyon, and the Panama Canal. The kids all grew up with an awareness of other cultures, thanks to their parents' love of travel, and several put this to good use in their chosen fields.

CHAPTER 15

HUNTING AND FISHING TRIPS

Earl grew up in a family of avid outdoorsmen and hunters. The Wood boys looked forward each fall to hunting, since pheasant, ducks, and rabbits were plentiful in Minnesota in the 1930s and '40s. The yearly calendar in the Wood household did not revolve so much around holidays, such as the Fourth of July, Christmas, New Year's, or Easter, but rather around hunting and fishing seasons. In the off-seasons, Earl took the boys out into the country to practice their shooting and marksmanship skills. Before any of Earl's sons could go hunting with their dad and uncles, certified hunter and firearms-safety training was an absolute requirement.

SPRING AND SUMMER: FISHING

With the warming spring temperatures and the ice melting off the lakes and streams came the anticipation of fishing season. Fishing was also something Earl was taught early in life, using a cane pole, a simple hook with a worm, to catch fish along the Blue Earth River near the 20 Acres, below the Rapidan Dam, and of course on Lake Washington. These waters were teeming with bluegills, crappies, sunfish, and walleyes, and there was the occasional northern pike.

Spring fishing meant long trips with friends and family into Canada over Memorial Day weekend, planned and organized by Chester Wood. Through Chester's research and connections, he found excellent areas for fishing on rivers, lakes, and streams north of the border in Ontario. All these locations were very productive; however, they were a challenge to reach. This made the journeys to these remote Canadian locations just as interesting and fun as the fishing.

One of the first Memorial Day fishing expeditions in Ontario was to Six Mile Lake. To get there, the crew had to catch a train near Sioux Lookout. They loaded their canoes and gear onto flat cars on the train, which transported them to a trailhead that led to Six Mile Lake. Once on the lake, they paddled to a campsite where they would spend the next several days. This provided excellent fishing for lake trout, walleye, and northern pike. Once, when they were returning from Six Mile Lake, the train was late getting to the appointed stop at the trailhead. The delay put them behind schedule; Mark and Guy needed to get back to school, and Earl, IJ Fox, Hi Marshall, and Don Hegland were needed back in the lab. Leaving Sioux Lookout in two cars loaded with canoes, tents, fishing gear, people, and a full limit of Canadian fish, they headed south toward Rochester. Earl, of course, was in the lead, driving his '55 Mercury station wagon with Hi Marshall desperately trying to keep up in his Studebaker. At about 3:00 a.m., while driving through Amery, Wisconsin, Hi was pulled over for speeding. As the policeman was writing out a warning ticket, he said, "If I ever catch that guy in the red Mercury station wagon, he will never pass through this town again!"

The favorite location for Memorial Day fishing expeditions was Obonga Lake, just south of Armstrong. At that time, in the late 1960s, access to Obonga Lake was via a small dirt road off the main gravel road to Armstrong. This side road was often muddy and rocky and occasionally washed out from snowmelt and spring rains, which sometimes required the four-wheel-drive capabilities of Earl's Land Rover. Once at the boat landing on Obonga Lake, the canoes and boats were removed from the vehicles and then loaded up to the gunwales with fishing and camping gear, plus food. The crew would then motor down the long, narrow lake to an inlet on the southwest side, where the fishing was good and there was an excellent campsite. The ten-mile trip on Obonga Lake to the campsite was long and somewhat treacherous, depending on the wind and waves. In addition, the water was very cold, since it'd been less than a month since the ice went out. Capsizing a canoe would be life-threatening. On one memorable crossing of Obonga Lake, the flotilla and crew endured not only high winds but also snow.

Fishing at the Obonga Lake inlet was good, but the Wood boys wanted to discover other areas. Portaging their canoes to a small pond upriver, they easily caught their limit of walleyes using just yellow jigs. Since there was a limit on the number of fish that they could bring back to the United States, they had to consume fish while in camp. That meant they often had fresh walleye fillets for breakfast, fresh walleye fillets for lunch, and fresh walleye fillets for dinner. The Woods returned to Obonga Lake for many years, bringing along many family members and friends.

FALL: DUCK, PHEASANT, AND GROUSE HUNTING

Cooling temperatures, changing leaves, the start of a new school year, and football season mean fall to most people. But to the Wood family, fall meant grouse, duck, and pheasant seasons.

The first weekend in October marked the opening of duck season. On the Friday night before the Saturday opener, Earl and the boys would drive over to Lake Washington, put the canoe on the car, and load up with decoys. On opening day, Earl got the boys up at 4:00 a.m. for a quick breakfast and then they climbed into the car to drive over to a slough near Saint Clair, Minnesota, about twenty miles south of Lake Washington. This slough was a favorite duck-hunting area that William C. Wood and his boys had hunted for decades. In the 1960s and '70s, this was still prime waterfowl habitat, right on the flyways of the birds headed south for the winter. On opening day, duck season started at noon. To get to a good location, they had to arrive very early. Still in the dark, the hunters would unload the canoes and fill them with decoys, firearms, and ammunition. To access the open water on the slough, they had to drag the canoes through cattails and muck, which could be waist-high. Once close to open water, they then paddled out to a point where ducks flew over. After setting out the decoys, the hunters wedged their canoes into the cattails and reeds to conceal themselves. Crouching down low in the canoes, the hunters started using their duck calls in hopes of bringing in a flock of mallards, bluebills, or teal, or even a flock of geese. After they'd spent about five minutes shooting, duck season officially opened at noon.

Pheasant season meant a mass hunter migration to western Minnesota and South Dakota. In the late 1940s and early 1950s, the ring-necked pheasant population in southern and western

Minnesota and the Dakotas was very high due to ample cover and food in the grasslands and cornfields in these areas.

One of Earl's first experiences hunting in South Dakota was a luxurious trip with Harry Harwick, the chief financial officer of Mayo Clinic. He had rented a private railcar that was attached to the Chicago and North Western's 400 train and pulled to Huron, South Dakota, where it was uncoupled and parked in the rail yard near the train station. From there, they rented a car and drove out to the fields in the Huron area to hunt. In the evening they returned to the railcar to eat dinner and sleep. A once-in-a-lifetime experience of luxury "gentlemen's" hunting, this was totally different from the roughing-it expeditions to which Earl was accustomed.

In the late 1970s, the Wood boys hunted on the John Gruntmeyer farm near Iroquois, South Dakota. John Gruntmeyer's son, Greg, had a congenital heart defect that was surgically corrected by Dr. Douglas Mair, who worked with Earl in 1969 and '70. The Gruntmeyer farm was about two thousand acres of corn and soybean fields, grassland, and some thinly wooded windbreaks. Since this was before the heavy use of herbicides, there was plenty of cover between the rows of corn, creating excellent pheasant habitat. The corn was less than six feet tall, providing a good view for shooting. A crew from Rochester would arrive for opening morning of the South Dakota pheasant hunt, including Dr. Doug Mair and his father, Lester; radiologist Dr. Pat Sheedy; Dr. Hugh Smith; and of course Earl.

LATE FALL AND WINTER: DEER CAMP

Deer hunting took center stage in November. For several seasons in the early 1940s, the Wood boys hunted along the

Manitou River in northern Minnesota, near the shores of Lake Superior. The hunting was good but challenging in the hilly terrain. In 1944, Chet found forty acres near the hamlet of Payne, about forty miles northwest of Duluth, which was flatter and better deer habitat.

Construction of the deer camp resulted in a basic shack placed on concrete blocks. Later, a larger living-room-type structure and other additions were added to the shack. Roof beams were cut from downed poplar and pine trees from the surrounding woods. The walls and floors were constructed using two-by-four and two-by-six studs nailed and bolted together and covered with tar paper to keep the elements out. The deer camp was heated by a fifty-gallon-barrel Yukon stove that was set up on concrete blocks in the living room. This provided heat for the building, thawing out of numb hands and feet, and drying off of wet, snow-covered clothes. Lighting was initially provided by kerosene lanterns and Coleman lanterns. These were later replaced by propane lamps.

The Wood brothers, their family members, friends, and coworkers who took part in the annual deer hunt called themselves the Deerslayers. The organization was jokingly called Deerslayers, Inc. It was not officially incorporated.

Just like at the 20 Acres or Lake Washington, when the Wood boys were at deer camp, they had their specific assignments. Chester, who lived the closest, in Duluth, was the project manager and probably had the most difficult job. He would cut the grass around the camp in the summer months, plus make needed repairs to the tar-paper palace. He cut down trees for firewood and made arrangements for meals during deer season. Chet also planned many of the deer stands in the area. Deer stands were tall trees, such as spruce, Norway pine, and poplar, that were strategically located near clearings or trails where deer could be sighted.

Delbert Wood was in charge of pumping water; he knew the ins and outs of the hand pump on the well. Upon arrival, he would screw it onto the wellhead, prime the pump, and pump up several gallons of water, enough to suffice a thirsty crew.

Harland was in charge of splitting wood and making sure the Yukon stove in the living room was continually stoked with ample firewood to keep the tar-paper shack comfortably warm and dry. On one particularly cold night, he threw several heavy logs into the stove, knocking it off the concrete blocks and filling the shack with smoke. With a yell, "We're in trouble, boys!" then, "All hands on deck!" they used long logs and two-by-fours to place it back on the blocks and resecure the stovepipe.

Another crucial member of the Deerslayers was Lester Krampitz, Earl's brother-in-law. When he was a student at Macalester, Lester worked as a short-order cook to earn money for tuition and support his young family. So when he went to deer camp, Lester was in charge of the kitchen and cooked breakfast for the Deerslayers.

William "Bud" Bennett was an executive at the 3M company in Saint Paul. His job at the deer camp was to prepare lunches for the crew at the camp or in the field. Bud was also the deer camp poet laureate.

David Clark, the president and owner of the David Clark Company, in Worcester, Massachusetts, and the manufacturer of the G-suit, attended deer camp for several decades. His job was transportation. In the early years of deer camp, the David Clark Company owned interest in Munsingwear, in Minneapolis. David would procure one of Munsingwear's company vehicles to use for transporting the Deerslayers from one part of the deer camp property to other hunting areas. Since the roads and the trails were not built for regular cars, these company cars proved inadequate and were returned to the Munsingwear headquarters extremely dirty and in need of substantial repair, particularly to the undercarriage and chassis, from going over rocks and logs and through the mud. Realizing that these automobiles were inadequate for the deer camp and their use there likely caused some consternation on the part of Munsingwear executives, Dave decided to give the Deerslayers a four-wheel-drive vehicle in 1960. It was a 1960 Land Rover, one of the first Land Rovers in Minnesota.

And then, of course, there was Earl. Earl was known as "the Coach" because he was the main organizer. Each evening he would come up with a game plan for the next day's hunt. This included assigning deer stands for each hunter, organizing drives, and establishing rendezvous times and places. Through his military contacts, he was able to get aerial maps of the area, which he used for developing the hunting plans. This was in the days before Google Maps, GPS, or Garmin. He developed his hunting plans with pinpoint accuracy and timing, with military precision to maximize the chance of sighting and bagging a deer. Earl was also the Deerslayers' record keeper and statistician. Each day he recorded the number of deer sighted and by whom, the number of deer shot at and from which tree or area, and of course the number of deer bagged and by whom. When he returned home from the deer camp, he would write up a summary that would have been the envy of any Minnesota Department of Natural Resources statistician.

Like any organization, deer camp—or Deerslayers, Inc.—had its specific rules. The governing body of the Deerslayers was called "the Kremlin." The Kremlin met the evening before the opening hunt, or when needed throughout the season to discuss policies, procedures, and strategies.

Like the scientific and academic laboratories where the Deerslayers spent their professional lives, the deer camp was run with scientific precision: by observation, intelligence gathering, data collection, analysis, precise planning, and execution that would make any military general proud. Maps were drawn and copied and handed out to all hunters. These maps were based on aerial photographs and then drawn in with pencil indicating specific landmarks, terrain, trails, roads, and of course deer stands.

Safety was paramount at the deer camp. On the walls in several rooms in the tar-paper shack, Chester nailed up hunting-safety posters he had procured through the Minnesota Department of Natural Resources as a reminder to all hunters as they left for their stand or drive. The veteran hunters insisted on wearing red clothing and were the first to use blaze orange when that color came out in the mid-1960s. All hunters were required to take into the field a functioning compass, a whistle for location, straps and rope to secure themselves into their deer stands, and candy bars for energy to get them through the day's activities or for survival in case they became lost. All younger hunters were required to take a firearms-safety course before they could hunt at the deer camp.

Firearms used at deer camp were low-tech by today's standards. The rifles used were lever action, bolt action, or pump. Will Wood used his beloved model 1892 38-40 Winchester, which he purchased in Texas in 1914. When he became too old to hunt, this rifle was passed to Earl's son Guy Wood, who shot his first deer with it. When Andy started hunting in 1966, he shot his first deer with the 38-40. Handguns at the deer camp were strictly forbidden due to multiple safety issues and their inherent lack of accuracy.

A TYPICAL DAY AT THE DEER CAMP

The first early-morning stirring at the deer camp was before or maybe just at 4:00 a.m. Earl and Lester were the first up.

Lester would start working on breakfast, while Earl would prepare oatmeal and mix up Tang orange drink. Harland would get up a short time later and start stoking the stove with wood to heat up the cabin. With a tray full of Dixie cups loaded to the brim with Tang, Earl would enter the bunkhouse and, at the top of his lungs, start singing,

Rise and shine
See if you can take it
Rise and shine
Life is what you make it

And then he would say, "Roust out, you bastards, there're deer in the swamps!"

There would be moans and groans as the Deerslayers got out of their warm sleeping bags into the chill of the cold cabin. Each member of the crew would don several layers of socks, long underwear, and wool shirts. It was cramped quarters, and a hunter did not want to lose any vital pieces of clothing, particularly in the bitter cold of a Minnesota November morning. Stepping outside to the outhouse, they got the first shot of the reality of the subzero environment.

Still half-asleep and half-clothed, the hunters would wander into the dining room, which was thick with smoke and steam from the stove's heat hitting the cool air. After they downed the Tang, the next thing to hit their taste buds was Lester's very strong coffee. The first course for breakfast was Earl's stick-in-the-mouth oatmeal. This was garnished with sugar or honey to make it more palatable. Lester cooked the main course. Being a short-order cook, he could make pancakes, scrambled eggs, or bacon quickly. However, if he was in a hurry or if there was a malfunction in the stove, the pancakes would be black on the outside and liquid batter on the inside. Regardless, the Deerslayers were happy to get something into their stomachs in anticipation of being out all day. Sometime during breakfast, the boys would start singing Lester's breakfast song to the tune of "Jesus Loves Me."

Lester loves us, yes we know
Cause our bellies tell us so
He is weak but his coffee is strong
For his deer he's waited long
Yes, Lester loves us
Yes, Lester loves us
Yes, Lester loves us
Our bellies tell us so

This was followed by Lester saying, "Flattery will get you nowhere!"

Following breakfast, the crew would get ready, making sure they had all the necessities to survive the cold Minnesota morning and the firepower to bag a deer. Equipment included warm gloves, knee-high boots, a blaze-orange jacket and hat, a compass, a whistle, a gun rope for tying themselves into a tree, ammunition, maps of the hunting area, and a gun. Final instructions were given by Chet, Earl, or Harn.

The hunters would load up in the Land Rover or possibly a two-wheel-drive vehicle, if the trip did not require being on a back trail. Once in the vehicle with "the Coach" at the wheel, they would roar down the road and then turn off onto an old logging road. Four-wheel-drive was used to go down these roads, and the headlights bobbed up and down as the Land Rover went through snow and underlying mud and sometimes corduroy-logged roads to the designated drop-off point, from where the hunters would then walk to their deer stands.

Disembarking the vehicles, the hunters would go through

the woods single file, led by Earl with a flashlight. Being as quiet as possible, yet walking at a rate that was almost running, Earl would suddenly stop, turn to one of the hunters, and give him directions to his particular deer stand. Directions would be like this: "You go east one hundred yards until you come to a clearing, then head north, and it's the fourth tree on your right side." They would end with Earl saying, "You can't miss it!" A single hunter would go off in hopes of finding the stand.

Once the hunter got to the stand, he would catch his breath from jogging, trying to keep up with the Coach. At the base of the tree, he would look up, eyeing the footholds on the branches or spikes to negotiate the ascent to the top. As he began the ascent, he would brush off the snow and ice that had accumulated on the branches he would be using as hand- and footholds. After what seemed like fifteen minutes of climbing, the hunter would look up and realize he had another twenty feet to go before reaching the top of the tree. Once on top, the hunter would straddle it, sort of like getting on a horse. This was a bit nerve-racking, since the tree could be forty to fifty feet high. The hunter could then take another breather and cool off before buttoning or zipping up his jacket to guard against the cold. Then he would use rope or nylon strapping to secure himself to the tree in case he lost his balance. Finally, he would unsling the rifle that he'd brought up with him. The gun was then loaded and a cartridge pumped into the chamber and the safety was placed on. When it was secured, he would start observing the area around the tree and clearings in the brush where he could get a shot at a deer. Usually at this time of day, it was still pitch-black. However, if they were running late, there could be some pink from the sun rising in the east.

The tree stand was usually fairly comfortable for the first fifteen minutes to half an hour. Then, slowly, the cold would set in. And occasionally a Canadian northwest wind would start to blow. Fingers and toes soon became numb, and the hunter would hunker down but still keep a wary eye on the various clearings surrounding the deer stand. As the sun came up, the hunter would realize that his deer stand was higher than any other tree in the surrounding area. In addition, the tree would swing and sway as a gust of wind hit it, making a fifteen-degree arc in the sky. Just like in a wheat field, one could observe the gust of wind coming in as the surrounding trees started to bend. The hunter would brace for the wind to hit, not only because of the cold but also because of the swaying of the tree. He would usually start shivering within a half hour of ascending the deer stand. A quick remedy to alleviate the potential symptoms of hypothermia was the sudden snap of a twig or branch, warning of an approaching deer or maybe another hunter. If a deer was sighted, Earl was adamant with all hunters, and particularly with his three boys, that they make that first shot count. They might not get a second shot.

After several hours of being on the deer stand, which could seem like days, the hunter had to wait to be retrieved by Earl or one of the other veteran hunters. Getting out of the tree also had its challenges. First, the hunter's hands would be numb, lacking the dexterity to empty the gun of ammunition and stow it in a side pocket. Second, it was difficult to untie the knots of the security ropes, which had invariably frozen since the hunter arrived four to six hours earlier. Once those were untied, the next challenge was that moving the arms and lower extremities, which had been still for that period of time, gave you the feeling of an arthritic ten to fifteen years older. Descending the tree, the hunter's challenge was having to put large boots onto the frozen branches blindly, since it was difficult to look down through the bulk of his clothing. Once on firm ground, he usually shook and jumped to get his blood circulating while he conversed with the hunter who retrieved him. Walking down the trail, invariably, he would see Earl with a freshly shot deer, knife in hand, cleaning it with the skills of a master surgeon. Once the deer was cleaned out, ropes were attached to it and tied to the waists of one or two hunters, who would drag it out to the waiting Land Rover. The deer was then tied to the top of the vehicle, and the hunters would load in and drive back to deer camp for lunch, which was usually soup and sandwiches prepared by Bud Bennett. The heat from the barrel Yukon stove felt welcome to all who had been sitting in the cold for the last four to six hours.

Returning from a successful day in the Payne Swamps in the Land Rover. Taken in the early 1960s. Pictured: Mark Wood, Earl Wood, Chester Wood, Buck Wood, and Willis Van Norman.

Over lunch, the Coach and other veteran hunters would discuss the strategy for the afternoon. Hunting drives would be organized in various areas surrounding the deer camp, including "the Broken-Down-Tree Drive," "the Slingshot Drive," and "North of 133." They might also have headed over to the Payne Swamps. One or two drives could be completed in half a day, depending on their length and the terrain. Heading back to camp at the end of the day with the Land Rover fully loaded with hunters and deer on the top, bouncing along the trails, the hunters would break into their old favorite song about Lydia Pinkham. This racy song brought many a chuckle to the Deerslayers.

Once back at camp, the hunters would stow their guns and ammunition and take off one or two layers of clothing. They then once again piled into the vehicles and headed into Payne and Roy Rask's general store. It was here the Wood boys could refresh themselves with a cold bottle of beer.

Following dinner, they would head back to deer camp, where they would briefly discuss the plans for the next morning. Harn would bring in enough firewood to last the night and stoke up the old Yukon stove to keep the cabin warm as long as possible, and they would settle into their bunks, totally exhausted. Within moments, even before total lights out, an orchestra of loud, guttural snoring would start. Champion snorers included David Clark, Chester Wood, and of course Earl Wood. The loud reverberation from the throats of these men was enough to drive some of the younger-generation hunters out of the bunkhouse and into sleeping bags they'd placed reluctantly in the back of the vehicles to spend a quieter night in the grips of the Minnesota cold. Within six to seven hours, the whole process would repeat itself. This routine lasted for eight more days, until the end of the deer season.

The Deerslayers of 1977

Back row: Ron Richardson MD, Dean Johlhaug, Hi Marshall MD, Don
Anthony PhD, Chester Wood EdE; Middle row: Les Krampitz PhD, Buck
Wood JD, Earl Wood MD, PhD, Erik Ritman MD, PhD; Front row: Mark
Wood MD, Abe Wood MD, Harland Wood PhD, Bud Bennett MBA

Once home and cleaned up, Earl would start working on the annual summary and report of the deer season. This was done in a scientific and academic manner, similar to the way he would publish data and results from experiments and observation in his laboratory. It included day-by-day tables and charts of the number of hunters participating per day, the number of deer sighted, and the number of deer harvested, along with time of day and location.

Throughout the years at deer camp, many interesting stories were told that are worth noting. Earl often invited his graduate students and fellows to join him there. Many of them returned year after year to participate in the camaraderie or, possibly, to impress the Coach.

During the forty years of hunting at the deer camp, there were no serious accidents; however, there were some very close calls. On one mild and warm morning, Earl was heading out to his stand in an area they called "the mid-swamp." The ground in this area was soft and mushy and full of moss. Earl started climbing up his stand and was almost at the top when a branch broke and he fell backward, hitting pine branches on the way down. He landed in the soft moss, creating a rather large divot. Realizing that he was not hurt, he brushed himself off and ascended the tree like nothing happened. This is reminiscent of the lucky fall he had on the 20 Acres as a young boy.

Deer season was tough on the home life, with Earl gone for ten days, then bringing home smelly hunting clothes and terrible body odor. A bath and a shave were required upon arrival. Ada was also not fond of venison, but she had the cooking skills to make a northern Minnesota swamp buck into a tasty meal. She put up with the hunting since it meant a lot to Earl. But that does not mean she liked it, as shown in the poem she wrote,

Wife's Lament
by Ada Wood

When the Earth's last deer has been eaten
And the Woods have passed from their
    stand
When old hunters are beaten
And gone to the Promised Land
We shall rest and gosh, we will need it
Quit cooking a season or two
Until the smell of venison has vanished
And lingers in hell with you

In 1984, the last deer harvested at the deer camp was bagged by Mark Wood. A final buffet dinner was held at a restaurant in Duluth. Bud Bennett had arranged to get a proclamation from then-governor Rudy Perpich celebrating the annual hunt of Deerslayers, Inc. Ada gave Earl a belt buckle with a deer on it, and a card on which she wrote,

> Here my Dear
> Is the only deer
> You old folks are going to see!
>
> So don't lament,
> But be content
> With the years
> You've spent in a tree!

This little poem brought tears to the eyes of the Coach. The next morning in the *Minneapolis Tribune*, outdoor writer Dennis Anderson described the forty years of gatherings of the Wood brothers and friends at the deer camp. Following the 1984 season, the deer camp was closed up for the last time and the property was sold to a group of hunters from the Duluth area.

The Deerslayers and the Wood brothers would always remember the camaraderie, the fellowship, the thrills, and the chills of waiting and chasing the elusive white-tailed deer, and being packed into the old Land Rover after a happy but weary day in the woods. Their spirits were high, and the optimism that prevailed will always be remembered. As Bud Bennett summed up in one of his poems,

> Near the shores of Gitche Gumee
> Where the white-tails are known to roam

Stands a tarpaper shack with many a rack
Known as the Deerslayers' home

Each day must be lived to the hilt
A chapter in itself as you see
And there is no better place to quicken
    life's pace
Than the shack south of 133

Hunting and fishing were a huge part of Earl's life. It gave him a chance to relive the rough-and-tumble lifestyle of his youth with his brothers and pass on his love of the outdoors to his colleagues (who dared join him in the wilderness) and his boys. Telling stories of what happened at deer camp brought him laughter and joy that lasted into his nineties. After listening to Earl, a visiting scientist once said, "I can't believe this guy is a Mayo Clinic doctor and a world-renowned scientist!"

CHAPTER 16

THE CAREER INVESTIGATOR

With the cardiac catheterization laboratory moving to Saint Marys Hospital and the clinical diagnostic procedures moved away from Earl's laboratory in the Medical Sciences Building, the Mayo Clinic administration began to wonder what to do with Earl Wood. Earl's career objectives and interest centered on investigation and education in the field of mammalian physiology, particularly in relation to the cardiovascular system, and he wanted to be relieved of the time-consuming clinical work that took him away from research.

To achieve this objective, Earl needed a source of funding and income. This was a bit unusual since his laboratory was located at Mayo Clinic and not a large university system. The Mayo Foundation, however, was affiliated with the University of Minnesota Medical School through the Mayo Graduate School of Medicine. One possibility to keep his laboratory running was to be nominated and apply for a career investigator award through the American Heart Association, which would provide a stipend for his salary and laboratory expenses. Initially, Earl was not interested in this award due to the potential lack of funding and loss of personal income, which he needed to support his growing family. However, with the urging of his scientific colleagues, in particular Drs. Morris Visscher, Gordon Moe, and Howard Burchell, the process began to nominate Earl for the career investigatorship.

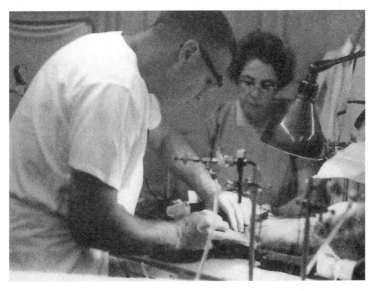

Earl performing a catheterization on an experimental
animal assisted by Lucy Cronin in 1963

The nomination process was spearheaded by Dr. Morris Visscher, Earl's former academic advisor at the University of Minnesota, and Dr. Gordon Moe, Earl's good friend and fellow graduate student at the University of Minnesota. Howard Burchell thought it was a good idea to have a career investigator affiliated with Mayo Clinic to enhance its research capabilities. Howard feared that Earl would turn down the appointment as a career investigator for financial reasons, since Earl told him he would not take it unless it was for more than $20,000. Gordon Moe, who worked with the American Heart Association, thought the award was close to $25,000.

In early 1960, both Drs. Visscher and Moe were urging their colleagues to write letters of recommendation to the American Heart Association endorsing Earl Wood for the career investigator award. Letters came from Dr. Charlie Code, Dr. Ed Lambert, Dr. Howard Burchell, and Dr. Jesse Edwards, who had recently left Mayo Clinic to work in the Twin Cities.

In a letter dated August 10, 1960, Dr. John Perkins, associate professor of physiology at the University of Chicago, summarized his recommendation to Dr. John Peters of the American Heart Association:

> I would guess Dr. Earl Wood has spent roughly half of his time and energy on basic physiological problems and half on physiology applied to clinical medicine. Whatever the portions have been, he has in my opinion contributed tremendously to both our knowledge of basic physiology of the heart and pulmonary circulation and our ability to treat the most serious disorders of these systems. In addition, he has been a great teacher and a trainer of many young physiologists and physicians. . . .
>
> I happen to be particularly familiar with the absolute reading of blood oxygen saturation by the oximeter developed by Dr. Wood, because of my own experience with this instrument. Originating [sic] by him in 1950, this device provided for the first time numerical readings of arterial oxygen saturation, even in cyanotic subjects. In the ensuing 10 years,

Wood oximeters have been used extensively throughout the world for studies on cardiopulmonary physiology and clinically during the evaluation of cardiac and pulmonary disease, during surgery and during convalescence.

His skill at developing an excellent cardiac catheterization laboratory and in improving the Gibbon pump oxygenator have undoubtedly greatly helped the progress of open-heart surgery at Mayo Clinic and elsewhere.

In another letter to Dr. Peters, dated August 15, 1960, Dr. Jesse Edwards wrote,

Dr. Wood's qualifications as investigator are so thoroughly known in the field that it seems hardly necessary to review these. In brief, however it might be stated that Dr. Wood organized the cardiac catheterization program at Mayo Clinic and the Mayo Foundation. In this work he was one of the pioneers. Included in this was the development of the oximeter, which now holds an invaluable place in every first-class cardiac catheterization setup. His original contributions to the field of dye dilution curves, both from the point of diagnosis and from the point of view of measuring blood flows and cardiac output, are classic in the field.

I would consider it a most logical move for Dr. Wood, as a means of his assuring more research time than he now has and,

from the point of view of the American Heart
Association, I am most confident that the appointment would result in accomplishments
of the finest hopes of the program of having a
career investigator.

On August 17, 1960, Earl wrote a long letter to Dr. Morris
Visscher outlining his accomplishments and future goals and
objectives for his laboratory, indicating that relieving him of
clinical duties would allow him more time to focus on physiological research.

By December 1960, rumors coming from the administrative staff of the American Heart Association confirmed that
Earl was to receive the career investigator award. This made
him essentially independent of Mayo Clinic's somewhat re-
strictive research policies at the time. Yet he had absolutely
no intention of leaving the unique cardiovascular and acceleration laboratories and technical staff he'd worked with at
Mayo Clinic for the last two decades.

In April 1961, Earl was named career investigator by the
American Heart Association. The award provided support to
enable him to work on research projects of his choice with
maximum freedom from other routine clinical duties. The
money provided by the American Heart Association paid his
Mayo Clinic salary and the salary for visiting scientists and
fellows, and it provided some funds to operate the laboratory
plus cover overhead expenses. It also provided a retirement
plan similar to compatible plans at a university. The career
investigatorship allowed him to continue doing his cardiac
physiology research in the catheterization laboratory and on
the centrifuge in the Medical Sciences Building, receiving additional funding from the National Institutes of Health, the
US Air Force, and NASA.

INTERNATIONAL LABORATORY

The late-1950s introduction of television fluoroscopy and X-ray angiography generated more accurate measures of cardiac output, blood volume, and the possibility of short circuits in the heart due to anatomical abnormalities. In addition, the development of the videotape recorder allowed for repeated intermediate playback of the images during the cardiac catheterization procedure so that different areas of the heart and vessels could be viewed.

In the early 1960s, Dr. Paul Heintzen, a pediatric cardiologist from Kiel, Germany, visited the Mayo cardiovascular research laboratory. He was also interested in video-fluoroscopy imaging for quantitative analysis of cardiac anatomy and function. Dr. Heintzen was born in Essen, Germany, in 1925 and served in the Wehrmacht on the eastern front and also in Italy. He was eventually captured by the American military in Schleswig-Holstein at the end of the war and held as a prisoner of war. After his release, he started his medical studies in Bonn in late 1945 and then worked at the Physiological Institute at the University of Münster. In 1954, he transferred to the department of pediatrics in Kiel, working in the pediatric cardiology clinic conducting cardiac catheterizations similar to what was being done at Mayo Clinic at the time. It was Dr. Heintzen's suggestion that multiple views of the structures were needed, plus analysis of the density of the video image as the dye was injected. This started a collaboration between Earl and Dr. Heintzen that lasted for years, even after Earl had to retire from Mayo Clinic.

In 1962, **Dr. Peter Osypka**, who came with a doctorate in biomedical engineering, started his fellowship in the cardiovascular laboratory at Mayo. Peter Osypka was born in Miechowitz, Upper Silesia, Poland. During the war, his father was an electrical engineer at Peenemünde, working on the guidance systems for the V-1 and V-2 rockets developed by Wernher von Braun. Teaming up with Ralph Sturm and Robert Hanson, a Mayo Clinic engineer, Peter developed a split-screen video display so that simultaneous X-ray fluoroscopic images taken at ninety degrees from each other—from both anterior-posterior (frontal) and lateral (side) positions—could be viewed. This allowed for better viewing of the heart and pumping action, with greater accuracy in calculating heart-chamber volumes, cardiac output, and ejection fraction (the percent of change in left ventricular volume from diastole, when the ventricle relaxes and fills, to systole, when the ventricle contracts). It eliminated the task of recording two separate images and then matching the timing for analysis. This was the beginning of viewing the chest and the internal organs from multiple angles at the same time, which within a decade led to the development of the Dynamic Spatial Reconstructor.

Dr. Wilhelm "Willy" Rutishauser started in Earl's lab in 1963. Willy earned his medical degree from the University of Basel, in Switzerland, and was working at the University of Zurich, where he had written a book on dye-dilution techniques to analyze blood circulation. He came to Mayo Clinic to learn the latest techniques in cardiac catheterization and about the latest research in analyzing cardiovascular dynamics and physiology. Much of Willy's time was spent participating in scientific experiments on the centrifuge, analyzing data from experimental animals subjected to different g-forces in various positions. Catheters were placed not only in the chambers of the heart but also within the pericardial sac, the pleural space between the lungs and rib cage, and the rectum and abdominal cavity to record abdominal pressure. These were tricky procedures, since any air introduced into the catheters would give false pressure data. Once the catheters were in place, the experimental animal, either a dog or chimpanzee, was placed in various positions to record the physiological responses during different exposures to gravitational forces on the centrifuge. Initially the data recorded was in analog form on paper or tape recording. It took Willy and others in the lab weeks to analyze the physiological data from just one centrifuge experiment. The data was used by both the air force and NASA to evaluate acceleration exposures for manned space-flight studies. Willy was one of many foreign fellows who participated in research that benefited the United States medical community, along with the military and space programs.

Other research fellows in engineering and medicine came to Mayo from all around the world to learn the techniques and about the latest physiological research in Earl's laboratory. Noted research fellows included Dr. Ernst Keck, from Germany; Dr. Arthur Kitchin, from Great Britain; Dr. Jack Sinclair, from New Zealand; Dr. Franz Bender, from Münster, Germany; Dr. Claude Puthon from Annecy, France; Dr. John Williams, from New Zealand and Great Britain; and Dr. Anastasios "Tasos" Tsakiris, from Greece. Each of them enjoyed one to three years working in research in the cardiovascular laboratory, learning the latest techniques in diagnostic cardiology and gravitational physiology and learning about and enjoying Midwest American life in the 1960s.

All of these individuals published their research in national or international scientific journals in addition to presenting at national physiology or heart association meetings. Upon returning to their homelands, many of these former research fellows became department heads at their universities, hospitals, or clinics. But before they left, they also became lifelong friends of Earl and the entire Wood family, participating in hunting, fishing, and skiing trips—and, of course, working weekends at Lake Washington. In the coming years, the Wood family visited many of these former fellows in their respective homelands.

This diverse laboratory, comprising individuals from different cultural and political backgrounds, came together in the quest for knowledge for the benefit of medical science and the patients they treated. Many of the nations represented there had been at war with each other two decades before these research fellows arrived at Mayo Clinic. Where else could Jews, Germans, French, English, Scots, Irish, Japanese, and Americans be found working in one location for a common goal? As Earl once said, "Good science has no borders." It is not known whether cultural or political differences were discussed in or outside of the laboratory during these fellows' stays in Rochester. One can only speculate.

CULTURE EXCHANGE

There was of course a language barrier for many of the fellows starting in the laboratory. One humorous incident occurred when Lucy Cronin was showing a new fellow the stopcock switch for flushing a catheter during an experiment. Lucy pointed to the valve and said, "On, off." The fellow thought the name of the valve was "on off." When it came time to flush the catheter, Earl directed this young man to turn the stopcock on. The poor fellow stood there totally confused. Lucy then intervened, turning the stopcock on to flush the catheter. She then took the fellow aside and showed him a light switch and said, "On," and turned the light on. She then switched the light off and said, "Off." The fellow repeated, "On, off," several times. They then walked over to the stopcock and repeated, "On, off."

Earl's position as a career investigator gave him, his staff, and research fellows a unique opportunity to share physiological and other scientific information, along with learning about other cultures and viewpoints—and having a lot of fun in the process. It also gave Earl the freedom to conduct research of his liking at Mayo and other research centers in Europe and Canada.

CHAPTER 17

SABBATICAL YEAR, 1965–66

Ever since Earl traveled in Europe in 1946 as part of Operation Paperclip, and then traveled with Ada to South America in 1957 and again to Europe in 1958, he and Ada had had a strong desire to introduce their family to other countries and cultures. Other members of the Wood and Peterson families who worked in university settings had taken sabbatical years in foreign countries.

Now that Earl was a career investigator with the American Heart Association, he could apply for fellowships to study and conduct research in a laboratory overseas. Earl still had a great interest in heart-muscle contractility, which stemmed from the research he conducted back in graduate school. He was familiar with the research being conducted on smooth and cardiac muscle in London and also at the University of Bern, in Switzerland. In 1964, Earl applied for a grant and fellowship through the Commonwealth Fund to study cardiovascular physiology, seeking to learn new techniques for recording transmembrane electrical potential of cardiac muscle cells and the influence of interstitial-fluid concentrations of calcium, potassium, and sodium. Earl proposed to work with a team of physiologists under Professor Alexander von Muralt, at the University of Bern. Earl had met von Muralt while visiting Bern back in 1946 as part of Operation Paperclip.

The Commonwealth Fund was initially slightly skeptical of Earl's request, due to their perception of his limited educational responsibility. This skepticism was set aside with a letter from Dr. Visscher indicating Earl's educational responsibilities while at the University of Minnesota, the University of Pennsylvania, and Harvard Medical School. In his letter to the Commonwealth Fund, Dr. Visscher wrote,

> I think in the field of cardiovascular physiology, Earl Wood is one of the top dozen investigators in the world in terms of productivity and general soundness of approach. He has already had a great influence in training younger men. There is no question whatsoever as to his high degree of initiative, originality, and creativity. He has these qualities to a degree found in a very small percentage of scientists. In other words, I would say you cannot go wrong.

In March 1965, Earl received notice from the Commonwealth Fund that his fellowship was approved for one year with an award of $5,825. Additional funds from the American Heart Association made the yearlong sabbatical for the whole E. H. Wood family financially feasible, and planning started in earnest.

Earl and Ada's kids were at an age where they were starting to depart the household. Phoebe was teaching school in Edina, Minnesota, and was starting on her master's degree in history. Mark was a freshman at the University of Pennsylvania, in Philadelphia, and was spending the summer in Waikiki as a bouncer at the Queen's Surf bar. Guy had just graduated from John Marshall High School in Rochester and was taking machine shop class during the summer. And Andy had just finished sixth grade at Lincoln Elementary School and couldn't figure out if he was going to Sweden or Switzerland.

The family's final evening in Rochester before leaving for Europe was spent at Michaels restaurant in downtown Rochester for a going-away dinner. Friends and coworkers from the lab attended too, including Ed and Louise Lambert, Ralph and Mildred Sturm, and Lucy Cronin. One very memorable moment during the dinner was Ada announcing that she had smoked her last cigarette. She snuffed out the menthol Kool in the ashtray and never touched another cigarette for the rest of her life. To the best of our knowledge, she did not suffer any withdrawal symptoms.

The family spent three days in New York City before boarding the ship to Europe. Earl had several meetings with Dr. William Manger, a former fellow in Earl's lab, while Guy, Mark, and Andy went to the top of the Empire State Building and then took the subway out to the 1965 World's Fair.

The day the SS *Independence* set sail for Europe was a day full of excitement. The pier was a beehive of activity, full of people, luggage carts, and porters yelling to passengers about assisting them with their heavy steamer trunks. At the ticket booth, boarding passes and passports were shown and the Wood family was escorted toward the gangplank leading to the entrance decks of the *Independence*. As they went through the turnstiles, the ship's photographer yelled out, "Let me get a picture of you all!" The Wood family quickly lined up, and in less than ten seconds the photographer snapped the best family picture of Earl, Ada, and the kids; it ended up on many Christmas cards and is still on display in the Wood kids' homes over half a century later.

The Wood family about to board the SS Independence, *September 8, 1965*

Money-wise, the mid-1960s was a great time for Americans to travel in Europe, since the exchange rate was in their favor: the Spanish peseta was twenty-five per dollar, the French franc was five and a quarter per dollar, the Swiss franc was five per dollar, and the German mark was four per dollar. At that time, you could travel in Europe for five dollars a day, which was the name of a tour guidebook popular with many students. The most expensive item was gasoline.

The family disembarked the *Independence* at the port of Algeciras, Spain. They drove north over the Sierra Nevada mountain range in southern Spain, ending up in the old Moorish city of Granada and then Madrid. They spent two busy days in Madrid, enrolling Guy at the University of Madrid and finding housing for his stay. This was a challenging endeavor, since so few people spoke English and Guy had only a limited working knowledge of the Spanish language from his high school studies.

They crossed the border into France, stopping in Carcassonne and Grenoble. Earl and family were invited to lunch with his former fellow and colleague, Dr. Claude Puthon in Annecy. Claude was a practicing cardiologist there.

The next morning, they crossed into Switzerland near Geneva. Entering the canton of Bern, they went from the French-speaking part of Switzerland into the German-speaking part. Both Phoebe and Earl noted that the dialect and accent were so strong that the language was almost unintelligible. This was their first exposure to *Schwyzertütsch* or *Schweizerdeutsch*, or Swiss German, which is a mixture of German and French with a singsong tone.

Arriving in Bern, they drove to the suburbs of Muri, where Earl and Ada had arranged for an apartment for the year sabbatical. At this point, the Wood kids went their separate ways, each to study a foreign language of his or her choice. Phoebe and Mark traveled together to Grafing, Bavaria, in Germany, where they had enrolled in the Goethe-Institut for studying the German language. Guy, on the other hand, had a very long train trip back to Madrid, with several transfers in Switzerland, France, and eventually Spain; he had no knowledge of French at all and a minimal working knowledge of Spanish. Earl stated that he was never so worried about any of his kids as he was for Guy when he boarded that train in Bern for the several-day trip back to Madrid. There was a real sigh of relief when Guy's first letter from Madrid arrived in

Bern a week and a half later. Andy was enrolled in a German-speaking school. This was a rather frightening experience for the twelve-year-old, being immersed into a preadolescent group of children without knowing a word of German, let alone Swiss German.

SWITZERLAND

Earl reported in to Professor von Muralt at the physiology department at the University of Bern. He was given a small laboratory with a desk and lab bench where he could set up his scientific experiments to study cardiac muscle contraction. He was working with a Dr. Silvio Wiedman, who also had a great interest in cardiac muscle contractility. The first several weeks in the laboratory were consumed with meeting other personnel, catching up on mail, and reading manuscripts Earl had received from Jean Frank and research fellows at Mayo to review and approve. It took another month to set up the equipment provided by the physiology department at the University of Bern and the equipment he had brought over from the United States. This equipment included an electrical device to stimulate muscle contraction, recording devices, an oscilloscope, a dissecting microscope, electrodes, surgical instruments, a small strain gauge to record the force of muscle contractions, and a small bath where muscle fibers would be studied. The goal of this research was to study cardiac contractility in various concentrations of electrolytes, including calcium, potassium, and sodium. Live cardiac muscle was supplied to the laboratory by a local butcher, who gave them pig hearts.

On the day of an experiment, a fresh pig heart would be delivered to Earl's laboratory. Earl would then dissect out a small section of the left ventricle and place it in a bath of saline solution. Each end was connected by small wires to a strain gauge and the electric stimulator. The concentration of the electrolytes varied, depending on the bath in which the muscle fibers were lying. Unlike the experiments with the centrifuge and cardiac catheterization back at Mayo, which lasted many hours and sometimes days, the physiological experiments conducted in Bern could be completed within several hours, giving Earl time for data analysis and correspondence with his laboratory back at Mayo, and, most important, precious time with the family in a foreign country.

Evenings in October 1965 were spent listening to the World Series on Armed Forces Network through a shortwave radio in the apartment. There was no television. The Minnesota Twins were playing the Los Angeles Dodgers at Metropolitan Stadium in Bloomington, Minnesota, and at Dodger Stadium in Los Angeles. The three Woods were glued to the play-by-play as Twins homerun sluggers Harmon Killebrew and Tony Oliva went up against the Dodgers' pitching duo of Sandy Koufax and Don Drysdale. The series was tied at three games apiece, but unfortunately the Dodgers won in the seventh game, leaving the Minnesotans disappointed.

Weekends were spent exploring Switzerland and the Swiss Alps. In the Bernese Oberland, they visited the town of Mürren, walked underneath the Trümmelbach Falls, and took the cog railway from Grindelwald up to the Jungfraujoch, where Earl had visited the high-altitude laboratory back in 1946. One side trip was to the town and castle of Gruyères. Here they learned how Gruyère cheese was made. They all developed a craving for this delightful cheese and became connoisseurs of Swiss cheeses, mastering the differences between Gruyère, Emmentaler, and Appenzeller.

By mid-December, the rest of the family had reassembled in Bern. Mark and Phoebe arrived from Munich by train.

Guy flew from Madrid to Geneva and then took the train to Bern. The small apartment in Muri was a hub of activity, as they exchanged stories from their experiences in Germany, Spain, and Switzerland. Christmas presents that year were skis, ski boots, poles, and a ski vacation in Klosters with Willy Rutishauser and family.

In March, Earl returned to Mayo Clinic for a week to see how things were progressing in the laboratory. At Ada's insistence, Earl invited Lucy Cronin to return with him to visit Switzerland for two weeks. Lucy had never been out of the United States and was thrilled to accompany Earl back to Europe. While in Europe, not only did Lucy get shown around Bern by Ada, but she also met up with Earl's former fellows back in their homelands, including Claude Puthon and Willy Rutishauser.

During spring break, the Wood kids once again assembled in Bern in preparation for an extended trip south into Italy and Greece, returning through Yugoslavia and Austria.

They arrived in Athens just as the Greeks were celebrating Greek Independence Day with a large military parade in front of the government buildings. The personal physician of King Constantine, who was a friend of Dr. Tsakiris, one of Earl's former fellows, invited Earl and family to view the parade from a hotel balcony overlooking the main square and parade route. This was a formal affair, and the family had to be dressed up in good clothes. The parade started with horses followed by a military band. Then came King Constantine, riding in a convertible Rolls-Royce. He stood up and saluted toward the balcony, acknowledging the doctor and his honored guests. This was followed by a flyover of the Greek air force and a parade of military hardware.

By August it was time to start packing the bags, since they had to get back to the United States in time for the start of the school year and college. The family gathered in Bern once again. The steamer trunks were repacked and shipped to Southampton, England, where they would be placed on the SS *France* for the return voyage to New York City. Their trip to England took them through Germany, Holland, Belgium, and France.

BACK HOME

Settling back into the routine at home was anything but routine. Earl had to catch up on everything that had been happening in the laboratory and Mayo Clinic. He also had many manuscripts from his fellows to review and edit before publication. In addition, he was under pressure to publish his scientific results from the experiments done in Bern. On the home front, clothes were washed and bags and trunks were repacked. Within a week, Mark was on a plane back to Philadelphia and starting his sophomore year at the University of Pennsylvania. Guy left for his freshman year at the University of Minnesota Duluth. And Andy started seventh grade at Central Junior High, in Rochester.

While in Europe, the Wood children all became independent, striking out on their own, traveling in strange countries, and making do by themselves when things got tough. These were the days before cellphones and helicopter and snowplow parents, which Earl and Ada were not. All the Wood kids became multilingual. Guy majored in Spanish and made a career out of the language, eventually ending up as a Spanish professor at Oregon State University. Phoebe taught history and German in the Denver schools for thirty-plus years, eventually earned a PhD in history, and ended up teaching German culture at the University of Denver. Mark went into medicine but still has a working knowledge of German. Andy took German from junior high through high school in order to boost his grade point average for an easy A. In college, he minored in German, and he still speaks and writes in fluent German to this day.

The sabbatical year of 1965–66 had a significant impact on Earl and Ada and their kids that lasted a lifetime. The European way of enjoying life by taking your time at a meal, walking or taking public transportation, and valuing history and the fine arts made them question the fast-paced American way of life. After a year of using the metric system of kilometers, meters, liters, and centiliters, they questioned the confusing and often cumbersome American/English measurement system of miles, feet, gallons, quarts, and pints. Earl noted that educators, professors, and researchers are far more respected in Europe than in America, since education and the teaching professions are more appreciated. He once stated, "I probably would have earned more money in Europe doing research than what I am [earning] back in the States." The whole family appreciated the high-quality education system with minimal or no tuition or fees, along with a universal healthcare system that they all used during their stay abroad.

CHAPTER 18

EXPANDING SCIENTIFIC
AND MEDICAL INSTRUMENTATION

When Earl returned from his sabbatical year in Europe in the fall of 1966, the laboratory was expanding in terms of both personnel and technological advances. NASA research continued on the centrifuge, using both dogs and chimpanzees as subjects, as well as more advanced usage of video analysis and simultaneous recordings of physiological data. Cardiovascular research continued and had expanded using multi-X-ray sources, video recordings, and higher-speed computer data analysis.

In 1966, **Don Erdman** joined the technical staff. Don had experience in radio broadcast technology, having worked with several radio stations in southern Minnesota. He also had experience in an aircraft engine machine shop and was noted for repairing just about anything in the laboratory. Don was to fabricate equipment and tools specific to the cardiovascular laboratory and the centrifuge. He was also put in charge of the safety countdown before all centrifuge runs and was always the last person out of the room before the centrifuge would start spinning.

Don Erdman, Donnie Hegland, Lucy Cronin, Willis Van Norman, Julijs Zarins, and Bill Sutterer, plus administrative assistant Jean Frank, were the key technological team that made the biodynamics research unit in the Medical Sciences Building function and produce groundbreaking research through the 1980s. Without these talented, knowledgeable individuals, Earl's laboratory would not have accomplished what it did. Earl often said, "MD and PhD fellows are a dime a dozen, but you cannot replace any of the technical team in the lab!"

New fellows to join the laboratory at that time were key in developing technological advances in diagnostic cardiology. **Dr. Barry Gilbert** joined the lab as a graduate student in the mid-1960s and was brought on for his expertise in computers, bioengineering, and data analysis. **Dr. Craig Coulam** completed his PhD at the University of Utah and started a postdoctoral fellowship at the lab in the spring of 1967. His good friend and fraternity brother from the University of Utah, **Jim Greenleaf**, started in the laboratory later that year. **Dr. Erik Ritman**, a physiologist and physician from the University of Melbourne, joined the laboratory in the late 1960s. **Dr. Donald Sass**, from the US Air Force and NASA, worked on the gravitational research being conducted on the centrifuge. **Dr. Richard Robb**, who had a PhD in computer sciences and mathematics from the University of Utah, joined the laboratory about 1970. All these individuals, from various backgrounds, were key in the development of advanced cardiovascular diagnostic techniques still used in many clinical laboratories today.

To study the movement of the heart, cardiac angiography involved injecting a radiopaque dye into the chambers of the heart and viewing the inside of the atria and ventricles on an X-ray fluoroscope. Initially this was recorded as a series of X-ray pictures, in an attempt to document a full cardiac cycle. Later the angiograms were recorded using movie films, which captured the dynamic movements of the heart from the fluoroscope. As time progressed, the angiography was recorded on videotape using a closed-circuit television system. Although film had higher spatial and temporal resolution than video, the film systems required more time for viewing and diagnoses, since the film had to be developed, whereas a video system offered quick playback.

At that time, the views of the chest and the moving heart were done in one single plane, or monoplane. To more accurately study the geometry of the cardiac chambers and the movement of the heart and chest organs, a biplane X-ray video system was installed in the lab so the images could be recorded on videotape at ninety-degree angles. Ralph Sturm, Dr. Peter Osypka, and Mayo engineer Bob Hanson designed and fabricated a method for simultaneously recording two fluoroscopic images and displaying both views of the heart on one television screen. This was a tricky procedure since the two X-ray cameras had to be exactly aligned at the same focal point on the anatomical structure. In addition, to reduce X-ray scattering, one camera had to shut off while the other one was turned on. The two cameras were pulsed at two-millisecond intervals. Each video line on the television screen was sampled sixty times per second, and the video line from one view had to match up at the same level as the second camera view. The two views produced by the biplane system were then projected in split-screen fashion on a television screen. The electrocardiogram and pressure waves in the atria and ventricles could be recorded on the audio portion of the videotape. Computer analysis of these two views was accomplished by transferring the videotape recording onto a stop-action videodisc, which was new technology used in broadcast television for instant replay during sporting events.

Before flat-screen video screens, a television image consisted of a stack of 250 horizontal lines refreshed every sixtieth of a second. In the laboratory, each horizontal television line was then displayed on an oscilloscope, creating a unique waveform for the specific line on the television screen. The waveform represented a cross section of the heart from two views. The location of the changes in brightness of each line on the television screen was used to compute the diameter of the chamber and the thickness of the walls in each biplane view. The values for all the cross sections of the heart chamber were summed up by the computer to get an estimated chamber volume. The system was calibrated by taking X-ray pictures of a ball of known volume from the two angles. If they could calculate the volume of the ball, they would be able to calculate the volume of the heart chambers. The two views were computer synchronized to more accurately measure the geometry and functioning of the heart.

Ralph Sturm also developed a method of measuring the opacity of the contrast medium in the chambers of the heart when viewed under fluoroscopy. This led to another version of dye-dilution curves using X-ray fluoroscopy. X-ray sampling windows could be placed upstream and downstream from where the radiopaque dye was injected through the catheter. For example, a window could be placed over the left ventricle and another window placed over the left atrium. When dye was injected into the left ventricle and then detected using the window over the left atrium, it would show the functioning or malfunctioning of the mitral valve. This technique became widely used to determine whether a patient needed to have a mitral valve replacement. This technique was further advanced to measure the blood flow in the coronary arteries.

The management of the borders of the silhouette under X-ray was called videometry, while the measurement of the density of small areas in the video picture is called videodensitometry. Using biplane X-ray, it became known as biplane Roentgen videodensitometry. Earl enjoyed using these long words and definitions with his peers, fellows, and family members.

LIQUID BREATHING

This was also the time of the Cold War and the height of the space race. Research continued on physiological responses to acceleration on the centrifuge. Research grants continued to come in from the air force as well as NASA. Further instrumentation was added to the centrifuge, including X-ray cameras, strain-gauge manometers, and dye injectors, which could be controlled remotely while the centrifuge was spinning. Special fiberglass casts were designed and manufactured by the David Clark Company to fit a dog or a chimpanzee placed in the cockpit of the centrifuge in a similar position as an astronaut in a spacecraft.

One of the most intriguing series of experiments involved the concept of liquid breathing. The concept was that if a human or animal were immersed in a liquid and they could breathe and exchange gases through the lungs with that liquid, they would be protected from increased gravitational or inertial forces, such as those encountered during airplane crashes, a spacecraft's uncontrolled reentry into Earth's atmosphere, or high-speed turns and other high-G maneuvers in an aircraft. In addition, breathing an incompressible liquid could possibly protect deep-sea divers from the excessive hydrostatic pressure of ocean depths. Liquid breathing would not only counteract the hydrostatic pressure applied to the chest wall but also maintain the partial pressures of the respiratory gases dissolved in the liquid equal to the partial pressures at sea level. The deep-sea diver would be able to quickly ascend to the surface without experiencing decompression sickness ("the bends") and without fear of nitrogen gas narcosis or oxygen toxicity and other hazards for divers breathing compressed gases.

Drs. Don Sass and Fred Bove had a great interest in this project from their background in the military and scuba diving. These experiments involved immersing the experimental animal in an enclosed tank filled with a saline solution, where it could breathe an oxygenated liquid fluorocarbon. Using an external pump to control the volume of the solution surrounding the experimental animal, the respiratory rate, tidal volumes, and residual lung volumes could be mechanically controlled by the amount of saline solution going in and out of the enclosed tank.

Intrathoracic pressures were recorded by strain-gauge manometers connected to fluid-filled catheters placed into the aorta, pulmonary vein, right and left atrium, left pulmonary vein, and the right and left pleural spaces. Cuvette oximeters measured oxygen saturation continuously from the thoracic aorta, pulmonary artery, and left pulmonary vein. This data was recorded while the animal was breathing room air and then again, in the same manner, when it was breathing the oxygenated liquid fluorocarbon. The experimental animal could breathe the oxygenated liquid for four hours or longer without signs of respiratory distress. They were exposed to various levels of G on the centrifuge while breathing the fluorocarbon. The evidence indicated that liquid breathing provided good respiratory gas exchange up to 6G. X-ray images showed that liquid breathing prevented inertial displacements of the heart and other chest structures while the body was exposed to acceleration. The results of these experiments indicated that, theoretically, liquid breathing could protect against pulmonary distress and injury due to acceleration and sustained extreme changes in environmental pressure, and minimize decompression problems associated with deep-sea diving and sudden changes of gravitational acceleration force.

Experiments on the centrifuge could be long and arduous, sometimes lasting up to two days. Experiment days started at 4:00 a.m. with Don Hegland, Don Erdman, Bill Sutterer, Julijs Zarins, and Lucy Cronin arriving to get the flywheels of the centrifuge turning and get the recording devices and surgical instruments prepared. Earl would arrive about 7:00 a.m., along with the other research staff, and start calibrating the instrumentation and preparing the experimental animal for the day's run; it was time-consuming to calibrate the instrumentation for accurate measurement.

The experimental animal was retrieved from Institute Hills and was properly anesthetized by Mayo veterinarian Dr. Paul Zollman. The animal was then placed in the cast in the cockpit of the centrifuge, and the X-ray cameras were lined up to focus on the chest. Preparation alone took most of the morning and sometimes into the afternoon. The experiment began with recording controls at 1G; that is with the centrifuge at a standstill and the experimental animal breathing room air. Centrifuge runs were then initiated by Lucy Cronin running off a safety checklist, like she did for the experiments during World War II. This checklist was double-checked by Don Erdman, who was assigned to be the last person out of the centrifuge room before the run was initiated. Once Don left the room, the doors were locked and the countdown began for a centrifuge run. The scientists, including Earl, were either in the control room or the data-recording room to observe the physiological recordings coming from the cockpit. Following the run, when the gantry had come to a complete standstill, Don Erdman was the first in the centrifuge room to lock down the gantry. Once the gantry was locked down, the scientists could enter the room to observe what occurred in the cockpit. This procedure repeated itself several times, depending on the experimental protocol and the number of G runs required.

When Dr. Hugh Smith started in Earl's lab in the late 1960s, he assisted in his first centrifuge experiment. By midday of the experiment, he phoned his wife, Ainsley, indicating that he would be late getting home for dinner. Later that evening, he phoned her again, indicating that he would not be home at all that evening and possibly the next morning. Obviously, these were unusual and unique physiological experiments.

During an experiment in the early 1970s, white smoke suddenly billowed out of the flywheel room underneath the centrifuge. Don Erdman did an emergency shutdown and the gantry came to a sudden, grinding halt. It turned out that the drive belts from the motor to the driveshaft for the flywheels had burned out. A replacement part was ordered from a supplier in the Twin Cities; it was to be driven down that evening, since the experiment was in process. Due to the expense and long preparation for the experiment, and since the flywheels were still spinning, they could not just stop the experiment for that day. So, they simply had to wait for the replacement part. To pass the time, Earl went out and ordered pizza for the entire crew and, against Mayo Clinic policy, came back with a case of Grain Belt beer, much to the joy of his hardworking crew. The new drive belt arrived from the Twin Cities and was installed, and the experiment continued on through the night and into the next day. The success of the liquid-breathing experiments was soon publicized in the media. Earl gave a presentation on liquid breathing to the Mayo Clinic Board of Governors, which at the time included former president Lyndon Baines Johnson.

One day a retired Navy SEAL showed up at the Medical Sciences Building and Earl's office, demanding to be the first human to attempt liquid breathing. Being a deep-sea diver, he saw its potential. After Earl showed the gentleman what was involved (some of which was still classified), including the potentially life-threatening risks, he still insisted on trying it. He was gently ushered out of the building. What was not publicly known, and had not been published at the time, was that several days after the liquid-breathing experiments, the animals died. This was very perplexing to all the scientists involved, since the animals were relatively healthy following the experiments. It was speculated that the cause of death was air embolism; however, it was later found out that the manufacturing process for the fluorocarbon created a small amount of a toxic substance, which over time caused the demise of the animals. For this reason, the liquid-breathing research was stopped.

OOPS!

One experiment on the centrifuge involved injecting a radioactive isotope to detect blood flow during G exposure. During one G run, a valve malfunctioned, spraying the wall of the centrifuge room with the radioactive substance. Following the experiment, radioactivity could be detected in the block walls where the substance was sprayed. The question was what to do about this potential environmental hazard. They could not tear down the supportive solid-brick walls of the centrifuge room, so the remedy was scrubbing them down and then applying many coats of thick paint. The radiation levels dropped to acceptable limits and gave the centrifuge room a bright, shiny look.

Centrifuge experiments continued through the mid-1970s. Despite the valuable scientific data coming from the acceleration studies for manned space flight and the air force, some engineers questioned the integrity of the aging G wheel. Some engineers would not enter the Medical Sciences Building when the centrifuge was running, for fear of a weld failing, a flywheel bearing going out, or metal fatigue. When not in use, the centrifuge room was used for meeting space during National Institutes of Health site visits, to remind visiting scientists of the significant research that had taken place in this historical laboratory.

Meanwhile, research continued on the development of electronic imaging techniques to study the structure and function of the heart and circulatory system. The biplane fluoroscopy technology was soon installed in the cardiac catheterization laboratory at Saint Marys Hospital. Clinical diagnoses and studies using the videometry techniques developed in the laboratory at the Medical Sciences Building were now being used clinically on patients. Following a cardiac catheterization procedure, a clinical technician would use a stop-action videodisc to evaluate the function of the patient's heart. The technician could outline the silhouette of the walls of the left ventricle in diastole, or when the heart chamber is filling, and then again at the end of systole, when the ventricle contracts. This was used to calculate left ventricular volume, ventricular wall thickness, the rate of wall thickening, and also the ejection fraction, which is the amount of blood pumped out of the heart per beat.

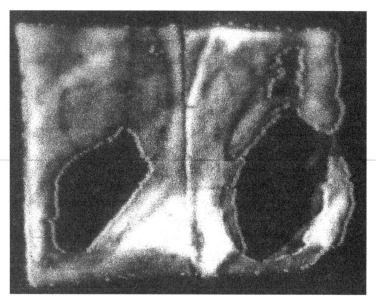

A biplane fluoroscopic image from a video, with left ventricular walls outlined by a videometry system

The biplane system, though state of the art at the time, was inherently inaccurate. The interior of the heart in computer-generated reconstructions from just two angles assumed an elliptical shape. Anatomically, the interior of the heart is not elliptical; instead, it assumes different shapes to include the papillary muscles and the heart valves. In addition, when the heart contracts, it not only compresses but also twists. Therefore, more views of the heart were necessary, along with faster computers to analyze the copious amount of data being generated from multiple views.

The solution was rapid digitization and digital storage of the X-ray video image data. Larger programmable digital os-cilloscopes were purchased, along with more powerful computers whose solid-state digital memory was similar to what was being developed at the time for video games.

One day in the early 1970s, Jean Frank was looking through some old scientific journals and came across a schematic of an electron microscope data-collection system for tomographic reconstruction of a virus using multiple density profiles. She brought this article to the attention of the scientists in the lab to get their thoughts on the possibility of tomographic reconstruction for the heart. Eventually, Dr. Garber Herman, a mathematician from the State University at Buffalo, started working with the lab to develop mathematical tomographic reconstruction from the video lines, creating a cross section of the anatomical structures in the chest cavity.

Initial experiments involved using an isolated cadaver heart and rotating it in front of an X-ray source, taking multiple video images. The video data was then processed from an analog to a digital format and a rough cross section of the heart could be mathematically reconstructed.

On Groundhog Day 1973, the X-ray fluoroscopic imaging system with heart rotation and video fluoroscopic image-recording systems were integrated to allow the laboratory's first tomographic reconstruction of an isolated heart. Earl was in London at the time, on his second sabbatical, and immediately realized the potential of this new diagnostic tool.

Not long after Earl's return to Rochester, multiple scans were taken of an anesthetized dog in a vertical position in front of the X-ray source. The researchers injected a radiopaque dye in the left ventricle, and the outline of the heart and the chest contents could clearly be seen on the video monitor and a graphic cross section of the heart could be digitally reconstructed. The system became known as the Single Source Dynamic Spatial Reconstructor, or SSDSR. Clearly, the next objective was to design and fabricate a multi-X-ray-source dynamic reconstructor for more accurate scanning and computer reconstruction of the moving organs of the chest and abdominal cavity. This involved faster computers than were available at the time and larger data-storage capabilities.

GRANT PROPOSALS

During the years 1973 through 1976, Earl and his research staff dedicated most of their time to writing grant proposals to the National Institutes of Health for funding the DSR (or Dynamic Spatial Reconstructor) project. This involved multiple written grant proposals in addition to site visits by NIH administrators and consulting scientists from all over the country. The proposals were thick books describing the latest results from the SSDSR, background references, projected costs, and potential benefits to medical science.

According to Earl, the written grant requests were larger than several volumes of Tolstoy's *War and Peace*. Medical device companies such as General Electric, 3M, Philips, and Raytheon were consulted on the design, construction, and funding of the DSR. The research, development, planning, and construction was a multimillion-dollar project. Earl voiced his frustration about asking for funds from some of the larger companies for the DSR. These corporations were unlike David Clark, who sacrificed time and money to develop the G-suit during the war. Earl came home one evening and stated, "These companies are only interested in making a profit, not assisting in the advancement of medical science." Meanwhile, research using the SSDSR was being continued by fellows and graduate students; this helped refine the design of the DSR. Finally, in late 1976 and after multiple NIH grant submissions and site visits, the design and construction of the DSR was funded for $5.2 million.

Unlike the CT scans of the time, which produced single cross sections, the DSR could do more. Theoretically, it could dissect the human body without breaking the skin. Earl called it "noninvasive vivisection." The image below is a reconstruction of a dog's heart using the SSDSR. The goal for the DSR was for a doctor to select an organ and then slice it up on the computer to make a diagnosis without surgery.

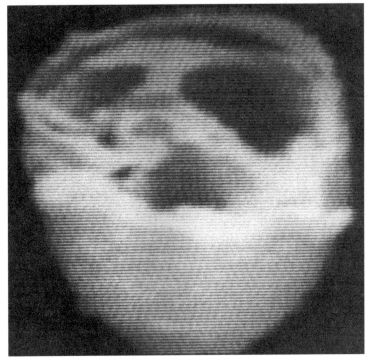

*Computer reconstruction and slicing of a live
dog's heart generated by the SSDSR*

The DSR funding and the launch of a huge new scientific project marked a transition in Earl's career. In 1977, Earl turned sixty-five, and he was required by Mayo Clinic policy at the time to relinquish the chair of the biodynamics research unit.

The chair was handed over to Dr. Erik Ritman, who had been in the lab since the late 1960s and was key in the development of the SSDSR and DSR projects. Earl continued on in the laboratory as senior consultant until his mandatory retirement at the age of seventy. Despite his title change, he continued to be "the Coach" of the team and was a critical contact for getting things done for the DSR project, both inside and outside of Mayo Clinic.

CHAPTER 19

SABBATICAL YEAR IN LONDON, 1972–73

As a career investigator with the American Heart Association, Earl had the opportunity to take a sabbatical every seven years. He wanted to return to Bern to continue his studies of cardiac muscle contractility in various concentrations of intercellular electrolytes. Ada, however, insisted on going to another location to experience a new culture and to an area where she could understand the language. Earl knew that similar studies were being conducted in the physiology department at University College London. In the fall of 1971, Earl was invited to give a presentation at an international aviation conference in Yerevan, Armenia, then a Soviet republic. On their return flight, Earl and Ada stopped in London and visited with the physiology department at University College. It was then decided that Earl would spend the academic year of 1972–73 working with Dr. Brian Jewell at University College. Housing arrangements were made for a flat in the London suburb of Hendon; it was owned by a professor who would be visiting another academic institution that year. Ada was thrilled with the opportunity to live in a large, international city with world-class museums, concerts, and of course shopping.

The Wood kids were also excited about another overseas adventure. Since the last sabbatical, they had all grown up and were pursuing college and advanced university degrees. Phoebe had spent another year in Europe following the 1966 year, taking several semesters at the University of Munich and then traveling to Ghana and South Africa. When she returned to the United States, she completed her master's degree in history at the University of Colorado Boulder and started her career in Denver teaching high school sociology, history, and German. Mark had graduated from the University of Pennsylvania and was enrolled in medical school at the University of Minnesota.

With the news that Earl and Ada were going to London, Mark arranged to do a medical clerkship at a hospital there. Guy had graduated from the University of Minnesota Duluth and was pursuing a master's degree in Spanish through New York University, but his classes were at the University of Madrid. He had already been there for a year when Earl and Ada announced that they would be in London. At the same time, Guy was in the process of filing for conscientious objector status to avoid the military draft; in this action, he had full support from his parents, the Unitarian Universalist Church, and local, state, and federal representatives. He was eventually granted that status. Andy had graduated from John Marshall High School and would be entering the Goethe-Institut in Murnau, Germany, to study German. Following his studies at the Goethe-Institut, he planned to enroll in the language institute at the University of Münster.

Once again, steamer trunks were packed and the house

was cleaned so it could be rented for the year. Passports were all updated with new pictures and visas. Since this became a contentious presidential election year after the initial reporting of the Watergate break-in, absentee ballots were procured and sent in for voting. Of note, all the Wood family members voted for George McGovern. Ocean passage was booked for Earl, Ada, and Andy on the *Queen Elizabeth 2* (*QE2*), which sailed from New York City to Southampton.

Earl and Ada had London to themselves and they loved it. Ada thrived in London. For once, she had Earl all to herself without the interruptions of her kids, relatives, or hunting and fishing seasons. Ada loved the British politeness, formalities, history, countryside, and humor. After Earl left the flat for work, she would tidy up and take the Tube by herself to downtown London. There she explored the history and culture of London and Great Britain. She also attended matinee concerts and, of course, window-shopped at the many fashionable department stores downtown, such as Harrods and Marks & Spencer. She spent a lot of time at the antique shops on Portobello Road. She did purchase silverware and silver napkin rings, which still grace the Wood family dining room tables to this day. Ada particularly enjoyed the Johann Strauss opera *Die Fledermaus*, which she saw several times. Often, Earl and Ada would meet for lunch or dinner in downtown London before heading back to the flat in Hendon. Weekends were spent driving through the English countryside, visiting historical landmarks, and hiking.

Earl got into the routine of getting up early, having breakfast with Ada, then driving downtown to University College, listening to classical music and *Thought for the Day* on BBC Radio. He would arrive at the physiology department before the peak of rush-hour traffic and the arrival of his colleagues. This gave him time to work on correspondence with the laboratory back in Rochester and review manuscripts written by graduate fellows for potential publication. This was also a time at Mayo when great progress was being made on the initial mathematical cross-section reconstruction imaging of the heart and lungs. Therefore, Earl needed to keep up with what was happening in the lab back home. About 9:00 a.m., his colleagues would arrive in the lab and physiological experiments would be planned and/or conducted.

LONDON

Earl was working with Dr. Brian Jewell and graduate assistant Dr. David Allen, studying the effects of calcium concentration on ventricular contractility and peak tensions of cardiac muscle. They conducted the studies by bathing the cardiac muscle in different concentrations of calcium solutions and electronically recording the action potentials across cellular membranes plus the tension generated by the muscles during contractions. These experiments, conducted in the physiology laboratory at University College, lasted only a few hours, which enabled Earl to enjoy the British culture and to accompany Ada to concerts and other events in London and other locations in Great Britain.

The Wood family had a holiday gathering in London that year. Ada arranged to get tickets for the entire family for a performance of *Die Fledermaus*, the London ballet starring the famous Russian dancer Rudolf Nureyev; the play *Sleuth*, starring the legendary British actor Sir Laurence Olivier; and, finally, main-floor seats to the rock opera *Jesus Christ Superstar*. They also spent several days at the Oxenham Arms pub and hotel in South Zeal, Devon, where they hiked on the moor and observed a fox hunt.

THE QUEEN'S GARDEN PARTY

After the holidays, Ada read about the queen's garden parties, which were held several times a year at Buckingham Palace. She came up with the idea of trying to get invited to one. This, however, proved to be a challenge: Earl and Ada had to be cleared through the American embassy and United States State Department with specific references for qualifications to meet the queen. As a visiting professor from the United States and from the standpoint of academic standards, Earl would qualify. The question was who in the US government would be a reference for him. The answer was easy: Supreme Court Justice Harry Blackmun.

As an attorney working with Mayo Clinic, Harry Blackmun had been responsible for the legal relationships between Rochester Methodist Hospital and Mayo Clinic as nonprofit institutions. His wife, Dorothy (or Dottie), was also a Macalester College graduate whom Earl and Ada knew from their years there. Harry Blackmun worked at Mayo for several years until he left in 1959 to take the oath of office as a judge in the United States Court of Appeals. He continued living in Rochester while on the court and served on the executive committee of Rochester Methodist Hospital until 1970, when he had to resign and go to Washington and don the robes of a Supreme Court justice.

After Earl and Ada filled out security clearances and submitted a letter from the United States ambassador to the Court of St. James's, the official invitation to the queen's garden party arrived.

Earl and Ada were not monarchists; in fact, just the opposite. Ada often said, "She's the richest woman in the world by birth only!" When the day arrived, they drove their car to downtown London and parked at University College. They then took a taxi to the Grosvenor Place Gate at Buckingham Palace. The gardens were packed with aristocrats, dignitaries, and commoners alike, all waiting to meet the queen, who had not yet shown up. Tea, small sandwiches, and tortes were being served from large tables under open tents. Earl and Ada wandered around, making small talk with other invited guests for about an hour. Finally, Queen Elizabeth II and Prince Philip emerged from the palace, and long lines formed to meet, bow or curtsy to, and shake hands with the queen and the prince. Earl and Ada watched in amusement but decided not to wait in line. As Earl said, "They are people like the rest of us, just in position by the luck of their birth!" Regardless, they both enjoyed the pageantry and having the opportunity to be on the grounds of Buckingham Palace and see the royalty from a distance.

Following the queen's garden party, Earl and Ada drove to Münster, where they met Guy and Andy at the Alsatia fraternity house. At the time, Guy was studying French in Strasbourg, France, and Andy had just returned from a monthlong bicycle tour of Germany with his German friend Eberhard Specker. Earl gave a lecture on the latest developments in cardiac-imaging techniques being done at Mayo Clinic to Franz Bender's cardiovascular division at the University of Münster. The next day they began an extended drive to Prague and Vienna and then back through Germany. Earl had to stop in the town of Köndringen to visit the Rebstock Restaurant, which was once owned by the parents of Dr. Otto Krayer, Earl's mentor at Harvard. Earl had visited this restaurant and met Dr. Krayer's parents in 1946, during his Operation Paperclip tour.

Earl finished his research at University College the last week of October. He and Ada boarded the SS *France* in Southampton and sailed to New York. Ada was a bit miffed at

Earl during the voyage because he spent the entire time working on data analysis and manuscripts and not enjoying ship
life with her. Earl was under some pressure to complete his
London projects, since he would need to give his full attention to what was happening at Mayo upon his return home.

After arriving in New York, they drove back to Rochester,
where Earl quickly changed clothes, packed his hunting gear
and rifle, jumped in his International Harvester Scout, and
drove up to the deer camp just in time for opening morning
of deer season 1973. The sabbatical year was over.

CHAPTER 20

THE DSR AND THE DEATH OF THE CENTRIFUGE

After Earl returned from the sabbatical year in London, he and the team in the biodynamics research unit started securing funding for the development of the Dynamic Spatial Reconstructor, or DSR, based on the data and experiments conducted on the Single Source Dynamic Spatial Reconstructor.

The DSR was planned as a large cylindrical machine with twenty-eight X-ray tubes pointed toward the center, where the patient would be lying horizontally. The DSR gantry would spin around the patient, taking multiple video images from multiple angles, thus creating enough data to accurately mathematically reconstruct the internal anatomical structures using a high-speed computer. Since the DSR could reconstruct an entire chest in three dimensions, even the smallest tumors had a better chance of being detected than with conventional X-rays.

The initial plan for the DSR was to have the patient lie on a radio-translucent table that would be inserted into a cylindrical opening in the wall of the examining room. In an adjacent room, circling the patient, was a three-ton wheel, fifteen feet in diameter—part of a fifteen-ton, twenty-foot-long data-collection device. Attached to the wheel in a semicircle, the twenty-eight X-ray guns fired in rapid succession as they circled the patient, all twenty-eight firing within a one hundredth of a second. The sequence was repeated sixty times every second. The giant wheel circled the patient once every four seconds, providing X-ray images from a wide variety of angles. Twenty-eight image intensifiers brightened the light several hundred times for scanning into twenty-eight special television cameras.

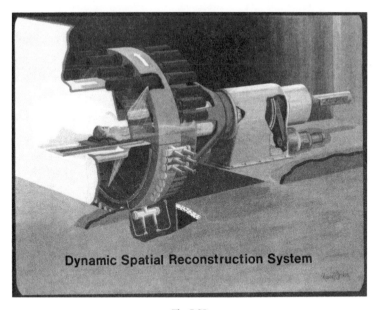

Dynamic Spatial Reconstruction System

The DSR

The images were then sent via special cables, recorded on videodiscs, and changed into numerical form by a high-speed computer. Each time one of the twenty-eight X-ray guns fired,

250 cross sections of data were collected. Each cross section was one fifteenth of an inch thick, which was less than the cross sections generated by CT scanners at that time. Since the sequence occurred sixty times per second, the data-collection gantry sent data for thousands of cross sections to the computer in four seconds, about four heartbeats. Data for sixty thousand cross sections were stored in numerical form for reconstruction as a three-dimensional image in real time or shortly thereafter. As Earl said over the dinner table at home, "That's a hell of a lot of data to be processed in a short period of time!"

The DSR had several advantages over conventional CT scanners, which in the 1970s were so slow they couldn't show the flow of blood through the organs, because they were unable to reproduce motion. In addition, patients had to hold their breath during a CT scan to record a single cross section of the chest cavity. Other advantages of the DSR included isolating and pinpointing tumors down to one fifth of an inch in size, giving accurate information on the extent of heart damage after a heart attack, diagnosing congenital heart defects, detecting and isolating coronary artery disease, and detecting aneurysms before a potential vascular rupture. The DSR was the most sophisticated, technologically advanced research project ever taken on by the biodynamics research unit and Mayo Clinic.

Development and construction of the DSR took experts in computer software programming, computer hardware, electronics, engineering, physics, physiology, and medicine. Dr. Richard Robb, a computer scientist, was in charge of coupling the high-speed video scanning images with mathematical formulas for quickly converting two-dimensional images into a digital format for reconstruction in three-dimension formats. Dr. Barry Gilbert was working on ways to speed up the processing of data coming from the DSR gantry. Initially, they tried using off-the-shelf computers, which could not handle the speeds and amount of data coming off the DSR. Eventually they modified and developed devices that could process seven hundred million arithmetic operations in a second, which no computer at the time could accomplish. Physicist Dr. James Kinsey worked on the image intensifiers first developed by Ralph Sturm, connecting and coordinating them on the DSR's gantry to collect video data to send to the high-speed computers. Dr. Lowell Harris worked on analyzing the information from the DSR and re-creating the images in digital form to display on a video monitor for physicians and diagnosticians.

Spearheading the DSR project, since Earl had to give up the chairmanship of the biodynamics research unit, was Dr. Erik Ritman. Erik was born in the Netherlands; received his medical degree in Australia in 1964, from the University of Melbourne in Victoria; and completed his residency in cardiology at Prince Henry Hospital in Melbourne. While there he developed an interest in aviation medicine. Through his boss at the time, Dr. Kenneth McLean, who had studied under Earl in the 1950s, Erik was able to make contact with Mayo and Earl. In 1968, Erik Ritman was invited to be a research assistant in physiology and biophysics, a position funded by the American Heart Association through Earl's career investigatorship. At that time, Erik assisted Ralph Sturm, who was completing work on a device to outline and measure cardiac angiograms automatically and then channel the information into a computer for analysis, which was the beginning of videometry. Erik completed his PhD in physiology from the Mayo Clinic Graduate School of Medicine in 1973 and joined the Mayo staff as a consultant for cardiovascular diseases.

STORMY STURM

And then there was Ralph Sturm. Without Ralph, the DSR never would have been planned, designed, or constructed. Ralph grew up in Indiana, the son of a country doctor. He wanted to be a doctor like his father. However, due to illness and lack of funding for medical school, he enrolled in the engineering program at Notre Dame. He developed an interest in aeronautical engineering, left Notre Dame, and enrolled in the University of Michigan in the aeronautical engineering. department. With his interest in flying, he got his pilot's license and shortly thereafter purchased a used open-cockpit biplane. He made money teaching flying lessons and also barnstorming at county fairs and other local events, performing loops and barrel rolls and giving people rides. He once described how he proposed to his wife, Mildred, while they were flying in his airplane: he'd joked that if she didn't accept, she could just step outside.

Ralph worked for a while for Stinson Aircraft, where he designed the electrical system for the Stinson trimotor low-wing monoplane, including the first electrical landing gear. After he was laid off from Stinson in 1935, Ralph worked with General Motors. At that time, scientists at Purdue University were working on a cathode-ray oscilloscope that Sturm thought would be useful in diagnosing ignition problems in automobiles. On a visit home, his father indicated the same electrical technology could be used in medicine for diagnosing medical issues. With renewed interest in the medical field, he developed a device called the Vibrocardiograph, which unfortunately did not sell. He then took a job with Bendix Aviation Corporation and was sent to Mayo on a secret military project for developing and installing instrumentation on the human centrifuge. That is where he met Earl Wood, Charlie Code, Ed Lambert,

Walter Boothby, George Hallenbeck, and Randy Lovelace. Following the war, he continued at Bendix, working on instrumentation and radio transmitters that could broadcast humidity, temperature, and air pressure from high-altitude balloons. He started a PhD program in physics at Johns Hopkins University, working on a research device that would amplify light from an X-ray fluorescent screen, giving higher-quality pictures of the gastrointestinal tract and chest. Bendix Aviation used this same technology, which they called the Lumicon, as a light amplifier to produce detailed astronomical photographs of the planet Mars. In 1957, the Lumicon was pressed into service when the Soviet Union launched Sputnik: the Lumicon image intensifier was linked to a television camera that tracked the Soviet satellite across the night sky and televised its progress nationwide. In 1959, Sturm was appointed director of research at New York City–based Dynamic Corporation. While Sturm was there, Earl phoned him and convinced him to come back to Mayo to work on the centrifuge and the new X-ray technology being installed in the cardiac catheterization lab. It is at Mayo that he combined his knowledge of physics and medicine and refined the image intensifiers in the development of video densitometry and biplane videometry products for better visualizing the beating heart and working lungs.

In the laboratory, Ralph was known as "Stormy Sturm." This came about not only from his barnstorming days, but also because he had a bit of a volatile personality. Some described him as "hell on wheels." Ralph was a chain smoker and would fill an ashtray within an hour at a meeting. He said what he thought in the most colorful language. Earl once said, "People think Ralph and I are fighting when they hear 'damn this' or 'damn that' coming from my office. We aren't arguing, but we do get into some heated discussions. It's never on a personal basis." Ralph's efforts were paramount to the development of the Dynamic Spatial Reconstructor. As Earl said, "Without Ralph there would be no DSR."

Equally important to the research scientists was the technical team. By this time, Lucy Cronin had retired. At Earl's request, Don Erdman became supervisor, a position he reluctantly accepted, being concerned about the politics between the various departments and personnel at Mayo Clinic. Earl had offered to handle the politics so Don could do his job with the technical staff. Don Hegland and Julijs Zarins were still maintaining the lab in room 456, where the SSDSR was, and the video and catheterization equipment needed for experiments using the SSDSR. Willis Van Norman continued working in both computer hardware and software. These were tremendously loyal and hardworking individuals that the biodynamics research unit was totally dependent on.

CHANGING TIMES

This was a time of change for Earl. Not only was he approaching the twilight of his career at Mayo Clinic, which didn't seem to bother him, but funding sources for research had changed. In Earl's early days at Mayo, research funding was solely institutional, with Mayo paying salaries and laboratory costs. Funding was also available through the American Heart Association, NASA, and the US Air Force. With a project like the DSR, Mayo relied heavily on government resources such as the National Institutes of Health.

It took several years to explain the research and intentions to government institutions, corporations, and scientific peers just to get recommendations for the DSR to be funded. It took numerous applications before grant money was awarded for its development. Earl's team at Mayo just kept putting in one grant request after another and having one site visit after another until the DSR project was eventually funded. During this long process, Earl spent the majority of his time writing grant requests rather than doing what he really enjoyed, what he called "blood and guts physiological research."

The research staff in his laboratory had also changed over the course of his career. In the 1950s, what some Mayo Clinic cardiologists call "the golden age of cardiac catheterization," the lab operated with research fellows who mostly had medical degrees. At that time, it was a matter of working hard and seeing patients and performing many cardiac catheterization procedures so that the fellows could learn specialized techniques to take back to their medical practices.

The list of these cardiology fellows that made up the Mayo cardiology department in the 1960s through the 1980s is extensive and includes John Shepard, Dan Connolly, Dwight McGoon, Harold Mankin, John Callahan, and Hugh Smith. But operating a sophisticated machine like the DSR took a different type of staff. The DSR required engineers, computer scientists, physicists, and mathematicians. As Earl stated, "It requires a mathematician and a plumber to run it! No MD can come over here and learn these techniques within a few months." People wondered what a diverse group with varying degrees like this was doing at Mayo Clinic. But with a project as technically advanced as the DSR, it required this team approach with a highly specialized staff.

With the DSR funded and the design on the drawing board, the question of where to put this large, heavy piece of equipment arose. To save time and money, fourteen cameras and the related imaging chain would be initially installed instead of the originally planned twenty-eight. The additional fourteen would be installed once the system was tested and additional funds were available. But this slight cutback did not change the size of the original design. The south side of the Medical Sciences Building was the logical spot to place the DSR. This was an open space that had outside storage tanks for compressed gases. These tanks could be easily moved, and a building addition could be constructed that would allow quick access to the computer rooms and laboratories. The NIH funding, however, was specifically for the construction and development of the DSR, but not for the brick-and-mortar building in which it would be housed.

THE END OF AN ERA

The initial plans for an addition to the Medical Sciences Building were met with resistance due to lack of funding and the Mayo administration not wanting to add more buildings. The suggestion was made to remove the centrifuge and place the DSR in that space. The centrifuge had not been used in four years, yet it was entirely functional. Earl soon found himself in a struggle to keep this unique historical and yet useful piece of equipment and still move into the future with a new-generation X-ray scanning system, which the National Institutes of Health called "revolutionary."

Multiple letters were sent and meetings held between the Mayo Clinic administration, the biodynamics research unit staff, and former scientists and fellows who worked on the centrifuge, including Charlie Code and Ed Lambert, to discuss keeping the centrifuge. According to the administration, it took approximately $250,000 annually to mothball the centrifuge. At that time there were no scheduled research projects to be conducted on the centrifuge, and it was not known if the device would ever be used again. It soon became evident that Earl was fighting a losing battle. "Once it's gone, it's gone," he said. "There's no going back, and one of the most unique research tools in the world will be gone forever."

Earl wrote letters and made phone calls to the Air Force Museum at Wright-Patterson Air Force Base in Dayton, Ohio, and also the Smithsonian Institution in Washington, DC, proposing to exhibit the centrifuge and display its major contributions to aerospace and clinical medicine. There was some interest, but no commitments. It was hoped that the superstructure and some related parts would be stored in a warehouse until a suitable museum exhibit could be found. Earl directed Don Erdman to call various military branches to find some Cosmoline to protect the superstructure from corrosion. In September 1978, the east circular wall of the Medical Sciences Building was bashed open. A welding torch cut the center shaft of the centrifuge, and the forty-plus-year reign of aviation-medicine research at Mayo Clinic came to an abrupt end.

The superstructure was eased out of the hole in the building by a crane, placed on a flatbed tractor trailer, and hauled to a storage facility outside of town. Soon after, the two twenty-ton flywheels were split apart and also removed, leaving a gaping hole in the Medical Sciences Building and, figuratively, in Earl's heart. About a year later, Earl got a call from someone who wanted a piece of the centrifuge. When he called the engineering department to inquire, he found out that the superstructure had been cut up for scrap. Earl felt totally betrayed.

THE DSR MOVES IN

Research continued using the SSDSR to refine the data-collection system and computer programming. The large circular gantry and base for the DSR was being constructed by

Raytheon in Waltham, Massachusetts. Construction crews were now building walls and forms in the new DSR room, and pouring the foundation for the heavy DSR structure. The base would be mounted on a concrete foundation on the floor, with four large bolts securing the DSR to the basement floor. The protruding bolts had to exactly match the machine's steel base. In addition, the threads could not be damaged when the heavy base was lowered onto the foundation. Don Erdman created several mock-ups of the foundation and mounting bolts to share with Raytheon designers to assure an exact fit. Parts of the DSR started arriving in Rochester, including X-ray cameras and the imaging chain.

One of the biggest issues for the project was how to get the fifteen-foot-diameter gantry through the hole in the Medical Sciences Building and eased into place on the rotating support bearing. This assignment was also given to Don Erdman. After taking careful measurements and consulting with architects, engineers, crane operators, and Raytheon, he noted that there was less than an inch clearance to ease the gantry into the building. Since it had to fit through the walls of the Medical Sciences Building, plus fit the base of the DSR, stress levels throughout the lab were extremely high. Under stress at the time due to the loss of the centrifuge and construction of the DSR, Earl told Don, "That damn thing better fit or you're fired!" This was the only time Don felt threatened in his career. Needless to say, he was going to make sure it fit. In addition, Don had to contend with building inspectors and also OSHA requirements to install guardrails.

On Friday, August 3, 1979, a flatbed truck from Massachusetts pulled up to the east side of the Medical Sciences Building. The fifteen-foot circular gantry was lifted off the flatbed very gingerly by crane and placed horizontally in front of the hole in the wall of the building. It was then eased through the opening very slowly, with millimeters to spare between the top of the gantry and the floor and ceiling of the DSR room. Don Erdman's careful calculations, blood, and sweat had paid off.

On Wednesday, October 8, 1980, the completed DSR was displayed to the press and the public for the first time at a nationally televised news conference showing the world's most advanced X-ray scanner, which had been under development for almost a decade, for everyone to see. The DSR was now undergoing testing and was basically on a shakedown cruise before being used on patients.

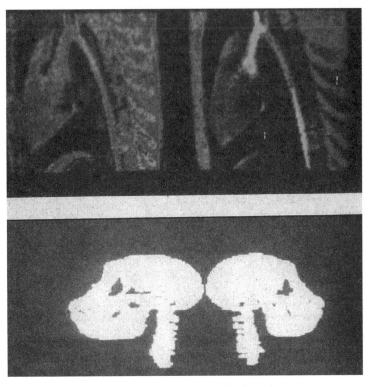

The first 3D reconstructions of a monkey from the DSR.
The video would show the movement of the lungs and heart.

THE LEGACY OF THE DSR

The first patient evaluation using the DSR occurred in April 1981 and was for a twenty-two-year-old man with coronary artery disease. After Earl's retirement in 1982, clinical research and patient examinations continued using the DSR. In the mid-1990s, a grant was submitted to the National Institutes of Health to upgrade the imaging systems on the DSR. Unfortunately, this project was not funded. Mayo Clinic decided to decommission the DSR in 1998 and have it removed from the Medical Sciences Building. Once again Earl wrote multiple letters as an emeritus staff member of the physiology department to convince Mayo administration to keep this unique scanning tool. Despite his best efforts, the DSR met the same fate as the centrifuge. It was cut up in pieces and removed, ending up as tons of recycled aluminum. Parts of the imaging chains were distributed to various investigators inside and outside of Mayo Clinic.

After a decade and a half of work on the DSR, clinicians found that images from commercially available CT, MRI, and PET scanners were somewhat better than the DSR. However, the speed and the wide coverage needed to accurately capture the beating heart and the breathing lungs were still only possible with the DSR. Even today, those DSR speeds and head-to-foot coverage are not achievable by a commercial CT scanner, let alone an MRI scanner. That being said, current CT and MRI scanners provide adequate data for clinical use but not always for research, which was the sole purpose of the DSR. The DSR data did live on in a digital format for several years after the technology's demise. The last scientific publication using DSR data was written in 2003.

CHAPTER 21

BIRCHWOOD AND CEDAR RIDGE

Earl and Ada always wanted a place in the country to hike, have picnics, hunt, and eventually build on. In 1975, they ended up purchasing seventeen acres of woodland east of Rock Dell, Minnesota. This strip of land overlooked the Zumbro River valley and was covered with oak and birch trees on the north-facing slope down toward the river. Due to the many birch trees, the property was christened "Birchwood." Just a twenty-minute drive on country roads southwest of Rochester, Earl and Ada spent many warm summer evenings and weekends hiking on Birchwood and, occasionally, bringing friends along to enjoy the fresh air and scenery. Of course, in the fall and winter there was hunting.

About a year after the purchase of Birchwood, Earl received a phone call from Clarence Fredrickson, a farmer near Rock Dell. Mr. Fredrickson inquired whether Earl and Ada would be interested in buying his farm, because he was getting older and wasn't physically capable of farming safely; in addition, his wife was in a nursing home. The property, which the Fredrickson family called "Cedar Ridge" due to the cedar trees and steep cliff above the Zumbro River, consisted of 160 acres, of which ninety were tillable cropland and the rest was forest.

Earl and Ada at Birchwood about 1977

Approximately a mile of the Zumbro River flowed through this property. Initially, Earl and Ada were skeptical; they weren't sure how they could afford to purchase such a large chunk of land. However, they were both intrigued by the idea of owning this property, particularly with the structures already built on the location, with a functioning well and electricity. There was no question the property would be a tremendous asset. The tillable land could be rented to a nearby farmer for crop production, and the forest area would be prime for recreation and hunting. Reviewing the abstract and the history of the land, they saw that the 160 acres was deeded originally to a Civil War soldier, and the deed was signed by Abraham Lincoln!

The question was how to finance such a large purchase, as Earl was quickly approaching retirement. To finance it, Earl and Ada cashed in their life insurance policies and mortgaged their house on Second Street. In July 1977, a purchase agreement was signed and Cedar Ridge belonged to Earl and Ada.

Now the owners of ninety-plus acres of tillable farmland, they had to search for a farmer who could rent, plant, and harvest crops on Cedar Ridge. After they canvassed neighboring farmers, Loren Scripture agreed to rent the tillable land. Loren was a big, jolly midwestern farmer who spoke with a rural Minnesota accent. After Earl explained that he grew up on a farm and understood the challenges of farming, he and Loren became very good friends. Earl was also introduced to neighboring farmers; these included Dennis Klinewort, Loren Wheeler, and Ken Offord.

Loren Scripture rented and farmed the tillable land on Cedar Ridge for several years. The crop yields in the main fields were mediocre at best due to the hilly terrain and rocky soil. The field on the north side of the river was subjected to occasional flooding but was very productive. Loren suggested to Earl that he enroll the hilly land into the Conservation Reserve Program, through which the US Department of Agriculture pays farmers to let the fields go fallow to reduce erosion and take some areas out of production to increase and stabilize crop prices. Since this was highly erodible land, it was easily enrolled into the Conservation Reserve Program with Earl's agreement to plant a food plot for wildlife and cut down any volunteer trees that might grow on the field.

Earl and Ada also had a great interest in planting trees in the river valley, which had previously been a pasture. At the time, walnut—particularly black walnut—was in demand for furniture and veneer trim in the building industry. Earl was able to receive cost sharing from the Minnesota Department of Natural Resources to plant several thousand black walnut seedlings on Cedar Ridge.

Late one night, Earl got a call from his neighbor Loren Wheeler saying he could see a fire at Cedar Ridge. By the time Earl and Ada arrived on the scene, the cabin had burned to the ground. Vandals, who probably set the cabin on fire, had also broken into the machine shed and stolen tools and some camping gear. Homeowner's insurance paid for the stolen items and to rebuild the wooden structure. However, Earl and Ada wanted more than just a wood cabin; they wanted something that would be sturdier and could be heated during the cooler months. They also wanted a basement for the utilities, such as the electrical panels and pressure tank for the water. The plan was to build a one-room cabin with a loft for sleeping.

FORT ADA

Construction started with the removal of the burned debris from the old cabin. Then an end loader was brought in to start digging a hole for the basement. They soon discovered that below the dirt was solid limestone. This limestone was chipped out and placed next to the hole for the basement. After viewing this beautiful stone, Ada came up with the idea of constructing a stone cabin. Plans were altered so the cinder block walls from the basement would continue up to the planned roofline. The limestone would then be cemented to the cinder block walls, forming the stone cabin. A wood-burning stove was placed in the center of the cabin to provide heat, and they added electric baseboard heating to supplement the stove if it ran out of firewood.

This solid, well-constructed cabin Earl affectionately called "Fort Ada." By the fall of 1981, the cabin was almost ready for occupancy, just in time for the fall hunting season. Although Ada did not want Cedar Ridge to turn into a "southern deer camp," Cedar Ridge did indeed become a hunting camp for the Wood family and friends for decades to come, in addition to a gathering spot for picnics and woodland projects, such as clearing trails and pruning trees.

Just like the deer camp north of Duluth, the tree stands were named by location and the hunter who preferred that particular tree. It soon was apparent that deer were more plentiful on Cedar Ridge and easier to hunt. Cedar Ridge became the gathering spot for Earl, his family, and their friends for the annual deer hunt.

Earl with his deer, which he harvested with his father's 38-40 Winchester

Earl, his boys, and their friends gathered at Cedar Ridge for the annual deer hunt for several decades. As Earl got older, his hearing started to fail. To compensate, he had to wear hearing aids. In order to be able to hear in the woods, he had to turn up the gain on the hearing aids; this produced shrill feedback. He could not hear the high-frequency feedback, but everyone else could, including the wildlife.

Cedar Ridge and Birchwood kept Earl and Ada active through their retirement years. After hunting season, they enjoyed hiking, cross-country skiing on the trails, and of course watching the wildlife. It was their getaway happy place for peace and quiet. In their twilight years, when Earl was still driving, they would simply drive out and sit in the car, sipping a cup of coffee and looking out over the Southeast Minnesota landscape. Eventually, Cedar Ridge did become their final resting place.

CHAPTER 22

SAILING FROM HONOLULU TO SEATTLE ON THE *DAISY*

In the mid-1970s, Dr. Homer Warner became very interested in sailing. He purchased a boat and learned how to sail on the Great Salt Lake. Homer would recruit sailing crews and race other boats between the Salt Lake harbor, Antelope Island, and other areas on the lake. The landlocked sailors had to learn how to trim the sails, how to tack, and how to navigate. After a couple of summers learning the ropes, they were excellent sailors. With limited sailing on the Great Salt Lake, Homer decided to purchase a larger boat based on Bainbridge Island, across the sound from Seattle. He and the Warner family would spend several weeks a year sailing in the Puget Sound area and up and around Vancouver Island. Becoming more confident in sailing and navigation, Homer traded in his boat for a brand-new forty-foot Valiant. The Valiant 40 was a very sturdy boat with a heavy keel capable of handling open-ocean sailing. The boat was christened the *Daisy* after Homer's mother-in-law, Daisy Romney.

In the summer of 1982, Homer decided to enter a trans-pacific sailboat race from Victoria, Canada, to Maui, Hawaii. The Victoria-to-Maui race included seasoned boats and crews, one of which was captained by Ted Turner, founder of Turner Broadcasting. Homer Warner's crew on the *Daisy* were family members and several colleagues from his lab. The sailing trip to Hawaii would take about three weeks. Most of the crew, with limited vacation time, needed to return to the mainland following the race. Therefore, Homer needed a crew to sail the *Daisy* back to Seattle. The invitation went to Earl and family.

Earl was available, having just retired from Mayo Clinic and still in the process of looking for new physiology research opportunities. He could not turn down this once-in-a-lifetime chance. He had done some sailing in the past, on Lake Washington. Andy, who was in graduate school at the University of Minnesota and had just finished collecting research data for his master's thesis, was also available for the trip. He had learned to sail at YMCA Camp Olson. Mark had sailed on Lake Washington and also in the San Francisco Bay Area, on larger boats. Unfortunately, Guy was not available, since his PhD dissertation was due at the University of Colorado. Phoebe was not interested in this adventure. Ada thought the whole thing was crazy.

Earl, Mark, and Andy met Homer at Honolulu Harbor and stepped on board the *Daisy* to stow their gear. The two other crew members for the eastern voyage had also just arrived. Steve Warner, Homer's oldest son, had sailed on the *Daisy* many times on Puget Sound. Ray Schracke worked in Homer's lab and was one of these individuals who could repair anything.

On the deck of the Daisy *in Honolulu Harbor: Homer Warner, Ray Schracke, Steve Warner, Earl Wood, Andy Wood, and Mark Wood*

The first night on the *Daisy* was spent learning the equipment, the rigging, and stowage for the various sails. They also learned how to use the stove, the fresh-water pump, and the head (the toilet). There was an autopilot on the *Daisy* named Fred, as in, "Let Fred do it." Programming Fred was relatively easy; it involved setting a course by compass, then flipping a switch, and Fred would automatically take over the helm. Unfortunately, Fred could not change sails or tack; the crew had to do that! Groceries were purchased and stowed in the compartments underneath the seats. Fresh fruit was hung in large nets above the galley and dining table, which would swing and sway with the rhythm of the boat. Fresh-water tanks were topped off along with several auxiliary water cans.

The diesel tank was also topped off. Diesel fuel was for the onboard engine for maneuvering in harbors or just plain motoring when becalmed; the stove; and a generator that charged the batteries for electricity to power the lights, radio, and Fred. In addition, there were several gallons of gasoline to power a portable Honda generator in case the diesel generator failed.

Sailing on the open ocean required at least two members on deck and at the helm twenty-four hours a day. The Swedish sailing watch schedule was adopted for the *Daisy*. Two sets of two crew members alternated watches, with one person getting a day off and the other person assuming the duties of the cook. The schedule was as follows, with traditional four-hour watches at night and six-hour watches during daylight hours:

First watch: 6 a.m. to noon
Second watch: noon to 6 p.m.
Third watch: 6 p.m. to 10 p.m.
Fourth watch: 10 p.m. to 2 a.m.
Fifth watch: 2 a.m. to 6 a.m.

Homer, the skipper, did not take watch since he was always on call for a sail change or in case of emergency. This would be their sleep-wake cycle until they reached Seattle. The night in Honolulu would be the only time all six slept on the *Daisy* until they made landfall in Washington State.

To help prevent seasickness, each crewmember was prescribed scopolamine. This medication was introduced through a transdermal patch worn behind the ear and changed every three days. Side effects included dry mouth, drowsiness, and heartburn.

At noon on August 1, 1982, the *Daisy* left Honolulu Harbor and set sail toward the island of Kauai with favorable winds. Soon Honolulu, the island of Oahu, and Diamond Head disappeared below the horizon. As they got out into the open waters of the Pacific, the swells grew to about ten feet high and the *Daisy* began rocking and pitching with the waves.

Once the sails were set, the crew rigged up a fishing line to troll for tuna or hopefully mahi-mahi. Fishing on the *Daisy* was easy. The crew simply set up a lure or bait on hundred-pound test line and dragged it behind the boat about fifty yards. Homer rigged up the line so that when it took some tension it pushed down on an air horn, signaling that they had a fish. When the alarm went off, the fishing line was wrapped around a winch and the fish was winched in. Their first evening at sea, they were lucky enough to catch a tuna, which they cleaned and had for their first dinner of the voyage. Within half an hour after dinner, both Steve and Andy were seasick.

LIFE ON BOARD THE *DAISY*

There are significant challenges involved in navigating and sailing east to the mainland from Hawaii, since the boat has to sail against the prevailing easterly winds. In order to sail east, you need to sail as far north as possible into the wind until the boat gets into the prevailing westerly winds. At that point, the ship takes a right toward the east as the prevailing winds shift from the westerlies. The trick is, if the crew turns the ship to the east too early, it may end up in Baja California, San Diego, or Los Angeles, and not Seattle. This meant pointing the *Daisy* as close to the wind as possible on a starboard tack without luffing the sails; in other words, without the sails flopping in the wind and not giving power to the boat. This also meant taking the waves head-on, tossing the boat and crew around. In heavier seas, the crew always wore life jackets and were tied in securely to the boat.

Since this was before GPS technology, navigation was done by sextant. Loran used radio navigation signals from land but did not work well in the middle of the ocean. Every day, exactly at noon, Homer got out his sextant and took a sun shot. Using the angle between the sun and the horizon, he was able to calculate latitude and longitude—the position of the *Daisy*—and approximate speed based on the previous shots. Several times on bright moonlit nights, he shot the moon at midnight. On cloudy days or when the seas were too rough, the crew went by dead reckoning, establishing their position through a series of running fixes on a chart.

Changing the sails was always exciting and challenging. Lowering a sail and catching it in the wind as it flopped around, without losing a halyard or line, could be frustrating. More challenging, however, was crawling up to the bow to release the old sail and raise the next, all while crashing up and down as the *Daisy* hit the crests and troughs of waves.

The day-watch schedules were nice because there was always someone available to consult with if there was a need to change course or sails. Nights were a different matter, particularly the 2:00 to 6:00 a.m. shift. It was all anyone could do to stay awake if the wind and rhythm of the boat were constant. Many times, the crew would set the autopilot (Fred) and doze off for a while.

On one early-morning shift, Earl was at the helm and dozed off, and for some reason, Fred decided to shut off too. *Daisy* slowly turned into the wind and came about with the wind hitting the sails, heeling her over about thirty degrees. No harm was done, but it woke up the whole crew. Watching the sun slowly rise in the east on the 2:00 to 6:00 a.m. shift was always a relief, since you knew your shift was almost over. But it was also the chilliest time of day, and with the added fatigue, shivering would start. The night-shift crew couldn't wait to go below deck for warmth, food, and sleep.

Being cook for the day gave everyone a real break in the sailing routine. The galley, or kitchen, was small, with a tiny sink on one side and a diesel stove-oven and counter on the other. The sink had two faucets, one that pumped up saltwater for doing dishes and cleanup, the other providing fresh water for consumption. They were clearly marked for obvious reasons. The cook had to strap himself into the kitchen so as not to be tossed around by the motion of the boat while cutting up fruit or kneading bread. The biggest challenge was pouring a liquid as everything moved around you. One mistake and you'd have a mess to clean up. Meals were much like those when camping. Early in the voyage they enjoyed fruit from Hawaii. This had to be consumed early, since fruit spoils quickly in the tropics. When they could, they had fresh tuna or mahi-mahi. Several times, they got creative in baking a pie or a coffee cake. By the end of the voyage, when provisions got low, it was meat loaf made from Spam, which looked more like dog food.

For the first ten days at sea, the *Daisy* remained on a course of 345 degrees, giving her a hull speed of about five knots. The wind direction was coming from the northeast at about thirty degrees, which was exactly the direction the boat needed to go to arrive in Seattle. Sailing as close to the wind as possible without luffing the sails, they were taking the full force of the waves, which made for a rough ride and slowed the boat down. On one rough-water day, after taking a sextant shot, Homer calculated that they had traveled 136 miles. However, only seventy-seven were toward their goal of the Washington coast.

Being on the open ocean was not all hardships and sleep

deprivation. There were scenes of great beauty not seen on land. Sunsets and sunrises were spectacular, depending on the cloud cover and weather. The sea was deep blue in the sunlight but could change to a cold gray on a cloudy or windy day. Watching an albatross glide just inches over the water, searching for scraps of food thrown overboard, was a lesson in aerodynamics. Observing porpoises playing on the bow wave below the *Daisy* was a total delight. One evening a killer whale surfaced right in front of the *Daisy*!

On a different evening, Mark and Andy were on the night shift, sailing through fog and mist at about five knots. The fog was so thick they could hardly see the running lights at the bow from the back in the cockpit. It was interesting that although they were in the wide-open space of the middle of the Pacific Ocean, the fog made them feel claustrophobic. This was a scary watch, since they could imagine a huge freighter coming out of the mist and fog banks, bearing right down on them with no time to react. They ended their shift without incident and went to bed. To their surprise, after they recovered from their shift, they awoke to a sunny morning with no wind; the ocean was flat as far as the eye could see. They had entered a high-pressure weather system with no wind, known as the doldrums. Without even a ripple on the sea, it was like floating on glass. They had no choice but to use the motor to proceed toward the goal. Just before lunch, they shut the diesel down to save fuel and the *Daisy* glided to a stop.

SWIMMING IN THE MIDDLE OF THE PACIFIC

The crew decided to go swimming in the middle of the Pacific Ocean. Diving into the sea a thousand miles from anywhere was unforgettable. The view of the world is relatively small, since your eyes are only six to eight inches above the water. Looking up at the sky from the ocean surface, you realize how insignificant you are. Although there was no wind, it appeared that there was some motion in the water. The swimmers soon realized there were currents that would separate the swimmer from the boat. Swimming alongside the *Daisy*, looking down through a mask, viewing the keel and the great abyss below, they soon realized that it was at least three miles down to the ocean floor. Getting back in the *Daisy* was a lesson in survival. Since the deck was at least four feet above the water level, there was no way they could get back into the boat by themselves. The crew used a ladder or were winched up using the ship's rigging.

ROUGH SEAS

The last two hundred miles west of the United States coast was the roughest ocean of the entire voyage. The *Daisy* hit heavy winds and huge waves that were higher than her mast. The sails were at a minimum, a storm jib about the size of a handkerchief to give the *Daisy* some helm control, yet they were still moving at a speedy seven knots. In these heavy seas, the *Daisy* would climb up a wave, and when she approached the crest of the giant wave, the wind would catch the mast and the *Daisy* would heel over to about forty degrees, washing seawater into the cockpit. There were times the crew thought they would capsize. Once on top of the crest, the heavy keel would right the boat and she would go sliding and speeding down the other side of the wave, much like a surfer. Occasionally the bow would hit the trough of the next wave, shooting water over the entire boat and soaking the crew.

The diesel engine could not be used; it was perilously low on fuel and it had a wet ignition. Battery power for the lights and radio was also getting low. By 8:00 p.m., Fred died due to lack of power. This meant someone had to be at the helm to control the boat while two other crew members had to cross over the pitching bow to get gasoline for the Honda generator, which was stowed below the deck, to power the navigation and interior lights. Mark entered the cockpit from below and had just strapped himself in as a large wave came crashing over the deck of the *Daisy*. The water and the pitching deck lifted him up, slamming him against the deck. He was only bruised, and he was very lucky his lifeline was tied on or he would have been washed overboard.

Mark and Homer crawled on the deck toward the bow as the *Daisy* pitched and heeled in the wind and the waves. Meanwhile, Earl and Andy took turns at the helm to keep the boat on course. Without lights in the darkness, and with the constant wash of water over the deck, they could not see Mark or Homer bringing the gas cans back to the cockpit. Earl and Andy were relieved once they were back and secured. Amazingly, the Honda generator started, and once again they had interior and navigation lights.

There were moments during that last night on the open sea that the crew did not think they would see the light of day again. About 7:00 the next morning, the wind started to die down. They changed the tiny storm jib to a small staysail, and the main had a double reef. Earl attempted to light the diesel stove to dry out the cabin and start breakfast, but with all the moisture, the stove created a smudgy smoke. Earl did manage to cook a breakfast of pancakes and canned bacon on a portable Coleman stove. The exhausted night crew crawled into their bunks with their rain gear still on and finally got to sleep.

LAND HO!

By noon, when the night crew woke up, it was a totally different day. The sun was out, the spinnaker had been raised, and the *Daisy* was cruising smoothly toward Cape Flattery and the Strait of Juan de Fuca at seven knots. Just outside the twelve-mile limit of international waters, they passed three Russian trawlers, obviously on a "scientific expedition." The coast of Washington and the Olympic Mountains were now in view. As the sun was setting over the Pacific Ocean, sails were dropped and the *Daisy* motored into the small harbor of Neah Bay on what little diesel fuel they had left.

Dinner that evening was at a local restaurant, where they had burgers and fries followed by apple pie and ice cream. This was the first night in twenty-three days on the high seas that the entire crew slept simultaneously on the *Daisy*. The next two days were spent sailing and motoring up the Strait of Juan de Fuca toward Seattle. The strait, of course, is a major shipping lane, so they saw ships of various shapes and sizes, including a nuclear submarine on the surface heading to the open ocean. That may have been the reason the three Russian trawlers were cruising just outside the twelve-mile international limit.

On the voyage, Earl had grown a beautiful white beard. When he stepped in the house back in Rochester, Ada took one look at him—she didn't even greet or hug him—and yelled, "Shave it off!"

The voyage from Honolulu to Seattle was one of the few times in Earl's life he was not the coach or leader. Homer Warner, Earl's former fellow and student, was the owner and skipper of the *Daisy*, and Earl and the rest of the crew took orders unquestioningly from him. Homer knew the boat and how to navigate, operate the radios, and change sails. The crew had depended on each other for the success of the voyage and safe arrival at their destination.

In an interview in the *Mayovox* about the sailing trip, Earl was asked if he would do it again. He hesitated, contemplating the recently completed voyage, then said, "Given the right boat and crew, I would do it again!"

CHAPTER 23

LIFE AFTER MAYO: THE VISITING PROFESSOR

Although Earl had reached Mayo Clinic's mandatory retirement age of seventy, he did not want to retire. After all, he was not a clinician interacting with patients, but a research scientist with still more to contribute. He enjoyed the challenging atmosphere working with his colleagues and scientists in the biodynamics research unit in the Medical Sciences Building. Expecting a gradual transition, he did start packing books and other items in his office for a potential move. One morning he entered his office and found, to his surprise, that the telephone had been removed. He knew then that the time had come for him to leave the Medical Sciences Building after forty-plus years of dedicated hard work and groundbreaking scientific accomplishments.

Reluctantly, he moved to a small cubicle in the emeritus staff room in the Plummer Building. This was not to his liking, since there was only part-time secretarial help and a small desk where he could write when he still had scientific articles that needed to be published. In addition, he did not like being interrupted by other retirees who wanted to discuss their tennis or golf games and talk about their winter vacation homes in Florida or Arizona, subjects in which Earl had absolutely no interest. At this time, he started looking for funding and institutions that could use his experience and expertise in physiological research.

In 1983, Earl was awarded a grant through the Humboldt Foundation, based in Germany, to work in Paul Heintzen's cardiovascular laboratory and clinic in Kiel. The foundation provided funding for his research activities, a stipend for living expenses, and the rental of a new BMW. In Kiel he was assisting in the pediatric cardiovascular laboratory, evaluating ventricular contractility and motion. He was also a guest lecturer at the Kinderklinik Kiel and several German universities.

Earl and Ada lived in a hotel not far from the university clinic where Paul Heintzen's lab was located, and also near a beautiful park where they could take long walks overlooking the Kiel Canal. On the opposite side of the canal were massive concrete submarine pens left over from World War II, which could be clearly seen from the walking paths. These well-constructed structures had survived the Allied bombings. Farther down the canal, going toward the North Sea, in the area of Laboe, was a submarine museum with an actual German U-boat on display.

They spent many weekends driving in the German countryside of Schleswig-Holstein, with travels to the Lübeck and to visit Franz and Maria Bender in Münster. At the recommendation of Paul Heintzen, they took an extended trip into Bavaria and stayed in a castle above the town of Arnsberg. This scenic castle, the Schloss Arnsberg, overlooked the Altmühl River valley, where there was ample opportunity for hiking and sightseeing.

Back in Rochester, Earl was able to obtain funding through DARPA (Defense Advanced Research Projects Agency) for an office on the fourth floor of the Harwick Building. This came with a full-time secretary with a word processor to help him compile a manuscript on the physiology and prevention of acceleration-induced loss of consciousness and vision in fighter pilots. When this office space was needed for other Mayo purposes, he had to move.

At Earl's urging, Mayo administration arranged and paid for an office for him on the second floor of the Norwest Bank Building, not far from the main Mayo campus. Here he could continue writing up the results of his scientific research conducted in Kiel, plus pursue his physiological interests in cardiac and aviation medicine. Barry Gilbert procured an Apple computer for word processing and email. Barry's son, Benjamin, taught him how to use it and gave him frequent "refresher courses." Earl marveled at the ability to send an email message across the world at the click of a button. He exclaimed, "This is a marvelous machine, unthinkable just a decade ago!" Earl was a great correspondent, emailing colleagues and family members about his latest activities.

In 1986, Earl was a visiting professor and lecturer at McGill University, in Montreal. During this time, he made connections with the Defence and Civil Institute of Environmental Medicine (DCIEM), based in Toronto. The DCIEM had a human centrifuge, and Earl immediately started to write grant proposals to visit and work there with Dr. Fred Buick.

In the 1980s, faster and more agile jet aircraft such as the F-15 and F-16 came into service in the United States and allied militaries. It became apparent that aircraft and pilots' lives were being lost due to high-speed maneuvers and gravitational loss of vision and consciousness. At the same time, pilots wanted to take high-speed, high-G maneuvers as a combat advantage over their opponents. Fighter pilots were spending time in the gym building up their upper extremities and core strength in an attempt to withstand the high acceleration and gravitational forces. As one fighter pilot stated in a CBS interview, "If I can take a 10G turn, I'm going to do it; if you can't, you are a grape!" All this even though modern fighter pilots were using the same type of cutaway G-suits that the fighter pilots used in P-51s and P-47s during World War II.

Earl started writing articles and letters to the editors of aerospace medical journals highlighting the World War II–era research done on Mayo's human centrifuge, research that seemed to have been overlooked by the air force and by the designers and pilots of these high-speed, maneuverable jet aircraft. He pointed out that at least ten catastrophic crashes were due to gravitational loss of consciousness and that these crashes could be limited with very effective full-coverage G-suits and properly executed straining maneuvers used with positive-pressure breathing, all of which was documented back in the 1940s. Earl speculated that the cause of many of these fatal crashes was jet fighters' increased capability to sustain accelerations of 7G to 10G for longer than thirty seconds, resulting in cerebral ischemia, blackout, and gravitational loss of consciousness. Another cause, he speculated, was improperly performed straining maneuvers by the pilots—the maneuver that Earl had developed and perfected at Mayo back in the 1940s.

In a separate report published in September 1988 for the United States Air Force School of Aerospace Medicine, Earl summarized the research from the Mayo human centrifuge during World War II and also came up with some potential solutions for avoiding fatal crashes due to gravitational loss of consciousness. One suggestion was to have the pilot in a fully horizontal prone position in the cockpit, essentially reducing the vertical blood column between the heart and the brain. After all, Superman flew in a horizontal position; why shouldn't they redesign fighter-plane cockpits and train pilots so they could perform like Superman?

STILL WORKING AT EIGHTY

In 1992, Earl and Ada turned eighty years old. To celebrate these landmark birthdays, the family gathered in Germany, at the Schloss Arnsberg, in June. During their stay in Germany, the family noticed that Ada had slowed down considerably due to acute arthritis in her feet and knees and hips. She tended to walk slowly, with a forward slump. In addition, they noticed that her short-term memory was quickly fading, compounded by age-related hearing loss, which Earl was also experiencing. The Wood kids and spouses were concerned about whether Earl and Ada could safely live in their current house in Rochester, in which they'd lived for forty-seven years. Their kids began to explore other possible living situations for them.

In December 1992, Earl began a one-year visit as a guest physiologist at the DCIEM, near Toronto. Working with Dr. Fred Buick, he would be repeating and expanding on some of the experiments conducted at Mayo on the human centrifuge. This time it was a Canadian human centrifuge using more up-to-date instrumentation. Fighter pilots' G tolerance was more important in modern aircraft than it was back in World War II. Earl wanted to be a subject in the experiments, but due to his advanced age and thoracic kyphosis, the Canadian scientist would not let him.

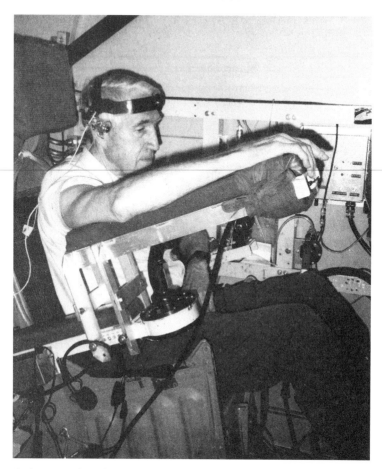

Earl posing in the cockpit of the Canadian centrifuge repeating the same experiments conducted on the Mayo centrifuge during World War II. Note that the same ear oximeter used on the Mayo centrifuge was used on the Canadian centrifuge.

Earl's daughter-in-law, Dr. Krista Coleman Wood, a bioengineer, suggested that the pilots wear an in-the-ear pulse oximeter. When zero pulse was indicated at head level after several seconds, the airplane's autopilot could take over the controls, thus avoiding a potential crash. The ear pulse oximeter was tested on the centrifuge in Toronto but never evaluated in flight tests. Earl and Ada called this new oximeter "the Krista," since it was her idea.[7] This was a trademark of Earl's: giving others credit for good ideas.

Earl continued to be invited to speak at national meetings in aviation medicine and cardiology. He became the elder statesman on those topics, giving several talks on perspectives of the aging scientist. In 1993, Earl was on a live teleconference panel discussing space medicine with the astronauts on the space shuttle *Columbia*, which included Mayo-trained physician Dr. Bernard Harris. Earl reminded the astronauts and audience that technology developed at Mayo almost a half a century earlier was critical to the safety of manned space flight.

EARL H. WOOD STRASSE

A further honor was given to Earl in 2002, when a street in Germany leading up to the offices and manufacturing plants founded by Earl's former fellow, Peter Osypka, was named after him. Peter Osypka was born in 1934 in Miechowitz, Upper Silesia, Poland. His father was an electrical engineer who worked in Peenemünde during World War II. Peter studied electrical engineering at the technical university in Braunschweig, completing his PhD in 1963. He was a postdoctoral research fellow in Earl's laboratory from 1963 through 1965. Following his stay in Rochester, Peter became the head of the biomedical electronics laboratory in the cardiology department at the Kinderklinik Kiel, Germany, working with Dr. Paul Heintzen. In the late 1960s and early '70s, he was a lecturer at the University of Zurich. In 1977 he

---

7.   This eventually led to the development of the pulse oximeter, which can now be found in every drugstore.

founded the Dr. Ing. P. Osypka Medizintechnik GmbH company in Loerrach, Germany. His company specialized in the development and manufacture of products for invasive cardiology and pediatric cardiac surgery. Peter was the inventor of the fixed screw for pacemaker electrodes and other implantable probes used in cardiology. In 1986, he developed a high-frequency ablation probe to treat cardiac arrhythmias. As his business expanded, he opened branch offices in Berlin and Palm Harbor, Florida.

In the early 2000s, with the expanding need for cardiac-implantable electrodes and pacemakers, Osypka needed to expand its offices and manufacturing capabilities. The decision was made to build a new corporate headquarters in Rheinfelden, Germany, just across the border near Basel, Switzerland. This was a large multiwing facility with state-of-the-art manufacturing capabilities that boosted the local economy and added almost forty more jobs, and Peter requested to have the name of the street leading to the corporate headquarters changed from Sengernstrasse to Earl H. Wood Strasse.

When Peter presented this idea to the local authorities and mayor, there was some initial resistance. First, they had no idea who Earl H. Wood was. Second, most memorials and streets are named after individuals who were deceased. Earl was alive and well at ninety. Peter presented Earl's credentials and scientific accomplishments through the decades. He also noted that without Earl's teachings, there would have been no Osypka medical technology center in Rheinfelden. The decision was made to change the name of the street to Earl H. Wood Strasse.

Soon invitations were sent to Earl, Wood family members, and Earl's former fellows to attend the grand opening of the new Osypka technology center and dedication for Earl H.

Wood Strasse in Rheinfelden on September 6, 2002. This also marked the twenty-fifth anniversary of the Osypka company.

The day of the dedication was marked with pomp and ceremony. Guests entered the main meeting hall with displays of Osypka Medizintechnik products, along with photos of Peter when he was a fellow in Earl's lab in the early 1960s.

The meeting hall was filled to capacity with employees, local dignitaries, politicians, architects, businesspeople, scientists, and Osypka and Wood family members. Tours were conducted of the manufacturing and office facilities of the Osypka headquarters.

Earl and Peter Osypka at the unveiling of Earl H. Wood Strasse

In 1993, Earl and Ada moved into the Charter House, a senior-living center owned and operated by Mayo Clinic. The Charter House provided apartments for individuals and couples that could care for themselves with little assistance. It also provided for assisted living and a full-fledged nursing home for people needing those services. After several months in the Charter House, Earl and Ada got used to a new routine and meeting former friends and colleagues from Mayo, including Ralph Sturm. Earl continued to work, writing articles and correspondence at his office in the Norwest Bank Building, which was within walking distance of the Charter House. Ada started doing short walks inside the Charter House and would have coffee in the Corner Cupboard, a small coffee shop and snack bar in the building. When funding for Earl's office ran out, he was forced to move into a small room in the Charter House to do his work. His former technicians, including Don Hegland, Don Erdman, and Willis Van Norman, assisted with the move. Earl was not thrilled, and he needed his old team there to help "calm the waters." Barry and Benjamin Gilbert provided computer support for Earl in his small Charter House office for about two years, until he was unable to follow directions. Drop-down menus were confusing to him, and he often got frustrated, resulting in multiple mouse clicks that caused the computer to crash. The physiologist was showing signs of slowing down.

CHAPTER 24

A LONG FAREWELL

Earl and Ada settled into a new life at the Charter House. Ada's short-term memory continued to deteriorate; she soon forgot the names of her grandchildren and daughters-in-law. Luckily, she could still recognize her own children, but she would mix up their names and where they lived. She also had progressive hearing loss, which did not help with communicating. At this time, Earl was writing notes and leaving them in various rooms of their apartment, reminding Ada what day it was and when he would return for lunch or dinner. Despite the many notes and reminders, sometimes he would return from work or a meeting to find Ada confused and agitated, wondering where he was and why he was gone so long.

In the spring of 1998, Ada woke up with a headache, slurred speech, and weakness on her left side. She was taken to Saint Marys Hospital, where she had a seizure. She was put on anticoagulants and antiseizure medication, but the stroke had already done its damage. With left-side weakness plus blindness in her right eye, she was now confined to a wheelchair and needed to move into the long-term care unit of the Charter House. Earl continued to live in the apartment; however he ate every meal with Ada. They spent the evenings together, sharing the newspaper and watching television before Earl went back to his apartment.

One evening Earl brought Ada up to the apartment for a visit. With Ada's left-side weakness and now profound memory loss, she forgot she could not get up and walk. When Earl was not looking, she attempted to stand up and walk, then fell and fractured her hip. She had a surgical hip replacement, but she was still nonambulatory and now totally dependent on skilled nursing care. Earl continued eating every meal with her, but she could no longer accompany him on rides to the farm or even visit their apartment in the Charter House. Due to the lack of mobility, Ada's health steadily declined.

Phoebe and her lifetime partner, Nancy, visited Earl and Ada in February 2000. With Ada's declining health, Guy and Mark flew in from the West Coast in March. Andy joined them from Minneapolis. To pass the time and to give Earl a break, the boys drove him to Cedar Ridge to prune the walnut trees. When they returned to Ada's room at the Charter House, her breathing was slow and shallow. Earl and her boys were in the room when she drew her last breath. A classy lady waited for all her men to be with her at her last moment.

In May 2000, the family held a private celebration of life on a chilly, rainy day in the cabin at Cedar Ridge. All the Wood kids, spouses, and partners were present, plus granddaughters Katie, Erika, and Karolyn and their family friend and adopted uncle, Hi Marshall. All the men in Ada's life wore blue blazers. She often said when advising the guys what to wear, "You can't go wrong with a blue blazer!" Many wonderful things were said about Ada; there were readings of her favorite poetry and sayings, and she was toasted with a gin and tonic, her favorite drink at cocktail parties and family gatherings.

Earl grieved deeply for Ada; sixty-four years of marriage, plus several years of dating during the Macalester years, left a gaping hole in his heart. After caring for Ada in her final years, he was left with his thoughts and little to do. His letters to the family included phrases like "living in a vale of tears" and "continued loneliness." Luckily, he could still drive out to Cedar Ridge to trim trees and visit the neighbors, Loren Scripture and Loren Wheeler.

Earl did keep himself busy in his small office in the Charter House, writing articles on aviation and medicine, as well as family correspondence. Earl also focused his attention on the old house at Lake Washington. The wraparound porch was falling apart. Using funds from the estate of his sister, Louise, Earl hired an architect and a carpenter. The old porch was torn off the main building and, over one summer, replaced with a three-season porch that was two feet wider than the original yet maintained its 1890s architecture. Earl frequently drove over to Lake Washington for a day to watch and monitor the new construction. He strongly felt that this addition would make the old house last another hundred years.

On January 1, 2002, Earl celebrated his ninetieth birthday. To commemorate this event, the whole E. H. Wood family, including grandkids, went on a cruise on the *Sun Princess* from Fort Lauderdale, Florida, to the Atlantic side of the Panama Canal. Earl's birthday dinner was a formal affair, with the ladies wearing evening dresses and the guys in tuxes. Cuban cigars and rum were passed around in honor of the occasion. This was the only time the family had seen Earl with a tobacco product and a stiff drink, which was totally out of character and produced hilarious laughter from the entire family.

Earl celebrating ninety years with a Cuban cigar and a shot of rum

As Earl aged, he became more stooped as he developed a rather prominent dowager's hump. This posture led to visual problems, particularly when he was driving. The mirrors on his Dodge Dakota pickup truck blocked his side-to-side view, and he could barely see over the steering wheel. As a result, he had several fender benders and scrapes and dents while maneuvering into his parking place in the Charter House garage.

In addition to Earl's visual issues with the truck, he could not hear the engine once it started overrunning the starter motor and chewing up the gears on the flywheel. On several occasions he placed the truck in gear while the engine was revving up, damaging the transmission. It soon became apparent to the Wood kids that Earl was a danger behind the wheel. When the keys were taken away, Earl had another set made and continued driving. Finally, Guy and Andy conspired and removed the cable from the coil to the distributor, so the truck could not be started. This resulted in a flurry of hate emails to his children, copied to various Wood relatives. Arrangements were made for a local agency to drive Earl and his former colleague, John Shepard, out to Cedar Ridge several times a week, trips he very much enjoyed, and his frustration at not having a car was soon forgotten.

Earl continued hunting on Cedar Ridge until his mid-nineties. However, he could not walk far from the cabin and was only able to climb a small ladder stand to watch for deer. On one of his last hunts, he shot several times at a herd of does and luckily missed, since it was a bucks-only season. He had lost a great deal of weight and was now very sensitive to cold weather. When he insisted that he must go hunting, Guy and Andy brought him out to Cedar Ridge and placed him in the front seat of Andy's Explorer, parked on top of the hill overlooking the prairie and woodlands. With his trusty Remington loaded with blank, spent shells, Earl could not hurt anything or anybody if wildlife or movement were spotted. Leaving Earl in the warm Explorer, Guy and Andy went out hunting. Returning an hour later, they found Earl sound asleep with his trusty shotgun across his lap—toasty warm and very happy to be enjoying a day's hunt with his sons.

Despite frequent visits, socialization, and activities around the Charter House, Earl's short-term memory started to deteriorate. He moved out of the apartment in Charter House and into assisted living. He could no longer operate his computer.

In 2008, Earl suffered a minor stroke, which made his balance and gait very unsteady. He now had to walk with a wheeled walker and was transferred into the skilled-nursing facility in the Charter House. His lung capacity had also diminished, and he had several bouts of pneumonia, which were treated with antibiotics and oxygen therapy. By this time, he could not orient himself in place or time and wondered where Ada was. He was put on medication to control his confusion and anger.

On a cold January morning in 2009, Andy got a call from Charter House stating that Earl had fallen in his room and had been transferred by ambulance to the Saint Marys emergency room. Andy found Earl there resting on an exam table, sedated. When Andy saw the X-ray of Earl's right hip on the monitor, his heart sank; there was an obvious fracture of the femoral neck. The question now: What was the best course of care for a ninety-seven-year-old man with right-side weakness, little balance, and minimal lung capacity? With minimal rehabilitation potential for a total hip replacement, the decision was made just to remove the femoral head.

After the operation, Earl was placed in the ICU for several days. His lung capacity actually improved somewhat due to the anesthesia, suctioning, and supplemental oxygen. After several days, he was transferred back to the skilled-nursing unit at Charter House. Phoebe, Mark, and Mark's wife, Molly, flew in from Colorado and New Mexico. Due to Earl's rapidly declining health, they decided to put him into hospice. Knowing that Earl was comfortable and in good care, Phoebe, Mark, and Molly said their goodbyes and left to return to their homes and work; Guy was on his way to Rochester. On the evening of March 18, Andy came to Charter House to see how Earl was doing. As Andy sat down next to his bed, Earl gave a small, weak cough and exhaled for the last time. The farm boy, outdoorsman, scientist, leader, and family man left for the happy hunting grounds. Unfortunately, Guy was still at the airport in Seattle; he did not get a chance to say goodbye to his father. Earl donated his body to Mayo Clinic to evaluate the long-term effects of exposure to g-forces on the body. Even after he passed away, he was still teaching.

In May, a celebration of Earl's life was held at the Unitarian Universalist church in Rochester. Former fellows, technicians, businesspeople, and relatives from all over the country attended. These included Craig Coulam, Jim Greenleaf, Erik Ritman, Don Hegland, Don Erdman, and Willis Van Norman, from Mayo Clinic; Loren Scripture, who farmed Cedar Ridge; the entire Wingert family from Lake Washington; and Dr. Jim Craig, retired vice president and company doctor at General Mills. Short presentations were given by Phoebe, Mark, Guy, Andy, and Dr. Hugh Smith.

When Mayo Clinic was finished with both Earl and Ada, their ashes were laid to rest according to their wishes, on the promontory overlooking the Zumbro River valley on Cedar Ridge. They were together once again, enjoying the sights and sounds of the change of seasons, the wind in the cedar trees, and the flow of the river as an occasional raccoon, deer, turkey, or pheasant passed by.

CHAPTER 25

SO, WHAT WAS IT ABOUT EARL?

The term *leadership* is thrown around a lot in the corporate and political worlds in the twenty-first century, to the point that it is almost meaningless. A local television news programs states, "Expect Leadership," when in reality they don't lead, but just read and broadcast the news and weather and give opinions. Thousands of books are written about leadership. Corporate human resources departments conduct extensive training programs in leadership for employees, yet the only ones leading the company are the CEO and vice presidents. It is common knowledge that the main reason good employees leave a company is not the company itself, but rather the employee's boss or department "leader." It is clear that Earl was a highly effective and inspiring, yet humble, leader. Employees in his laboratory were all very loyal to him, staying there for thirty or forty years. Employee turnover was nonexistent in his department. Research fellows stayed longer than they originally planned; one was dubbed "Fellow

Emeritus." Even the Deerslayers came back decade after decade to brave the cold, unpredictable weather of northern
Minnesota. Extended family members always wanted to be
with Earl during family reunions and events.

Loyal members of the lab
Back row: Julijs Zarins, Ralph Sturm, Earl Wood, IJ Fox, Bill Sutterer;
Front row: Don Hegland, Lucy Cronin, Jean Frank, Don Erdman, Irene Donovan

In his book *The 8th Habit*, Stephen Covey defines leadership as "communicating to people their worth and potential
so clearly that they come to see it in themselves." He points
out that most of the world's work is accomplished through
organizations. Earl worked with many formal and informal
organizations, including the 20 Acres, Wood's Hilltop Beach,
the University of Minnesota, Mayo Clinic, the Deerslayers,
Cedar Ridge, and of course the Wood family. Just as Covey
describes in his book, Earl enabled each person in all of those
organizations to sense his or her innate worth and potential

to contribute his or her unique talents, passion, and voice to accomplish the organization's purpose and goals. Although Earl was a highly effective leader, he never read any of Stephen Covey's books or any other business management or self-improvement books. He had absolutely no interest in them. His leadership skills came from his natural abilities and his experiences with people.

So, what was it about Earl that made him such a good leader? This was an individual who could relate to anyone, regardless of their background, nationality, race, political views, religion, education, the number of degrees (or lack of degrees), or sexual orientation. A neighboring farmer near Cedar Ridge described him as "just a good ol' boy, we didn't know who he was." Loren Scripture recalled visiting with Earl after planting corn on Cedar Ridge and remarking to his wife, Janice, "That guy is going to be famous someday!" Later Loren read an article about Earl in the newspaper. "I found out he already was famous!" he said. Loren always considered Earl his "buddy."

What made Earl and Ada tick? The formative years for the Woods, as well as for the Petersons, were the 1910s and '20s. Both grew up in large families by today's standards. The kids had to depend on each other to sustain a living, whether it was helping in the drugstore, delivering papers, milking cows, cleaning stalls, planting the gardens, preparing meals, or building a bathhouse for the beach business at Lake Washington. Teamwork was a requirement to survive. Working diligently was a way of life to overcome the hardships of the day. Work was actually fun, a mindset that lasted long into the careers of all the children.

One significant moment in Earl's early life may have been while the family was on their way to Texas in 1914, when their Model T Ford got stuck in the mud on a cold, rainy evening (see chapter 2). Inez Wood walked in the cold mud with young Abe, Earl, and Louise to a nearby farm and asked for help. The well-to-do owners told them to go away. They then walked to a sharecropper's cabin, where they were fed and spent the night. The impressionable youngster never forgot the generosity and compassion of that African American family on that cold, miserable night.

When the Great Depression hit in 1929, they got second jobs in construction or washing dishes to make ends meet. As Tom Brokaw described it in his book *The Greatest Generation*, "This generation was united not only by a common purpose, but also by common values—duty, honor, economy, courage, service, love of family and country and above all, responsibility for oneself." When times were tough, this generation got going. As a result, America thrived in the late 1940s through the 1960s, with the passage of the GI Bill; the building of the Interstate Highway System; breakthrough technological, scientific, and medical innovations; and, eventually, landing men on the moon and returning them safely to Earth. The Woods and Petersons all came of age during this generation, and these factors certainly helped shape Earl's and Ada's character.

In addition, Earl's and Ada's parents insisted that all their children go on to get a higher education. When working jobs in construction during his high school and college years, Earl developed a lot of respect for the carpenters and bricklayers he worked with. He noticed that these laborers were very smart, but he realized he did not want to do hard labor for the rest of his life. That gave him the incentive to pursue a college degree like his older siblings.

Earl's career in cardiovascular physiology was exemplary, and that's because it was more like a vocation. As David Brooks writes in *The Road to Character*, "A person choosing a career is looking for something that will provide financial and psychological benefits. A vocation is a calling." In other words, Earl's life would have been very different if he hadn't pursued that calling. When and where Earl got his calling, one can only speculate. It may have been on the dock at Lake Washington in the early 1930s, when he and brother Abe were discussing their futures. Or it may have been when he was sitting in a duck blind on a cold, wet morning, waiting for a flock of mallards to land in his decoys.

In January 1979, the *Mayo Clinic Alumni* magazine interviewed Earl in their introduction to the development and construction of the Dynamic Spatial Reconstructor (DSR). Much of this interview revolved around his past accomplishments, but he also discussed how his career evolved and his philosophy about leading a scientific and technical staff in the advancement of aerospace and clinical science. What follows are some highlights from that article.

The article describes a lecture Earl gave in Judd Hall in the Medical Sciences Building, a presentation on the future use of the DSR. One of Earl's slides featured a drawing of the space shuttle, which had not yet orbited Earth. In the payload bay of the space shuttle was a futuristic-looking DSR. Even though the Mayo DSR was still under construction at the time and weighed far more than what the space shuttle could handle, Earl still envisioned a DSR-like instrument in orbit, studying the effects of zero gravity on the astronauts. He stated, "It is certain that the effects of long-term duration exposures of zero gravity in man will be of considerable scientific, technological and military importance to both Russia and the USA. The Dynamic Spatial Reconstructor is so ideally suited for the study of the physiological effects of zero gravity I am certain as its unique capabilities become progressively more evident to the biomedical community, that it will eventually be used in the life sciences, flight studies made practical by NASA's space shuttle developments and required for interplanetary or other very long duration flights for scientific or military purposes. I think we are forced to keep abreast of the Russians as far as space is concerned."

The author of the *Mayo Clinic Alumni* article asked Earl what it was like when he joined Mayo Clinic. Earl said, "I figured that I would be a classical physiologist, but the centrifuge changed that. It soon became apparent that there was no good animal model that existed for studying the effects of acceleration in comparison to a live human. We had to experiment on ourselves. I became convinced that if you paid enough attention to instrumentation and technique, you could make almost any measurement on humans that you could make on animals. It changed my life from that of a classical animal physiologist to that of a human physiologist." The author commented that Earl had probably blacked out under controlled circumstances more than anyone in the world, and yet he was still healthy at the age of sixty-seven, when the interview was conducted. Earl responded, "We had pretty strict rules in our laboratory; one of them was that we would never do anything on any subject that we didn't first do on ourselves."

The article continued, indicating that Earl's research goal was the understanding of the mechanism by which the human heart, lungs, and circulation adapt to stress, whether it is imposed by disease, exercise, or aerospace flight. In citing the accomplishments of the lab, Earl preferred to give credit to his colleagues and technical staff—he referred to them as "team members." As a result of their work, the lab became the most completely instrumented and technologically advanced in the world studying the effects of blood flow through the cardiovascular system. Despite Earl's many honors and professional affiliations, the interviewer indicated that he remained friendly, approachable, modest, and faultlessly unassuming. Earl stated, "We just kept doing what came naturally. It was just the logical thing. Most of what we've accomplished has been the result of prior work. Take, for example, cardiac catheterization, which was initially done in the United States in 1946 in New York City. What we did was improve the instrumentation that gave us the information we needed while the examination was still in progress. Before the procedure was over, we knew what the diagnosis was or we knew that we couldn't get the diagnosis. Many of our firsts have been in applying things. One first, for example, was our use of the strain-gauge manometer to record blood pressure. It was initially designed to measure air pressures in airplanes. Again, we just kept doing what came naturally; if we had a problem, we found a way to solve it."

"Another example," Earl went on to say, "is videodensitometry and Roentgen videometry techniques which led to the development of the spatial reconstructor. There was a need to measure the true shape and dimensions of the heart very rapidly. Although we should have realized it from the start, it took the incisive mind and hard work of Erik Ritman to demonstrate beyond a doubt that videodensitometry wouldn't give us the information we wanted, so we began working on ways to do that.

"That in turn got us interested in converting the electronic video images into digital numbers. Conversion of an X-ray image into numbers suitable for input into a computer was a basic must for building the spatial reconstructor. Shortly thereafter, with help from mathematician Gober Herman, we started reconstructing the heart of a dog using digitized pictures. It is just one and one makes two."

Although he had the stature of a world-class scientist at Mayo Clinic, many of Earl's colleagues in the biodynamics research unit, plus members of his family, simply called him "Coach." The famous UCLA basketball coach John Wooden and coauthor Andrew Hill describe what a coach is in their book, *Be Quick—But Don't Hurry: Finding Success in the Teachings of a Lifetime.* They say the coach has to be in the role as a teacher, not the boss. Wooden breaks down teaching into four components: demonstration, imitation, correction, and repetition. Earl demonstrated these components with his fellows in the lab and his boys when teaching them how to safely shoot and hunt. John Wooden was tough on his players in practice, with constant correction and repetition. The confidence built up in practice gave the UCLA basketball players the independence to think on their feet and win the game. The same can be said about Earl when his fellows left the lab for other clinical or academic institutions, or when the Deerslayers left the cabin for their deer stands on a cold November morning in Minnesota.

In the magazine article, Earl also noted that hard work and enthusiasm are the key ingredients for success, perhaps more important than native intelligence. He stated, "I know a lot of people who I think are a hell of a lot smarter than I am, better at mathematics, know more about physics, have more textbook knowledge. Too often, scientists get good ideas and sit around and figure out 1,000 reasons why the ideas won't work. One of the most important things every researcher can have, beyond the desire to work hard, is enthusiasm to drive ahead and take risks."

Early in his career, Earl developed his well-known open-door administrative policy, and he noted, "I wanted to encourage people to air their problems." But time and again, because of interruptions created by this policy and a busy schedule during work hours, things did not get done. Because of family responsibilities, his success rate working at home during waking hours was low. So Earl decided he would accomplish what he could during unconventional hours; he would go to bed early and get up early each day, using the hours between 4:00 and 8:00 a.m. for tasks requiring intensive, sustained thought. Biologically he was an early riser.

Those who worked with Earl knew him to be a good listener and a person who had great faith in his associates at all levels. As he said, "I think if there's anything that is characteristic about our laboratory, it is the tremendously loyal technical people who work here, such as Don Erdman, Julijs Zarins, Willis Van Norman, Lucy Cronin, Merrill Wondrow, Bob Hanson, and so on. They are tremendously loyal. They have been here for years. They are the people who really make this lab work. I have the greatest respect for all of them." He continued, "I don't want anybody working for me. I want people working with me. That attitude is important. I don't want to be boss. You have to lead by example. You have to convince people that you really do respect them for their intelligence and enthusiasm, and you have to work as hard as they do and work harder at the common goal. People must know that you will treat them fairly, that you regard them as valuable members of the team, that you appreciate their efforts and most importantly, that you are interested in their problems. There is a hell of a lot of good in people. And boy when you bring it out, the good it will produce!"

Over and over during the interview, Earl returned to the team theme: "A project like the Dynamic Spatial Reconstructor can only be accomplished by a multidisciplinary team. In this type of team effort there is a good deal of creativity as specialists interact with each other. If you ask me who in this laboratory had the original idea to build the

DSR, I could not answer the question. I don't know whose idea it was. I defy anybody to know. It was just a natural evolution that came from a laboratory where people can express and discuss their ideas freely and work together towards a solution of challenging, mutually interesting problems. The ideas came out of this environment."

In 1950, Inez Wood received the Mother of the Year award in Minnesota due to the extraordinary accomplishments of her children. In a tribute to Inez, a family friend named Mary June described the unique parenting style she observed in Earl's parents:

> If there is any recipe in child rearing, it is that the parents share their lives with their children in whatever they did. They [Will and Inez] always counted them in. It was no sacrifice, just more fun. It was sort of a golden rule behind everything that went on at the 20 Acres, or Hilltop. Love your children and share your life with them and they'll turn out all right. Share the work, the sacrifices, the burdens and the joys, everything, and you don't have to worry. Above all, Mother and Dad Wood shared their interests and ideals with their children, creating ambitions to do just about anything. In their sharing their interests, they treated their children as adults. Harn stated, "Mother always listened to us. She and Dad always counted us in to share their ideas around the family table, asking for our ideas and respecting them." The children

learned to listen, ask and learn. Inez said, "I always believed if you listen to what happened at school and play and other things, children will want to confide in and be really interested. Then you always have their confidence. But if your mind wanders to your own problems, and you don't listen and be interested in your children, they will skip away from you. It is certain if you don't listen to your children at the age of eight, you will not have a chance at sixteen."

The active listening skills of Earl's parents carried into his leadership skills as a teaching scientist and parent. He was known for his open-door policy, his willingness to hear about an individual's issues, whether it was a professional or a personal matter. This is clearly revealed in conversation with his former students and fellows, such as Drs. Richard Robb, Erik Ritman, Jim Greenleaf, and Barry Gilbert, who were interviewed by the author of the *Mayo Clinic Alumni* article.

Several colleagues who were close to Earl described him as a genius at human relations. Dr. Robb put it this way:

The key to his success as a scientist and human being is the way he is able to relate to other people. His first and primary concern is human relations. Even his research efforts and personal feelings about what can and should be done in research can be related to his concern for his fellow man. His office door is always open, no matter what he is doing at the time. You can walk in and talk with him about a personal domestic problem as well as a scientific problem. His professional and paramedical colleagues know and appreciate that. He has paramedical staff members who have been with him for over 20 years. That says something.

It is telling that, upon hearing this, Earl chuckled and said, "I don't think it's genius; maybe it's just growing up in a large family, one that enjoyed working and playing together. I like to work with people."

All Earl's former fellows and laboratory technicians said he was incredibly honest. They also commented that he did not like models; he tended to make judgments based on quality data. Both Erik and Jim characterized Earl as a taskmaster. However, if things did not go well with an experiment or data collection, he encouraged them to improvise to get the job done and still do it well. He was data driven, using accurate measuring techniques resulting in quality data. But due to being data driven, he stopped doing cardiac catheterizations on pediatric patients because of the stress put on the kids during repeated measures to get the quality data he needed for both clinical diagnostic procedures and research.

Despite his full schedule as a researcher, Earl published more than eight hundred scientific papers in peer-reviewed journals such as *Circulation, Journal of Applied Physiology,* and *Mayo Clinic Proceedings* and numerous chapters in physiology texts. Erik and Jim laughingly said his writing style included very long run-on sentences. An entire paragraph may be one or two sentences. And somewhere within the description or conclusion in his manuscript would be the word *heretofore.* Earl knew that presenting at national and international meetings was equally important to getting their latest results out to the scientific community. The evening before national scientific meetings, each fellow had to present and practice their talk for the next day. The "bigwigs" in the room, which included Earl and one of the senior fellows, such as IJ Fox, would critique the presentations, making changes and/or suggestions. On a couple occasions, the bigwigs would sit back in their chairs, sharing a bottle of Scotch or bourbon. The young fellows soon discovered that those who presented last had fewer changes and/or criticisms as the level in the bottle decreased.

Erik said that Earl rarely berated someone in public, but if he did, it had a devastating effect on all concerned, especially the guy in the crosshairs. One such incident was when a research fellow gave a presentation at the Mayo Foundation House about a research project. The problem was, it was not his work and he did not acknowledge the person whose idea and data he used. Earl let the speaker and audience know. That was the end of this individual's stay at Mayo and his research career. Another notable case was during an NIH site visit, when a grant was being reviewed for scientific worthiness. After one of the reviews, a scientist presented some questionable data. Earl responded and gave him hell. It may have made Earl feel good at the time to set the record straight, but it did not sit well with the NIH reviewers. To sum it up, Earl ventured where angels feared to tread, sometimes to his own disadvantage.

This concern for what was right also informed Earl's approach to his research involvement with the military. Barry Gilbert noted that during the development of the F-16 fighter jet, several high-ranking air force officers and designers came to Mayo Clinic to discuss the angle of the seat in the cockpit. They proposed that it be reclined at a twenty-three-degree angle. Earl gave an extensive presentation on the data and the results of the studies on the centrifuge from World War II up to the present time, indicating that the safest position for a pilot to sustain maximum G, but also in the event of an ejection, was straight up and down.

If the pilot is reclining at a twenty-three-degree angle when subjected to G or in the event of ejection, Earl explained, his heart would be compressed onto his spinal column. After a day and a half of Earl's lecture, the air force personnel indicated they were going to design the seat at twenty-three degrees anyway, to fit the taller pilots. After having spent so much time presenting the scientific data on why the reclining seat would be dangerous to pilots, Earl was infuriated. He told the air force brass that they would lose several pilots each year due to this positioning. This is indeed what happened, and many years later one of the decision makers came back to Earl admitting that he was right; the man had video images of fighter jets auguring into the ground due to pilots' loss of consciousness. It wasn't until recently, with proximity technology, that computer controls will take over to keep a jet from hitting the ground.

Earl not only held himself to high standards but also encouraged those he worked with to do the same by developing their expertise. To that end he tended to give assignments in the laboratory. For example, Barry Gilbert's assignment was to create a supercomputer for analyzing the multitude of data coming from the centrifuge experiments, cardiac catheterization, and eventually the DSR. Barry wanted to measure anatomical structures during motion, such as a heartbeat. But when he indicated that he had no experience in computers, Earl said, "You've got a degree in electrical engineering, so therefore you should learn about them." Learn he did, ultimately becoming an international expert.

Earl's management style brought out the best in the

people he worked with. Barry said Earl was always compli-
mentary as long as he knew the individual did the very best
he could. In his book *Be Quick—But Don't Hurry,* Coach
John Wooden offers a similar definition, saying that success
is "peace of mind, which is a direct result of self-satisfaction
in knowing you made the effort to do the best of which you
are capable." In contrast, some other scientists in the Medical
Sciences Building might say, "The best just isn't good enough."
This would lead to interesting conversations between the lead
scientists and showed the difference in management styles of
department heads.

In 2017, a video interview was conducted with Earl's former lab technicians Don Hegland, Don Erdman, and Willis
Van Norman. These were long-term employees who worked
downstairs in the Medical Sciences Building. They referred
to Earl either as "Dr. Wood" or simply "EH," for Earl Howard.
The following are excerpts from that interview.

Don Hegland, who started in the lab in 1955, stated, "I
operated the recording apparatus of all the experiments they
did, and it was very old equipment. But it was the only equipment like it in the world." Willis Van Norman, who started
there in 1962, described his initial work in the lab as follows:
"I primarily worked in the cardiac lab. Dr. Wood would be
sterile, of course, and I would flush the stopcocks or do whatever he wanted. I learned how to do dye curves by hand, recorded on paper. The first programming class I went to was
with Dr. Wood and Ralph Sturm. As soon as we got out of
the class, Stormy Sturm says, 'Well, those computers aren't
here to stay, I've had enough of that!' Then Dr. Wood said,
'Willis, you understand that stuff?' . . . Fortran, that was the
new computer language, so I said, 'Well, yeah, I guess so.' So
Dr. Wood says, 'OK, you're in charge of computers!'" This was
an opportunity and a career change given to Willis by Earl.

Don Erdman started in 1967, replacing an X-ray technician, but was assigned special mechanical projects for the studies Earl wanted. In the interview, Don said of Earl,

> Oh, he was one of a kind, in my book. I worked for forty-two and a half years before I retired, and I never had a boss like him. I don't know about you guys, but to me he was tough but in a loving way. When you were in the lab and you made a mistake, boy, I tell you, you heard about it. And he had a loud voice if you really messed up, but the nice thing about him is he always came back at the end of the day and wherever you were, came up, patted you on the back, and said, "OK. We had a good day. Don't take anything I yelled at you personally." And that's what made him unique. He was a very good man.

Erdman went on to say, "Every now and then it was kind of fun just to sit and pick his brain. . . . He had that ability to allow people to use their own abilities, imaginations, whatever. He always considered that part of the research. EH was dead serious about what he was doing, but there was also a lot of laughter too now and then. And I think that's what made it so pleasant for me to work for thirty years with him."

Over the years, other lab employees, Jim Greenleaf and Erik Ritman, joined Don Hegland and Willis Van Norman on fishing and hunting trips with Earl. Jim described deer camp as "insanity." Erik described it as "hunting on the industrial level. Very well organized and orchestrated." Don Hegland described taking almost every mode of transportation available to get to the fishing lake of choice in Canada. He also noted that he used the kitchen table as a bunk when at the deer camp. Barry did not participate in hunting or fishing, but he said the only time he saw Earl get a little angry was when he missed a plane in Germany due to a pilot and air traffic control strike and they had to cancel a fishing trip.

The biodynamics research team

We'll end where this book began, at the Earl H. Wood Scientific Symposium, a celebration of a brilliant career at Mayo Clinic, in September 1981. In a presentation, Dr. Charles F. Code summarized Earl's leadership qualities this way:

> Earl Wood is a great man. What makes a man great? Different things in different people. Some men have greatness through being mean and nasty. Earl is great through being wonderfully kind and considerate. What makes Earl so outstanding? He is bright and exceedingly intelligent. He always uses his head and when his head has reached its

limit, he recognizes it and goes to someone else who knows more. Oh, Earl knows more than anyone else about some things, but he is unusual because he knows when he doesn't! He has humility. He has complete and total integrity. When he has found he was wrong, to me at least, he was always admitting it. We have both been wrong a number of times.

How do I know all this about Earl? Because I've known him for forty-three years. Early on, Earl began to knit us into a team. He saw the jobs to be done and identified the proper priority. He set up the data-collection apparatus. I helped with some bioassay principles, and Lambert topped off the enterprise with the centrifuge of the air [the G-Whiz]. With Dave Clark at the sewing machine and Ed Lambert in the airplane, we devised an anti-blackout suit which our pilots used at the end of the war and still do today. We could not have done it without Earl.

You must ask, Isn't there something wrong with this man? Surely, he picks his nose? No. The harshest thing I can say of Earl is you are on his team or you are not. At the end of the war, Ed Lambert and I recognized this, and we went our separate ways. When you leave Earl's team, that does not mean he will be against you. Earl understands if you go your way. He still loves you. He has helped me whenever I have asked and sometimes without my knowledge. There is nothing vengeful in this man. There is no eye for an eye or tooth for a tooth.

He is a noble man. I am on his side, always
have been and always will be all the way.

Out of the laboratory, Earl approached home projects
and hunting and fishing trips in the same manner. He was
a methodical list maker. He would organize hunting drives
with precision timing and give exact directions to his fellow
hunters going into the deep northern Minnesota forests way
before sunrise, compass in hand, with this last expression of
encouragement: "You can't miss it!" When someone bagged
game or caught a fish, Earl was the first to congratulate them
with a "Way to go!"

In 2013, an anonymous benefactor gave a substantial do-
nation to Mayo Clinic to name the cardiac catheterization
laboratory in Saint Marys Hospital after Earl. Many from
Mayo Clinic's executive branch attended the dedication, including CEO Dr. John Noseworthy. Dr. David Holmes, the
laboratory's director, gave a presentation called "Stained
Glass and Other Stuff," relating to the stained glass windows
of the Chartres Cathedral, in France, suggesting that the cardiovascular laboratory and Mayo Clinic were also standing
on the shoulders of a giant.

At the dedication, Andy was asked to give the Wood family's perspective. Here are his remarks:

> Dad was not a self-promoter, unlike many
> in today's business world. He did not value
> profit, market share, or the bottom line. He
> valued knowledge, the quest for knowledge,
> and the proper use of that knowledge. He
> often said to me when discussing compli-
> cated scientific concepts when I was in col-
> lege and graduate school, "Science is a bunch

of simple concepts just piled on each other, which makes it complicated." Dad had a way of breaking down the complicated and making it . . . well, more understandable. He also had the unique quality to capitalize on an individual's strengths and totally ignore their weaknesses. This made him an extraordinary leader, teacher, and parent.

Another one of Dad's values was his technical "crew" in the lab. These were his heroes. He often said to me and my siblings, he would not trade any of these people for all the MDs and PhDs that have gone through here. These were the people that got things done. They knew the science, technology, and were the "go-to" people that made the lab run. These people include Bill Sutterer, Ralph Sturm, Lucy Cronin, Jean Frank, Willis Van Norman, Julijs Zarins, Don Erdman, Don Hegland, Jim Fellows, Irene Donovan, Merrill Wondrow, Bob Hanson, and many, many more. These are the unsung heroes of Mayo Clinic and the catheterization laboratory. Earl often acknowledged that without them, many innovations that occurred in the catheterization laboratory in the 1950s, '60s, and '70s would not have happened.

Last, but not least, I do have to mention my mother. She had to put up with Dad being in the lab for long hours. You have to remember the experiments on the centrifuge in the catheterization laboratory lasted for days! And then there were the long business trips. But it was she who insisted he take the sabbatical years overseas. Incidentally, when they met at Macalester College in the 1930s, Dad spoke with poor country-boy grammar and apparently had terrible table manners. It was Ada who gave Dad sophistication.

Did Earl Wood invent the G-suit? The answer is no. Wilbur Franks was working on a water-filled suit and David Clark had one of his prototype air-bladder suits available before Earl started at Mayo Clinic. What Earl and the Aero Medical Unit did was have the instrumentation, tools, measurements, and data available to make the G-suit better and usable for the army, air force, and navy. Besides making the G-suit better, Earl developed a straining maneuver, which would increase G tolerance with or without a G-suit.

Did Earl Wood invent cardiac catheterization? The answer is no. What Earl and his team did in the 1950s and 1960s was make cardiac catheterization better through the instrumentation used on the centrifuge, for accurate physiological measurements, data analysis, and perfecting cardiac catheterization techniques for quicker, more accurate clinical diagnosis.

Often overlooked is Earl's greatest contribution to clinical medicine, which was the development of oximetry and the oximeter. Today, every emergency room and operating room and most hospital rooms and clinics throughout the world have a working pulse oximeter that can be clipped to the finger for quick measurement of blood-oxygen saturation levels. The pulse oximeter was one of the key medical devices used to measure pulmonary and cardiac function during the COVID-19 pandemic. Now pulse oximeters are even available in many pharmacies.

Family, education, love of the outdoors, and a sense of vocation developed Earl's character. David Brooks describes character as including qualities such as courage, honesty, and humility that endure over the long term. People with character, like Earl, are "anchored by permanent attachment to important things . . . they stay attached to people and causes and callings consistently through thick and thin . . . they have permanent commitment to tasks that cannot be completed in a single lifetime." Earl's character lives on in the hearts and minds of his family and former fellows, students, and technicians. His physiology contributions live on in every clinic, hospital, and air force in the world.

Dr. John Williams, from New Zealand, worked in Earl's laboratory in the 1960s. He is quoted as saying, "Someday they should put on Earl's tombstone: 'Here lies a man who knew how to measure.'" It is perhaps ironic that the man who devoted his life to figuring out how to measure to the most exacting degree possible eludes measurement himself. We can chronicle Earl's background and his contributions to medical research, aviation medicine, and public health; speculate about his influences; praise his character, his clear leadership, his belief in teamwork, and his willingness to take risks; and even acknowledge his occasional human failings. But none of this gives the true measure of the man, Earl H. Wood. Perhaps great men, like Earl, are beyond measure.

As our culture evolves, may Earl's example live on for those who follow. Today's society is constantly challenged by "alternative facts" and "fake news." We can only imagine what Earl (and particularly Ada) would have said about what is happening today. We can only hope that through this chronicle of Earl's life, the unique nature of his leadership will inspire others, and that there will be other Earls out there to take the helm.

ACKNOWLEDGMENTS

First, I would like to thank Earl's former "crew" and laboratory technicians, Don Hegland, Don Erdman, and Willis Van Norman, who gave me a wealth of information on what happened downstairs in the Medical Sciences Building in preparation, construction, data collection, and data analysis for the physiological and cardiovascular experiments that were conducted from the 1950s through the 1990s. Our every-other-week breakfasts at Perkins and Denny's were a total delight, and it was a thrill for me to rub shoulders with "Earl's heroes"!

I have to extend a thank-you to Earl's former fellows, Dr. Erik Ritman, Dr. Jim Greenleaf, and Dr. Barry Gilbert, who assisted in gathering articles and shared what it was like to work with Earl on the centrifuge and during the transition to the DSR project.

Thank you to Dr. Jan Stepanek and Dr. John Lynch for reviewing the manuscript for scientific accuracy.

Most of the Wood family history was compiled by Earl's oldest brother, Chester Wood, who wrote and self-published *The Wood-Goff Family Chronicle*.

A huge thank-you goes to the staff of the W. Bruce Fye Center for History in Medicine, including Renee Ziemer and Emily Christopherson, and to David Coleman, Mayo

Clinic Media Support Services, for retrieving the historical documentation and photographs that made this book possible. Thank you to Matthew Dacy, Jeanne Klein, and Nicole Babcock from Mayo Clinic Heritage Days.

Thank you to the University of Minnesota Archives and the alumni center at Macalester College for retrieving the historical and scientific articles that document Earl's post–high school years in college, graduate school, and medical school and throughout his scientific career.

I would like to thank my initial editor, Ms. Holly Hughes, for taking what was initially a 180,000-word manuscript and paring it down to a more readable document for publication. The hours we spent on Zoom calls during the COVID-19 pandemic made difficult times more tolerable.

I have to acknowledge Elayne Becker, Katherine Richards, and the editors at Girl Friday Productions for the final editing of the manuscript and fact-checking the names and historical references discussed in this book.

Thank you to my siblings, Phoebe, Mark, and Guy, who have encouraged me throughout my life to explore history, stay current on world events, work and study hard, and, of course, find time to play and enjoy life.

I have to thank my parents, Earl and Ada Wood, who taught me perseverance, showed me how to work hard, and encouraged me to explore different cultures and languages—and, at the same time, to have fun in life. They had incredible patience while helping me cope with severe dyslexia, staying up late at night and making time on the weekends to assist me with schoolwork from the time I was in grade school all the way through high school. I would have never succeeded academically without them.

Thank you to the Dyslexia Institute of Minnesota's Reading Center in Rochester, which provided professional reading tutors and gave me the ability to complete high school, college, and graduate school.

Last and most important, I would like to thank my wife, Krista, and daughter, Karolyn, who encouraged me to write this biography about a true twentieth-century scientific icon, leader, teacher, coach, parent, and grandparent.

ABOUT THE AUTHOR

E. Andrew "Andy" Wood is the last of four children born to Earl Howard and Ada Catherine (Peterson) Wood. He is a graduate of Hamline University and the Mayo Clinic School of Health Sciences and has a master's degree from the University of Minnesota. Andy spent over twenty-five years at General Mills as the manager of health promotion and ergonomics and two years as director of ergonomics and corporate solutions at Muve Inc., a joint venture with Mayo Clinic, where he was responsible for developing and implementing activity-based ergonomic and wellness programs for corporate clients. Andy was an ergonomics consultant at Ferguson Risk Management, where he provided ergonomic and wellness strategies for corporations, including Land O'Lakes, Bayer, Bosch, Dairy Farmers of America, and CVS Health, and several government agencies until his retirement in 2021. Andy has authored several articles on the development and assessment of ergonomic and health promotion programs in industry. A graduate of the Dyslexia Institute of Minnesota's Reading Center, Andy is now a spokesperson for the institute.